Proving the Unprovable

Proving the Unprovable

The Role of Law, Science,
and Speculation in Adjudicating
Culpability and
Dangerousness

Christopher Slobogin

OXFORD
UNIVERSITY PRESS

2007

OXFORD
UNIVERSITY PRESS

Oxford University Press, Inc., publishes works that further
Oxford University's objective of excellence
in research, scholarship, and education.

Oxford   New York
Auckland   Cape Town   Dar es Salaam   Hong Kong   Karachi
Kuala Lumpur   Madrid   Melbourne   Mexico City   Nairobi
New Delhi   Shanghai   Taipei   Toronto

With offices in
Argentina   Austria   Brazil   Chile   Czech Republic   France   Greece
Guatemala   Hungary   Italy   Japan   Poland   Portugal   Singapore
South Korea   Switzerland   Thailand   Turkey   Ukraine   Vietnam

Published by Oxford University Press, Inc.
198 Madison Avenue, New York, New York 10016

www.oup.com

Oxford is a registered trademark of Oxford University Press

Library of Congress Cataloging-in-Publication Data
Slobogin, Christopher, 1951–
    Proving the unprovable : the role of law, science, and speculation in
adjudicating culpability and dangerousness / Christopher Slobogin.
        p. cm.—(American Psychology-Law Society series)
    Includes bibliographical references and index.
    ISBN-13 978-0-19-518995-7
    ISBN 0-19-518995-7
    1. Evidence, Expert—United States.   2. Criminal liability—United States—Psychological aspects.
3. Criminal liability—Social aspects—United States.   4. Violent offenders—United States.   5. Criminal
psychology—United States.   6. Forensic psychology—United States.   7. Forensic sociology—
United States.   I. Title.   II. Series.
    KF9674.S59 2006
    345.73'067—dc22   2006007048

9 8 7 6 5 4 3 2 1

Printed in the United States of America
on acid-free paper

To Richard Bonnie,
who started me down this path

Foreword

This book series is sponsored by the American Psychology-Law Society. APLS is an interdisciplinary organization devoted to scholarship, practice, and public service in psychology and law. Its goals include advancing the contributions of psychology to the understanding of law and legal institutions through basic and applied research, promoting the education of psychologists in matters of law and the education of legal personnel in matters of psychology, and informing the psychological and legal communities and the general public of current research, educational, and service activities in the field of psychology and law. APLS membership includes psychologists from the academic research and clinical practice communities as well as members of the legal community.

APLS has chosen Oxford University Press as a strategic partner because of its commitment to scholarship, quality, and the international dissemination of ideas. These strengths will help APLS reach its goal of educating the psychology and legal professions and the general public about important developments in psychology and law. The focus of the book series reflects the diversity of the field of psychology and law, as we will publish books on a broad range of topics.

Professor Christopher Slobogin's book focuses on evidentiary standards for expert testimony by mental health professionals in two key areas: culpability and dangerousness. These two inquiries, one asking clinicians to evaluate past mental states and the other asking them to predict future behavior, are arguably the most difficult legal issues behavioral scientists are asked to assess. They place mental health professionals front and center in decisions that affect the lives of many, as their opinions often carry considerable weight in court decisions about whether a defendant should be held responsible for a criminal act, or whether an offender should be preventively detained or put to death.

Professor Slobogin begins by evaluating the reliability and validity of these opinions, focusing on whether they meet the criteria established in *Daubert v. Merrell Dow Pharmaceuticals* and *Kumho Tire Co. v. Carmichael*. After an extensive review of the research demonstrating the difficulty of assessing past mental states and future behavior, he concludes that interpreting these decisions to require scientifically verifiable expert testimony would produce a criminal justice system that is both less fair and less reliable. Instead, Professor Slobogin argues, more relaxed evidentiary standards should apply. For culpability testimony, experts should have to show evidence of content validity (which Slobogin defines as the extent to which clinical opinion addresses the factors the law considers material) as well as add to the information that the trier of fact would normally use in making decisions about responsibility. For prediction testimony, he argues that, although testimony based on empirically derived probability estimates should be the norm, the *defense* should also be able to rely on less "scientific" clinical predictions if they are founded on the risk literature and on generally accepted professional evaluation procedures.

Proving the Unprovable is a book that will be of considerable interest to both researchers and clinicians. Professor Slobogin reviews the extensive literature on culpability and dangerousness in a clear and highly readable style. Experts preparing for court testimony on these topics will be well prepared to respond to questions about admissibility after they have carefully reviewed the material in this book. Indeed, Professor Slobogin's framework for analyzing the admissibility of clinical testimony—requiring consideration of materiality, probative value, helpfulness, and prejudicial impact—can be applied to virtually any area in which mental health professionals might serve as experts. As editor of the American Psychology-Law Society series, I am very pleased to add this impressive and thoughtful book to the series.

Ronald Roesch
Series Editor

Preface

Culpability and dangerousness. These are the two central issues raised by any sensible societal attempt to deal with antisocial behavior. We punish people who have committed a criminal act with a blameworthy state of mind. We enhance people's criminal sentences or commit them to psychiatric hospitals and detention centers when we think they are likely to harm others. Other criteria for determining when people will be deprived of life or liberty are secondary to these two crucial determinations.

Unfortunately, both determinations are very difficult to make. It is hard enough in many cases simply figuring out whether a person has committed an antisocial act. It is harder still to determine the extent to which he or she intended the act, and why he or she committed it. And most difficult of all is divining whether a person will harm again.

The law has increasingly turned to mental health professionals to help address these issues, particularly the last two. Because of their familiarity with and study of human behavior, psychiatrists, psychologists, and other clinicians are thought to possess special expertise in assessing culpability and dangerousness. As a result, members of these groups routinely furnish the courts with evaluations of insanity and other issues regarding mental state at the time of the offense, even more frequently proffer predictions about future behavior, and occasionally even provide insight into whether a particular individual is the type of person who could have committed a crime at all.

Although this expertise has for the most part been welcomed by the courts, it has also been maligned. Critics deride clinical testimony about culpability as disguised storytelling and tar expert prediction by comparing it unfavorably to coin flipping. Syndrome and profile evidence—battered woman syndrome, Vietnam veteran syndrome, rapist profiles—have been particular subjects of scorn and are often labeled "junk science." Numerous commentators have proposed severe limitations on, or even outright prohibition of, the testimony of psychiatrists and psychologists in criminal and commitment proceedings.

These critics have been aided in their efforts by a series of influential decisions from the U.S. Supreme Court in the 1990s that appear to impose a relatively high threshold for expert testimony, one that requires that the testimony's underlying assumptions be verified as "reliable" through scientific or other testing. The basis of much clinical opinion about culpability and dangerousness may not meet this test if it is applied rigidly. Although many courts have yet to consider that possibility or its implications, an increasing number of lower court decisions suggest that a more restrictive evidentiary regime is in the offing.

This book is an effort to sort out whether that development would be a good thing. It does not provide an answer that can be summarized in a sentence or two. How we should go about proving culpability and dangerousness depends on a number of variables, including the governing substantive law, our ability to answer the questions that law generates, the extent to which judges and juries can arrive at sensible conclusions without the help of experts, and whether the testimony proffered is from the government or from the person whose liberty is at stake. In other words, contrary to the explicit assertions of the critics and the implicit message from the Supreme Court, proving "facts" that are sometimes unprovable requires a nuanced approach that is not focused simply on the reliability of the evidence presented. Culpability and dangerousness are socially constructed concepts that probably cannot, and in any event should not, be determined solely through the scientific method.

In developing these ideas, this book relies heavily on the law of evidence, which is the primary set of rules governing admissibility of expert testimony. But it also looks closely at the laws defining culpability and dangerousness, because they tell us when mental health professionals have something legally useful to say. And of course any effort to gauge the usefulness of testimony by behavioral scientists must also examine the worth of the behavioral science on which they rely. Thus, this book is an interdisciplinary attempt to provide an analytic framework for deciding how we identify who should be punished and preventively detained.

As such, this book is a sequel to *Minding Justice: Laws That Deprive People with Mental Disability of Life and Liberty* (Harvard University Press), a previous work of mine that discussed the criteria for determining who should be punished and who may be preventively detained. *Minding Justice* tried to define the categories of people who can be deprived of life or liberty. This book addresses how we decide which individuals belong in those categories.

For their help in working through the ideas in this book I would like to thank Richard Bonnie, Thomas Cotter, Mark Fondacaro, Stephen Friedland, Donald Judges, Tom Lyon, Rick Matasar, John Monahan, Joelle Moreno, Randy Otto, Norman Poythress, Michael Seigel, and Andrew Taslitz. I would also like to acknowledge the indicated journals for granting me permission to use portions of articles I have authored, cited here in the approximate order in which they are relied on in the book: "Psychiatric Evidence in Criminal Trials: To Junk or Not to Junk?," 40 *William & Mary Law Review* 1 (1998); "Doubts about *Daubert*: Psychiatric Anecdata as a Case Study," 57 *Washington & Lee Law Review* 919 (2000); "The Admissibility of Behavioral Science Information in Criminal Trials: From Primitivism to *Daubert* to Voice," 5 *Psychology, Public Policy & Law* 100 (2000); "Pragmatic Forensic Psychology: A Means of 'Scientizing' Testimony from Mental Health Professionals?," 9 *Psychology, Public Policy & Law* 275 (2003); "The 'Ultimate Issue' Issue," 7 *Behavioral Science & Law* 259 (1989); "The Hartman Hotz Lecture—Race-Based Defenses: The Insights of Traditional Analysis," 54 *Arkansas Law Review* 739 (2002); "Dangerousness and Expertise," 133 *University of Pennsylvania Law Review* 97 (1984); "Dangerousness and Expertise Redux," 55 *Emory Law Journal* 1 (2006); "The Structure of Expertise in Criminal Cases," 34 *Seton Hall Law Review* 105 (2003).

Contents

Proving the Unprovable

1

Introduction: The Need for Nuance

The government's two most invasive exercises of power are criminal punishment and preventive detention. Criminal punishment imposes sanctions for antisocial conduct that is considered "blameworthy" because it is intentional or grossly negligent and is neither justified (as in self-defense cases) nor excused (by insanity or other impairment). Preventive detention—detention of persons thought to be "dangerous"—can either be an aspect of punishment, as when a court extends a sentence to protect the public, or take place independently of it, as occurs when people with mental disability are committed to mental hospitals. Both punitive and preventive interventions frequently result in prolonged deprivation of liberty and can sometimes result in the deprivation of life.

In determining who should be punished and preventively detained, the American legal system has increasingly relied on mental health professionals, mostly psychiatrists at first, but more recently psychologists, social workers, and others with behavioral science training.[1] This development is probably largely the result of two factors: first, a belief among lawyers and society at large that the most plausible claims of lessened culpability and heightened dangerousness involve people with "mental disability," and second, the fact that the definition of the latter term is continually expanding. Whatever the cause, clinicians (a word I use interchangeably with mental health professionals) today routinely proffer expert opinions in criminal trials, sentencing proceedings, and commitment hearings. The goal of this book is to assess the value of these opinions to the extent that they address culpability and dangerousness questions.

The subject matter of this book thus represents the intersection of two very important debates. The first debate is about the appropriate scope of government's power to deprive its citizens of life and liberty. To what extent are an offender's subjective beliefs and motivations relevant to a determination of criminal liability? How much risk must a person pose to society before government may detain him or her, and must that risk be due to some sort of mental abnormality if government wants to engage in pure preventive detention rather than pursue some form of punishment? These are the types of questions I addressed in my previous book, *Minding Justice*, but they will need to be briefly resurfaced here (albeit not resolved), because an assessment of whether mental health professionals have something to offer the legal system depends on what they are being asked to assess.

The second debate that underlies this book is epistemological in nature: Is it possible to be certain about anything having to do with past mental states or future events? If not, how does a legal system that needs answers to these questions cope? In short, how do we prove the unprovable? Similar questions might be raised about many other areas of the law in which mental health professionals participate, including child custody disputes, personal injury claims, and disability evaluations. This book's focus, however, is solely culpability and dangerousness assessments, partly to keep the topic manageable, partly because those assessments have more riding on them than any other forensic issues addressed by the courts, but mostly because, this book argues, the admissibility analysis is different in these two contexts.

The primary goal of this introductory chapter is to canvass the law that frames these debates over government power and legal epistemology: the substantive law that defines when opinions about culpability and dangerousness are legally relevant and the rules of evidence that govern how facts can be proven in a court of law. Section B describes the insanity defense and related doctrines having to do with culpability assessments and sentencing and commitment laws to the extent they call for assessments of risk. Section C outlines the evidentiary rules that govern expert testimony.

With this description of current law as a backdrop, section D lays out a framework for analyzing expert admissibility issues, a framework that provides the organization for the remainder of the book. Based on the Federal Rules of Evidence, the four factors that make up the framework allow for a more nuanced assessment than most courts have provided to date. This section also gives a brief preview of the primary themes in the book.

Before addressing any of these points, however, it is necessary to rehearse briefly the current controversy over the admissibility of clinical testimony, a task undertaken in section A. Almost every type of expert testimony has been the subject of scorn, but the most virulent complaints about experts seem to be directed at forensic mental health professionals.

Several commentators have even suggested that, in the two areas of concern here, clinicians have so little valid information to offer that they should be barred from the courtroom. Because these criticisms of clinical testimony are a large part of the motivation for writing this book, we must begin with them.

Of Storytelling and Coin Flipping

Clinical testimony in criminal cases has long been the butt of jokes, but 1995 may have been the first time the humor was officially endorsed, in a New Mexico statute setting out licensing requirements for psychiatrists and psychologists. The law, which passed both houses of the New Mexico legislature before it was vetoed by the governor, provided that a mental health professional who testifies in a criminal case "shall wear a cone-shaped hat that is not less than two feet tall. The surface of the hat shall be imprinted with stars and lightning bolts." Additionally, the proposed legislation stated, the expert "shall be required to don a white beard that is not less than eighteen inches in length, and shall punctuate crucial elements of his testimony by stabbing the air with a wand." Finally, during the testimony, "the bailiff shall dim the courtroom lights and administer two strikes to a Chinese gong."[2]

At least this statute permitted mental health professionals to testify. A number of commentators have suggested that forensic clinicians should be barred from the courtroom, regardless of how they are dressed. During deliberations on the federal insanity test in 1983, Jeffrey Harris, deputy associate attorney general during President Reagan's administration, stated: "What amazes me is that in any trial I've ever heard of, the defense psychiatrist always says the accused is insane, and the prosecuting psychiatrist always says he's sane. This happened invariably, in 100 percent of the cases, thus far exceeding the laws of chance. You have to ask yourself, 'What is going on here?' The insanity defense is being used as a football and quite frankly, you'd be better off calling Central Casting to get 'expert psychiatric testimony' in a criminal trial."[3]

These types of sentiments might be written off as posturing by politicians. But academics have made similarly strong statements. Stephen Morse, a well-respected law professor who is also a psychologist, has stated, "the categories and theories of mental health science are at present too imprecise and speculative to help clarify legal questions" raised in criminal and commitment proceedings. He has also asserted that "without hard, methodologically sound quantitative data, the guess of an expert is unlikely to be better than the guess of laypersons," and he has been particularly critical of Freudian-based psychodynamic testimony offered to mitigate criminal culpability, which he considers "story-telling" based on guesswork.[4] Morse concludes that, in the absence of hard data, mental health professionals in the courtroom should describe only behavior they have directly observed; inferences drawn from those observations should be prohibited.[5]

Other academic professionals reach similar conclusions. Professor David Faigman, another law professor with a social science background who is also coauthor of a widely used reference work on scientific evidence, compares clinical testimony to Dostoyevskian novelists spinning tales about criminal motivations. He has suggested that much clinical testimony is merely "suppositional"—by which he means untested by the scientific method—and thus should generally not be admissible.[6] Perhaps most famously, David Faust and the late Jay Ziskin, both psychologists and professors, argued in *Science* that most, if not all, testimony offered by psychologists and psychiatrists should be excluded from the courtroom because it cannot be offered with "reasonable medical certainty"—which they equate with "pretty likely accurate"—and because it does not improve the accuracy of the fact finder's decision.[7]

Even psychiatrists, who are generally the *focus* of much of the criticism (because they resort to softer testimony more often than research-oriented psychologists), have joined the chorus. For instance, in his book *Reign of Error*, psychiatrist Lee Coleman provides several examples of fanciful testimony in insanity cases and argues that, because "psychiatrists do not have the tools to find out what an accused person was thinking at the time of the crime," they should not be allowed to testify about insanity or any other past mental state issue.[8] In *Law, Psychiatry and Morality*, Alan Stone, a past president of the American Psychiatric Association, lamented the inability of mental health professionals to answer the law's questions about the relationship of mental illness and culpability and said of psychiatrists who testify in courts "they know not what they are doing."[9]

While most of the foregoing comments were directed at testimony about insanity and related issues, equally vigorous criticism has been aimed at clinical predictions of dangerousness. Most memorable in this regard is the article written by Bruce Ennis (a well-known civil liberties lawyer) and Thomas Litwack (a psychologist) entitled "Flipping Coins in the Courtroom."[10] Arguing that these predictions are no more accurate than random choice, Ennis and Litwack opined that they should never be introduced as evidence in court. A large number of other commentators, with both legal and clinical training, have agreed that clinical prediction testimony should be inadmissible or severely circumscribed.[11]

If these critics had their way, judges would suddenly feel very lonely at commitment hearings, lawyers would have to scramble for new types of evidence in insanity, preventive detention, and sentencing proceedings, and a large number of mental health professionals would be looking for work. To begin evaluation of their claims, we need to look more closely at how the law defines culpability and dangerousness and how it determines when opinion evidence is expert enough to be admissible. That is the task of the next two sections.

B. Substantive Law: FAQs about Culpability and Risk That the Courts Direct at Clinicians

Because the consequences can be so serious, we try to be (or at least say we try to be) very careful in deciding whom to punish and whom to target for preventive purposes. As noted earlier, we punish only those who commit an antisocial act, and usually also require some showing that the way they committed the act renders them blameworthy. We preventively detain someone through a sentence enhancement or civil commitment only if concrete evidence of the danger exists, and also often require proof of some sort of mental abnormality as well. The doctrines that implement these general principles are numerous and complex. The following discussion highlights those doctrines most likely to call for testimony by mental health professionals.

The Law of Culpability

Even in medieval times "madness" was a defense. Since then assessments of blame have become increasingly fine-tuned. Today, for instance, our criminal courts often make subtle differentiations between premeditation and recklessness, frequently ask how a person "in the actor's situation" would act, and increasingly rely on judgments about subjective mental states en route to deciding whether and how much to punish an individual.

The criminal law doctrine that most obviously calls for clinical participation is the *insanity* defense. By the time the mental health professions began organizing (in the middle of the nineteenth century), most American jurisdictions abided by the so-called M'Naghten test for insanity, which excuses people with a "mental disease or defect" that prevented them from knowing "the nature and quality" of their criminal act or from knowing that it was wrong.[12] Some jurisdictions also permitted an excuse when the mental disability produced an "irresistible impulse." By the mid-twentieth century, a number of competing insanity formulations, all of them broader in scope, had surfaced. The most popular reform test was the American Law Institute's, which combined M'Naghten and the irresistible impulse standards and expanded on them. The ALI's test, which appears in its Model Penal Code (MPC), excuses people whose "mental disease or defect" at the time of the offense resulted in "a lack of substantial capacity to appreciate the wrongfulness [criminality] of the conduct or conform . . . conduct to the requirements of the law." A second formulation, even more expansive and thus less attractive to most lawmakers, is the so-called product test, which excuses those whose crime was the product of mental disorder.[13]

The insanity defense has always been controversial. Many people believe, quite erroneously, that it is routinely asserted, frequently successful, and results in little or no time in confinement when it prevails.[14] After John Hinckley's acquittal on insanity grounds in 1981, several states and the federal government narrowed their insanity tests, and at least five states have now eliminated the defense altogether.[15] To some extent, the current hostility toward mental health professionals is a by-product of antipathy toward this much maligned defense. But it remains on the books in most states (usually as some form of M'Naghten or the ALI test), and has been stoutly defended by numerous courts and commentators as a necessary means of identifying that small group of people who do not deserve punishment and are not deterrable because of their mental disability.[16]

Even more controversial is the *diminished capacity* defense, more accurately described as proof that the defendant does not have the required mental state (or *mens rea*) for the offense as a result of mental disability. This defense, which first appeared in the mid-twentieth century and is recognized in some form in roughly half the states, is conceptually distinct from the insanity defense.[17] Most people who are found insane—John Hinckley, for instance—clearly intend to commit their crimes and thus have the mens rea for their offense. Some offenders, however, are sufficiently impaired due to mental disability that they do not meet the requisite mental state element. For instance, a person with mental retardation might not be able to premeditate a murder (depending on how much planning is required for premeditation under the law of the jurisdiction). Or a person with delusions may honestly believe that the car he takes is his, and thus not be guilty of theft in a jurisdiction that requires the prosecution to prove a thief knows the stolen property belongs to another. If successful, a mens rea defense will normally not result in acquittal, but rather conviction for a lesser included offense that does not require the same degree of mens rea. In the first example, for instance, the mentally retarded individual would still be convicted of second-degree murder. On the other hand, the car taker might not be liable for any crime, unless the jurisdiction permits conviction for a lesser degree of theft on proof that he *should* have been aware that the vehicle was someone else's (a negligence or "general intent" mens rea).

A third doctrine that might call for clinical testimony is often called the *diminished responsibility* defense. This doctrine differs from insanity because it does not require the same degree of impairment as that defense and differs from diminished capacity because the offender concedes that he has the mens rea for the charged crime. It is usually restricted to homicide cases and takes the place of the old common law "provocation" or "heat of passion" doctrine, with the most common formulation tracking the ALI's language in its Model Penal Code (MPC).[18] The Code provides that murder charges are to be reduced to manslaughter even if the killing is intentional, if the homicide was "committed under the influence of extreme mental or emotional disturbance for which there is reasonable explanation or excuse," with "reasonableness" to be determined "from the viewpoint of a person in the actor's situation under the circumstances as he believes them to be." The last phrase of this provision calls for some assessment of the offender's subjective perceptions and perhaps his or her motivations as well.

The MPC uses the same sort of language in its definition of self-defense and duress. According to the Code, "The use of force upon or toward another person is justifiable *when the actor believes* that such force is immediately necessary for the purpose of protecting himself against the use of unlawful force by such other person on the present occasion." And duress is a defense when a person is "coerced" to commit a crime "by the use of, or a threat to use, unlawful force against his person or the person of another, which a person of reasonable firmness *in his situation* would have been unable to resist."[19] This kind of language seems to invite clinical input to the extent that it can bolster a defendant's claim that he or she felt threatened by the victim or a third party.

Admittedly, the MPC's subjectification of defenses has not attracted many followers. Most states continue to adhere to the traditional formulations of provocation and self-defense, which are phrased in objective terms; that is, would a "reasonable person" have felt threatened by the victim? According to a leading criminal law treatise, although a "very distinct majority" has adopted the MPC's approach to duress, only a "substantial minority" has copied its extreme mental or emotional stress language, and only a "few" states have endorsed its approach to self-defense.[20] The important point for present purposes, however, is that the potential for subjectification exists and that some jurisdictions have moved in that direction.

When one looks at sentencing law, as distinct from criminal defenses asserted at trial, that movement is even more apparent, especially in death penalty cases, where the Constitution requires individualization.[21] For instance, virtually every death penalty statute recognizes as mitigating factors whether the murder was committed "under the influence of extreme mental or emotional disturbance," "under circumstances which the defendant believed to provide a moral justification or extenuation for his conduct," and "under duress or under the domination of another person."[22] Many noncapital sentencing regimes permit sentence reductions on similar grounds.[23] Absent from these formulations is any reasonableness restriction. The inquiry focuses solely on the defendant's motivations and beliefs.

A last culpability issue of relevance to this book is character. Sometimes a defendant will introduce character evidence for the purpose of disproving mens rea, admitting that she killed someone but arguing that she's not the type of person who would do so intentionally. More frequently, character evidence is meant to suggest that the defendant, because of her innate goodness, her passivity, or similar factors, could not have committed the criminal act at all, intentionally or unintentionally. Whereas at one time this type of testimony was limited to "community reputation" evidence, today, under the Federal Rules of Evidence and the evidence rules of many states, the witness's *own* opinion about a person's character is permitted.[24] Here again, the door is open to clinical testimony.

The Law of Dangerousness

The mental health professions have recently begun using the term "risk assessment" when describing the dangerousness inquiry. That term probably is a better way to conceptualize the work of experts involved in violence prediction. But this book uses the term "dangerousness" to refer to the *legal* issue involved because it better captures the various considerations that concern courts: not just the probability of a given risk, but its magnitude, imminence, and frequency and the extent to which this combination of factors represents a danger to society.

Sentencing courts and parole boards have long considered dangerousness (along with culpability and other factors) in determining the appropriate duration of punishment for a convicted offender. In the past two decades, however, the federal government and many states have abolished parole and moved toward sentences based solely on backward-looking culpability assessments.[25] A determinate sentencing regime of this sort eliminates the need for risk assessment at the dispositional stage of criminal cases. However, recent Supreme Court decisions may move sentencing back toward indeterminate terms.[26] More important, several states, including those that have determinate sentencing in noncapital cases, make the risk of future violent crime an aggravating circumstance in death penalty cases, and mental health professionals have been conspicuously involved in addressing that issue.[27]

In contrast to the sentencing context, dangerousness still plays a pervasive role in justifying pure preventive detention (preventive detention unrelated to punishment) of people with mental disability. This role is a long-standing one. In colonial times, for instance, persons with mental illness could not be locked up unless they were "dangerously distracted," "furiously madd," or "so far disordered in their senses that they may be dangerous to be permitted to go abroad."[28] With the advent of asylums in the nineteenth century commitment tended to be easier, merely requiring proof of a need for treatment. But civil liberties litigation in the 1960s, which aimed at narrowing the scope of commitment, resulted in a concerted movement toward criteria requiring dangerousness to self or others. Today the civil commitment laws of virtually every state focus on the likelihood of imminent serious bodily harm.[29] Similar provisions authorize commitment of those found not guilty by reason of insanity, although these criteria often do not require proof of *imminent* danger and may be more relaxed in other ways as well.[30]

Beginning in the early 1990s, a third type of commitment, more of an adjunct to punishment than a means of forcing treatment, has come to the fore. Codified in so-called sexual predator laws, this version of preventive detention does not require the sort of serious mental disability associated with traditional civil commitment, but rather may rest on any "mental abnormality" that predisposes a person to commit sex offenses, which many courts equate with garden-variety personality disorders.[31] An earlier version of this form of preventive detention, the mentally disordered sex offender (MDSO) statute, was popular in the first half of the twentieth century but almost disappeared in the face of claims that treatment did not work and that the predictions that led to the treatment were suspect.[32] The new incarnation of these laws has been greeted with more favor, perhaps because it allows commitment not only in lieu of sentence, as occurred under the MDSO laws, but also *after* an offender's sentence has expired. These laws now exist in roughly twenty states, and the courts have upheld them against due process, double jeopardy, and ex post facto challenges, as long as the state proves the existence of a mental abnormality that makes the person "dangerous beyond [his or her] control" and makes some effort to provide treatment (even if it is unlikely to work).[33]

The Role of Mental Health Professionals

This brief exposition of the relevant law makes it is easy to see how mental health professionals became so heavily involved in culpability and dangerousness assessments. Many of the criminal law doctrines that define when an individual may be punished contemplate inquiry into the defendant's mental state and motivations at the time of the offense. Because mental health professionals study and treat mental states and aberrant behavior on a daily basis, criminal defense attorneys and prosecutors naturally gravitated toward them when these types of questions were raised. Similarly, it is not a big leap from making a forward-looking treatment plan for someone with a mental disorder, which is the bread and butter of clinical practice, to forecasting whether, without treatment, the person will hurt another person in the future. Mental health professionals first performed the latter function in civil commitment hearings, but courts naturally turned to them in connection with sex offender statutes and sentencing as well.

One might argue that the criminal law should not subjectify culpability, or even that it should not concern itself with culpability at all.[34] Similarly, it has been contended that dangerousness should never influence sentencing or form the basis for commitment.[35] Although these arguments might be furthered by an inquiry into the validity of clinical opinion (because difficulty in proving culpability and dangerousness might be one reason to eschew them as legal criteria), the issues they raise are beyond the scope of this book. This book takes current law for granted because it seeks to examine whether mental health professionals can contribute to the questions the law is asking *now*.

On that assumption, the agenda is to figure out whether clinicians can usefully address culpability and dangerousness issues, or whether instead the law should rely on other means of proof. The critics argue that the courts' reliance on clinicians in criminal and commitment cases is misguided because mental health professionals have little or no expertise on the questions raised in these proceedings. Whether the critics are correct depends on how one defines "expert" for legal purposes, which is the province of the rules of evidence.

―

C. Evidence Law: The Definition of Expert

The law defining when a witness is transformed from a *fact witness*, who is limited to reporting perceived events, into an *expert*, who can offer opinions about matters in a legal dispute, has gone through several incarnations. Before 1975, the usual threshold requirement for opinion testimony was that it be based on specialized information "beyond the ken of [the] jury."[36] In theory, then, expert opinions about something the typical layperson could grasp were not admissible. Testimony that did meet this threshold might also be subject to two further limitations. It could not rely on information, such as hearsay, that was not independently admissible, and it could not address the ultimate legal issue in the case.[37]

Coexisting with these rules, at the federal level and in many states, was the *Frye* test. This test came from a 1923 case, *Frye v. United States*, which held that the results of polygraph examinations were not admissible because the scientific underpinnings of the polygraph were not "sufficiently established to have gained general acceptance in the particular field in which it belongs."[38] In many jurisdictions, this "general acceptance" test became the primary means of evaluating the admissibility of scientific evidence, especially novel scientific evidence in criminal cases.[39] Indeed, many courts evaluating such evidence relied entirely on *Frye*, without any explicit inquiry into whether evidence was "beyond the ken of the jury."[40]

In 1975, the Federal Rules of Evidence went into effect. On their face, the new Federal Rules governing expert testimony, widely copied by the states, relaxed previous restrictions. Under Rule 702, opinions based on "scientific, technical or other specialized knowledge" need only "assist the trier of fact to understand the evidence or to determine a fact in issue." Although the difference between evidence that "assists" and evidence that is "beyond the ken" may be subtle, the former language suggests a greater willingness to classify an opinion as expert, and courts have so held.[41] In more obvious contrast with previous practice in many jurisdictions, Rule 703 permitted opinions to be based on otherwise inadmissible information such as hearsay if the information is "of a type reasonably relied upon by experts in the particular field." Finally, again in contrast to the law in at least some jurisdictions at the time it went into effect, Rule 704 permitted qualified opinion testimony to "embrace an ultimate issue to be decided by the trier of fact" (although this rule was amended nine years later to prohibit ultimate issue testimony on issues of "mental state or condition").[42]

Note that Rule 703's "reasonable reliance" language resonates with *Frye*'s general acceptance test. But the commentary to the rule and the other

Federal Rules governing expert testimony made no reference to that case. Nonetheless, many courts continued to apply *Frye* to scientific evidence, with or without reference to the Federal Rules or the analogous state rules.[43] Other courts developed their own separate screening tests for scientific testimony. For instance, one test looked at whether there was "substantial," as opposed to general, acceptance of the subject matter, and another focused on whether the opinion was "the product of an explicable and reliable" system of analysis.[44]

Still other courts, with the support of most commentators, rejected these separate screening tests for expert testimony, including *Frye*.[45] Instead, these jurisdictions adhered to the Federal Rules' "helpfulness" analysis, supplemented by the balancing test applicable to any proffered evidence; under this regime, any relevant specialized knowledge from a qualified expert is admissible unless its potential for confusing the jury, unfairly prejudicing one of the parties, or wasting time substantially outweighs its probative value. This approach might be called the 401/403 balancing test, in reference to the Federal Rules that deal with the definition of relevance (Rule 401) and the delineation of countervailing factors such as prejudice to one of the parties (Rule 403).

In short, even at the federal level, the scope and effect of Rule 702 and its companion rules were unclear for many years. Then came the Supreme Court's 1993 decision in *Daubert v. Merrell Dow Pharmaceuticals*. In that case, the Court concluded that Rule 702 was meant to reject what it called the "austere" *Frye* standard as the sole test of admissibility in favor of the multifactor "liberal" regime of the Federal Rules. But the liberal regime the Court had in mind was not the pre-existing balancing test focused on Rules 401 and 403. Rather, the Court explained, federal courts are to judge the helpfulness of proffered expert testimony by looking at "whether the reasoning or methodology underlying the testimony is scientifically valid and . . . whether that reasoning or methodology properly can be applied to facts in issue." According to the Court, validity (which the Court usually described as "reliability") can be determined by whether the theory and methodology underlying the opinion has been tested through attempts to "falsify" it, the error rates thereby obtained, the extent to which the theory and procedure have been subject to peer review and publication, and the extent to which they are generally accepted by the relevant field.[46] Although the last factor obviously echoes *Frye*, the difference under *Daubert* is that general acceptance is neither necessary nor sufficient for admissibility. About half the states have followed the federal lead and adopted *Daubert*; most of the rest adhere to *Frye* or its equivalent.[47]

A question left hanging in *Daubert* was whether its reliability threshold for expert testimony applies only to "scientific" evidence or to "technical and specialized" knowledge as well (recall that these are the three types of knowledge to which Rule 702 refers). Because the evidence in *Daubert*—involving epidemiology studies of the drug Benedictin—was scientific in nature, *Daubert* specifically deferred applying its holding to technical and specialized knowledge, a fact that several courts noted in deciding not to apply *Daubert* to evidence from social scientists.[48] However, six years after *Daubert*, in *Kumho Tire Co. v. Carmichael*,[49] the Supreme Court explicitly applied *Daubert* to all types of expert testimony, meaning that clinical testimony must also meet its dictates.

Kumho Tire itself is subject to some second-guessing, however. Despite its refusal to exempt specialized and technical knowledge from the reliability inquiry required of scientific knowledge, the majority opinion in *Kumho Tire* emphasized the flexibility of the *Daubert* test.[50] It also clearly contemplates that "personal experience" as well as "professional studies" can form the basis for expert testimony under some circumstances.[51] Thus, *Kumho Tire* can be read to permit expert testimony that is not based on research. At the same time, *Kumho Tire* firmly requires that experts demonstrate the validity of their opinions, which is usually difficult to do without resort to some sort of scientific methodology.[52]

Partly in an effort to clear up the ambiguity, the Federal Rules committee drafted, the Supreme Court promulgated, and Congress endorsed amendments to Rules 702 and 703 shortly after *Kumho Tire* was decided. In 2000, the italicized portion of Rule 702 was added: "If scientific, technical, or other specialized knowledge will assist the trier of fact to understand the evidence or determine a fact in issue, a witness qualified as an expert by knowledge, skill, experience, training, or education, may testify thereto in the form of an opinion or otherwise *if (1) the testimony is based upon sufficient facts or data, (2) the testimony is the product of reliable principles and methods, and (3) the witness has applied the principles and methods reliably to the facts of the case.*" For readers with a social science background, it should be pointed out that "reliability" as used in this amendment is meant to be synonymous with what a scientist would call validity or accuracy, rather than replicability, which is the scientific meaning of the term. That distorted usage is necessary given *Daubert*'s initial misapplication of the word. Except where indicated, I follow *Daubert*'s lead in this regard as well.

Also in 2000, Rule 703, having to do with the data underlying the expert opinion, was changed to read:

> The facts or data in the particular case upon which an expert bases an opinion or inference may be those perceived by or made known to the expert at or before the hearing. If of a type reasonably relied upon by experts in the particular field in forming opinions or inferences upon the subject, the facts or data need not be admissible in evidence *in order for the opinion or inference to be admitted. Facts or data that are otherwise inadmissible shall not be disclosed to the jury by the proponent of the opinion or inference unless the court determines that their probative value in assisting the jury to evaluate the expert's opinion substantially outweighs their prejudicial effect.*

This language is an attempt to prevent the parties from using experts to describe to the fact finder evidence that is otherwise not admissible.

D. A Proposed Analytical Framework

More will be said throughout the rest of this book about how the new Federal Rules, *Daubert/Kumho*, the 401/403 balancing test, and *Frye* should be interpreted. For now it merely needs to be noted that most critics of clinical testimony prefer some version of the *Daubert/Kumho* test (which I generally abbreviate to "the *Daubert* test") and assert that, under it, mental health professionals who offer opinions about culpability and dangerousness often or always fail to meet it. Several commentators have suggested that, applied literally, *Daubert* would exclude virtually all behavioral science opinion testimony.[53]

To date, the courts have largely ignored these assertions. But there are signs that they are starting to listen. Ironically, that development comes during an era when responsibility and propensity assessments are more important than they have ever been in the criminal justice system. Given these developments, the time is ripe for a detailed examination of the role mental health professionals should play.

The framework I propose for analyzing the admissibility of clinical testimony requires consideration of four issues: materiality, probative value, helpfulness, and prejudicial impact. *Materiality* analysis requires a determination of whether the testimony logically relates to the relevant substantive law. *Probative value* is a measure of the accuracy of expert testimony, with respect to both its general principles and its specific application to the case at hand. *Helpfulness* refers to the extent to which the testimony adds something to what the fact finder can accurately figure out for itself. And the *prejudicial impact* factor permits assessment of whether testimony that is material, probative, and helpful nonetheless should be excluded because it will most likely be misused by the fact finder.

This four-factor framework is consistent with the structure of the Federal Rules of Evidence. Under Rule 401, all evidence, lay and expert, must be "relevant," a concept that combines an assessment of whether the evidence is material to a matter in dispute with an evaluation of whether it is probative because it actually tends to prove that fact.[54] When the evidence is expert testimony, Rule 702 requires, as indicated earlier, that the evidence help the fact finder. And Rule 403 provides that even relevant, helpful evidence should be excluded if its probative value is substantially outweighed by the likelihood that it will confuse or mislead the fact finder. My framework realigns the Federal Rules' factors somewhat, in particular by integrating the reliability analysis mandated by the amended Rule 702 into the evaluation of probative value. But this manipulation merely changes labels, not the content of the analysis. The framework is similar to the 401/403 balancing test, but it more explicitly bows to *Daubert*'s requirement that expert testimony demonstrate reliability.

In the following chapters, this four-factor analysis is applied both to clinical testimony about culpability (part I) and to prediction testimony from mental health professionals (part II). Chapter 2 describes in more detail both the nature of clinical culpability testimony (which has become increasingly imaginative) and the courts' response to it (which has been very generous, even post-*Daubert*, except with respect to some types of syndrome testimony). The chapter ends by criticizing this judicial nonchalance to the extent it is explained by inattention to the substantive law of culpability. More specifically, it applies the materiality factor to culpability testimony and finds that many of the more novel claims made by clinicians should be excluded even if they are assumed to be reliable, because they are not responsive to the questions the law asks.

Chapters 3 and 4 then tackle the key issue in this area, the probative value of clinical culpability testimony that *is* material. In chapter 3 I take issue with the critics, arguing that, even though this testimony often is, at best, informed speculation, much of it should nonetheless be considered sufficiently reliable, given the lack of viable alternatives and the criminal accused's right to voice. However, I also make a distinction between opinions about past mental state (e.g., insanity, diminished capacity, and diminished responsibility) and opinions about conduct (e.g., character used to prove innocence) because the latter is more amenable to the type of scientific study that *Daubert* mandates.

Chapter 4 proposes that, when the testimony is about past mental state, probative value should be measured in terms of "generally accepted content validity," which equates *Daubert*'s reliability test not with accuracy (which I argue is impossible to gauge), but with the extent to which clinical opinion addresses the factors the law considers material. As a possible method of implementing this means of measuring probative value, I discuss the recent suggestion of pragmatic psychologists that forensic specialists maintain a database of reports that the courts have considered useful. This database could be used to identify those clinical factors that courts deem important to assessing culpability and should accelerate the production of structured interview formats designed to address that issue. Chapter 4 also examines the expert's obligation to assure the reliability of information that forms the basis for clinical opinions, a topic that the courts have neglected despite the amendments to Rules 702 and 703, yet one that is just as important as the limits on inference drawing that have been the focus of the critics.

Chapter 5 concludes the discussion of culpability issues with an examination of the helpfulness and prejudicial impact factors. The helpfulness inquiry, I contend, should involve a determination of the extent to which clinical testimony challenges lay conceptions of human behavior, by looking at what I call "factor-based incremental validity." In practice, this requirement would tend to reinforce the admissibility of expert evidence proffered by the defense, because that evidence is more likely to rebut lay assumptions that offenders intend the natural consequences of their acts and are sane when they commit crimes. The helpfulness requirement also has implications for the manner in which testimony is expressed. Here I discuss when experts may use ultimate issue language, concluding that whereas legal conclusions should always be avoided, use of test language (e.g., the M'Naghten wording) should depend on the extent to which the proceeding is adversarial and otherwise structured to enable the fact finder to understand the issues. Finally, this chapter discusses the assessment of prejudicial impact, both on the parties to the dispute and on groups in society that, some have argued, might be pathologized by certain types of culpability testimony.

The two chapters in part II deal with the admissibility of prediction testimony proffered by mental health professionals. Chapter 6 begins by describing the current state of prediction science, which is improving but is still almost as likely to produce inaccurate judgments as accurate ones. It also makes the crucial distinction between clinical prediction testimony and prediction testimony based on empirically derived probability estimates (which includes not only actuarial prediction testimony but might also encompass testimony based on what has come to be called "structured professional judgment"). The chapter then canvasses judicial decisions concerning the admissibility of prediction testimony, decisions that, despite the high error rates associated with predictions, are even more welcoming than the decisions dealing with expert opinions about culpability. Finally, the chapter begins my own evidentiary analysis of prediction testimony with an assessment of its materiality, a concept that raises particularly interesting issues in connection with prediction testimony based on group data and demographic information.

Chapter 7 applies the final three admissibility factors—probative value, helpfulness, and prejudicial impact—to expert prediction testimony. Despite false-positive rates approaching 50 percent, prediction testimony should usually be considered probative because, contrary to the critics' insinuation with their coin-flipping analogy, both clinical and actuarial predictions produce results better than chance selection would. Furthermore, in contrast to culpability testimony, we at least have error rate information about predictions, which provides the fact finder with a way of gauging its worth. Prediction testimony is also generally helpful, at least when it avoids ultimate issue language, because it identifies risk factors that laypeople might not otherwise consider.

Where prediction testimony is most likely to fail in evidentiary terms, chapter 7 concludes, is with respect to the fourth factor, prejudicial impact. When the government proffers expert testimony that someone who has just been convicted or charged with an offense is dangerous, it is merely confirming what the fact finder already strongly suspects. When this testimony is presented in clinical, as opposed to actuarial, form, even aggressive rebuttal evidence normally has minimal impact on the fact finder. Thus, this chapter argues that the decision as to whether clinical expert testimony on dangerousness will be presented should be left up to the subject of the prediction. This *subject first* rule is analogous to the well-known character evidence rule, which bars evidence of bad character, despite its probativeness on the issue of whether the defendant committed an offense, unless and until the defendant opens the door by presenting evidence of good character.

Chapter 8 concludes the book by reviewing the previous chapters and offering two key observations about the structure of expertise in criminal and preventive detention cases now that *Daubert* has been handed down. The first is that a rigid application of *Daubert*'s positivist approach will, in the long run, be good for prosecutors and bad for criminal defendants and those subjected to commitment. The second is that the result of this differential impact will be a justice system that is less just. A more nuanced approach to clinical testimony on culpability and dangerousness is essential if we care about fairness and appropriate outcomes.

Part I

CULPABILITY

2

Diagnoses, Syndromes, and Criminal
Responsibility

If nothing else, the interaction between the criminal courtroom and the mental health profession has produced some memorable nomenclature. "The abuse excuse," "battered woman syndrome," "child sexual abuse accommodation syndrome," "XYY chromosome abnormality," "false memory syndrome," "premenstrual stress syndrome," "television intoxication," "urban survival syndrome," "posttraumatic slavery disorder"—these are just a few of the colorful appellations describing claims that mental health professionals have bolstered with their testimony over the years.[1] From reading the tabloid press, one could easily come to the conclusion that this testimony is spurious psychobabble that will eventually swallow up our justice system. Even a more tempered observer is likely to wonder whether this type of opinion evidence is worthy of consideration in courts of law. In a nicely ironic turn of phrase, Ian Freckleton has used the term "forensic abuse syndrome" to capture the popular (and academic) sentiment about novel psychiatric claims.[2]

This chapter begins, in section A, by describing in more detail the various types of diagnoses and syndromes that clinicians have offered on culpability issues. Contrary to the impression one might get from press reports, for the most part this testimony has relied on traditional diagnostic categories. However, at the margins it has gradually changed in character. Specifically, it has become more nomothetic, more scientific in appearance, and less linked to the medical model of mental disorder. It has also increasingly been offered to support novel legal claims outside the traditional bailiwick of the insanity defense.

Section B describes how the courts have applied the evidentiary tests described in chapter 1 to this testimony. The bottom line is that under both *Frye* and *Daubert*, as well as under the 401/403 balancing test, diagnostic testimony has pretty much been left alone, whereas nontraditional syndrome testimony has been subject to somewhat more (but still not very intense) scrutiny; furthermore, contrary to what one might expect after *Daubert*, reliability does not seem to be the linchpin of the analysis. The chapter then offers some generalizations about the factors that do drive the courts' attitudes toward clinical culpability testimony. The most significant generalization is that the substantive law of culpability plays a major, usually unacknowledged role in admissibility decisions, with testimony that pushes the doctrinal envelope much more likely to be excluded.

The latter observation leads to section C, which begins the analysis of whether the law's current approach to expert testimony about culpability makes sense. This part of the chapter links chapter 1's recitation of the substantive law of culpability to the rules of evidence and emphasizes that the first criterion for admissibility must always be materiality—a determination that the testimony addresses a proposition that the criminal law considers germane. It turns out that, despite the movement toward subjectively defined culpability recounted in chapter 1, in many jurisdictions a considerable amount of clinical testimony that purports to be about culpability is in fact immaterial. In such cases, courts need not even address whether the evidence is reliable because, whether it is or not, it is not logically relevant to the questions the law asks.

A. A Half-Century of Expert Testimony about Culpability

The following description of testimony from mental health professionals in criminal cases is in two parts. The first part describes the testimony from a clinical perspective and compares it to testimony of yesteryear. The second part describes expert clinical opinion from a legal perspective, again taking a historical view.

The Substance of Psychological Testimony

Psychological testimony about culpability comes in all shapes and sizes: opinions based on official diagnoses; psychodynamic formulations derived from Freud and other explorers of the unconscious; descriptions of organic or genetic abnormalities; theorizing about the impact of childhood and other social traumas; and, of course, testimony about syndromes, which are usually composites of symptoms that are not officially recognized by the profession but combine all or some of the previous sources. Any further effort to develop a taxonomy of clinical testimony about culpability is probably futile because, as will become clear in the following discussion, this testimony can be categorized along so many different, overlapping spectrums. Instead, the following discussion briefly describes some of the more conspicuous specimens.

As noted in the introduction to this chapter, syndrome evidence has occasioned much of the current ferment over clinical testimony. The most prominent example of this type of evidence may be the battered women syndrome (BWS). In its original version, since modified somewhat, BWS describes the state of "learned helplessness" allegedly visited on women who suffer through cyclical battering from their spouse or significant other.[3] The syndrome was at one time quite popular with defense attorneys and is still used to support insanity, provocation, and self-defense claims.[4] The child sexual abuse accommodation syndrome (CSAAS) and the rape trauma syndrome (RTS) purport to identify psychological symptoms experienced by people who have been subjected to sexual abuse and are relied on by prosecutors to bolster testimony by alleged victims whose injuries are otherwise hard to discern.[5] The Vietnam veteran syndrome, like the three syndromes just discussed, is an application of the posttraumatic stress disorder diagnosis, this time to those who experienced the trauma of war.[6] It is usually introduced in insanity cases to support the argument that the defendant experienced a flashback to his or her war days at the time of the crime.[7]

Other types of syndrome testimony are less common, but no less familiar to those who peruse the media. Urban survival syndrome, which posits that black ghetto youth are also in a war zone—an urban one that makes them particularly fearful of other black youths—received considerable publicity some years back even though it has been advanced in only one case to date.[8] Also rare, but particularly controversial, are prosecutions for decades-old child abuse bolstered by psychological evidence that people can repress memories and then discover them years later; these claims may be rebutted by what has been called the false memory syndrome.[9] Another example is the abuse excuse, popularized in the trial of the Menendez brothers, who claimed that they killed their parents because, conditioned by years of abuse by their father, they feared that otherwise they would be killed.[10]

With such a wide array of new and sometimes bizarre-sounding psychiatric claims finding their way into criminal trials, it is no wonder that many commentators charge that modern-day psychological testimony often appears to be made-to-order junk science unfit for a court proceeding. The legal ramifications of these challenges are addressed later. For now, a few observations about the nature of psychological testimony will help to put them in perspective.

First, and most important, the bulk of criminal trials in which mental health professionals testify do not involve any of these dramatic claims. Rather, the typical expert psychiatric opinion is rather humdrum, usually concerning whether the defendant was evidencing symptoms of schizophrenia, manic-depressive psychosis, antisocial personality, schizoid personality, or some other traditional diagnosis found in the American Psychiatric Association's *Diagnostic and Statistical Manual of Mental Disorders* (*DSM*).

The battles of the experts, if they occur at all, are over whether the defendant fits into diagnostic categories that have been well established for decades.[11] The issue is often whether the defendant suffers from an Axis I disorder (e.g., a serious psychotic disorder such as schizophrenia), an Axis II disorder (e.g., a less serious personality disorder), or no disorder at all. Rare is the forensic professional who has ever offered syndrome or other novel opinion testimony.[12]

A related observation is that, contrary to the innuendo of the anti–junk science literature and the press, psychiatric innovation in criminal cases is not at an all-time high. Thirty years ago, the psycholegal landscape was no less dotted with gaudy claims (although, again, these claims were rare). In the 1970s, defendants based exculpatory defenses on "television intoxication," cultural upbringing, "brainwashing," "rotten social background," and the possession of an extra Y chromosome.[13] Going back even further, a number of criminal defendants in the 1960s relied on claims of multiple personality disorder, "psychic disintegration," and other manifestations of the unconscious.[14]

At the same time, the nature of nontraditional testimony does seem to have changed at the margins over the past few decades, in at least three ways. First, such testimony is more likely to be explicitly *nomothetic*, as opposed to *idiopathic*, in nature. Instead of individualized descriptions based on an intimate interview with the subject of the testimony, which was the usual fare thirty years ago, the newer brand of nondiagnostic evidence tends to rely on off-the-rack data or impressions about a group of people, presented by an expert who may never have seen the defendant or witness to whom it is applied.[15] John Monahan and Larry Walker have called this type of testimony "social framework evidence" because it provides background information that must then be tied to the case at hand by other submissions.[16] For instance, framework testimony in a child abuse case might describe the typical psychological characteristics of a victim of child abuse. Other evidence is then needed to link those characteristics with the child in question. All psychological testimony fits this pattern to some extent; for instance, even traditional testimony that the defendant was hearing voices at the time of the offense is usually bolstered by references to the typical symptoms of schizophrenia. The new syndrome testimony, however, is more explicit about focusing on "group character" as opposed to the character of the subject.

A closely related difference between the recent and more distant past is that today's nontraditional testimony is more likely to be presented in a self-consciously scientific style. This is not to say that today's testimony is necessarily based on better science, just that it is more commonly framed in scientific terms. For instance, experts who testify about BWS or RTS often talk about studies purporting to show specific symptoms to be sequelae of battering and rape.[17] In contrast, testimony of the 1960s and 1970s about unconscious conflicts, brainwashing, and rotten social background, as well as unusual defenses of the early 1980s, such as pathological gambling and premenstrual syndrome, rarely referred to concerted scientific research; instead, the usual basis of the opinion was experience and theory.[18]

A third difference between psychological testimony today and that of thirty years ago is that more of it departs from the medical model of mental disability. Psychodynamic testimony and claims about extra Y chromosomes, premenstrual conditions, or pathological gambling attribute mental problems primarily to biological or intrapsychic causes.[19] In contrast, claims based on urban psychosis, war-induced trauma, or cultural differences (the last of which have become much more frequent in the 1980s and 1990s)[20] place primary blame for mental disturbances on the environment. The abuse excuse, a label encompassing a wide array of claims to the effect that previous abuse caused particular criminal behavior, also focuses on exogenous etiological factors.[21]

Not too much should be made of these tendencies regarding psychological evidence at criminal trials. Certainly some nontraditional testimony from the 1970s was nomothetic and explicitly research-based (e.g., concerning the effects of watching television), and some of the specific claims made in that decade focused on environmental causes (e.g., television intoxication, rotten social background, and brainwashing testimony).[22] Nonetheless, these three minitrends are worth noting; as developed below, they may bear some relationship to judicial analysis of psychological evidence.

The Legal Focus of Psychological Testimony

Psychological testimony has changed not only in content but also in purpose. In the old days, such testimony was offered almost entirely in support of an insanity defense, with occasional attempts to prove lack of mens rea or diminished capacity.[23] Today, psychological testimony is used to ground self-defense, provocation, duress, and entrapment claims,[24] as well as more traditional insanity and absence of mens rea arguments.

In each of these newer areas, the testimony takes advantage of, or tries to get the courts to adopt, relatively recent substantive reforms in the law that subjectify inquiries into the defendant's mental state at the time of the offense. For instance, as chapter 1 indicated, in some jurisdictions for some types of crimes, self-defense no longer depends on whether the force used by the defendant was reasonably necessary, but on whether the defendant honestly believed the force was necessary. Similarly, in many jurisdictions, a manslaughter instruction must be given not only when a reasonable person would have been provoked, but also when, to use the Model Penal Code's much copied formulation, the provoked reaction was reasonable in light of the actor's situation under the circumstances as he or she believed them to be.[25] Subjectifying blameworthiness in this way opens the door wide to psychological speculations.

Nor has clinical testimony in criminal cases been limited solely to assessments of mental state. Courts also have allowed such testimony in support of a claim that the defendant does not meet the act requirement of an offense. Usually, the testimony is framed in terms of the defendant's character; someone with the defendant's personality, the expert opinion suggests, could not have (or could have) committed the offense in question. The first reported appellate opinion sanctioning such testimony was handed down during the 1950s, but the phenomenon appears to have become much more prevalent in the past twenty years.[26]

Still another way in which innovative lawyers have used psychological testimony in recent years is as a method of addressing the credibility of a witness, which is an indirect way of proving or disproving culpability. In a sense, this issue arises any time a mental health professional testifies in support of or against a psychiatric defense. An opinion that the defendant is insane suggests that the defendant's claim of insanity is true, and a contrary opinion suggests the opposite. The type of credibility testimony of concern here, however, is testimony that is explicitly framed in terms of whether a witness other than the defendant is telling the truth about some event. Perhaps the most famous example is the psychological testimony presented in the Alger Hiss trial, which asserted that Whittaker Chambers, Hiss's prime accuser, was a psychopathic liar.[27] That trial, like the first character evidence cases, took place during the 1950s, but it seems to have been well ahead of its time. Most appellate cases dealing with expert testimony about the truthfulness of a witness have come in the past three decades, many of them in cases involving child abuse and rape.[28]

A related, relatively recent use of behavioral scientists is helping the trier of fact determine whether a witness is accurate, as opposed to truthful. The most obvious example of this practice is expert testimony about the foibles of witnessing and remembering an event, which suggests that the testimony of an eyewitness, though not an intentional fabrication, may be erroneous. The eyewitness expert points to phenomena that can affect one's registration of an event (e.g., weapons focus), memory of an event (e.g., time), or recall of an event (e.g., suggestions by the police).[29] The jury then may consider this nomothetic information in deciding whether a particular eyewitness identification is correct. A variant is testimony about the theoretical basis for repressed memory, designed to support the validity of a sudden remembrance of an event that occurred years earlier.[30] Here, however, the expert not only provides information about the theory of repressed memory but also tends to vouch for the accuracy of the particular memory in question.[31]

B. The Impact of Evidentiary Law on Psychological Testimony

How have the courts reacted to these various types of expert testimony? Does the reaction vary depending on the evidentiary test used: *Frye*, the balancing test, or *Daubert?* The short answer to these questions is that, regardless of the test applied, courts rarely reject clinical testimony, and that the few exceptions to this rule appear to be based not on an assessment of reliability but on other concerns.

The Relative Irrelevance of the Screening Tests

Frye and its progeny resulted in the exclusion of polygraph evidence and several other types of expert testimony based on the physical sciences. *Daubert* and *Kumho Tire* have had an even bigger impact on expert testimony, leading to exclusion or serious limitations on opinions from crime lab scientists, economists, epidemiologists, and others.[32] Given the assertions of the critics about the weak basis of forensic clinical testimony, one might expect similar results in that area.

The reality is quite different. Most forensic mental health professionals who testify in criminal cases have never had their testimony excluded or significantly limited.[33] In particular, mental health professionals who testify about insanity and who rely on a diagnosis found in the *DSM* (what I call "diagnostic" or "traditional" testimony) have been able to say virtually anything they want in criminal court, post-*Frye*, post-*Daubert*, and even post–*Kumho Tire* and amended Rule 702. Daniel Shuman documented that, as of 2001, there had been "no reported *Daubert* challenges to retrospective psychiatric assessments of criminal responsibility" that rely on the *DSM*.[34] That conclusion is probably still true today.[35] The only significant limitation on diagnostic opinion has been the general prohibition on ultimate testimony concerning mental state, introduced in the federal system in the wake of the *Hinckley* trial in 1984, and even that limitation has had very little practical effect.[36]

When considering syndrome testimony and other novel opinion evidence, the courts have been somewhat more willing to scrutinize admissibility issues, especially when offered on an issue other than insanity. Thus, opinions about pathological gambling, the effect of an extra Y chromosome, BWS, RTS, CSAAS, and eyewitness accuracy have all been subjected to one of the evidentiary screening tests described in chapter 1.[37] Even here, however, the tests are often left in the shed, usually on the ground that this type of testimony does not really involve science. One review found, for instance, that "many *Frye* courts decline to follow *Frye* in considering evidence regarding various psychological syndromes, such as battered woman syndrome or rape trauma syndrome, and argue that *Frye* has traditionally been applied in cases that concern 'novel scientific devices or processes involving the evaluation of physical evidence.'"[38]

Daubert jurisdictions are not necessarily any different. For instance, based on a survey of judges that took place circa 2000, Veronica Dahir and her colleagues concluded, "It appears that *Daubert*'s influence on judicial admissibility decisions for [profiles and syndrome] evidence is insignificant, leading us to conclude that one reason that psychology is still considered part of the 'soft sciences' is that judges seldom hold the discipline to the same rigorous methodological standards as the 'hard sciences.'"[39] A similar study found that the proportion of cases in *Daubert* jurisdictions admitting expert evidence about such subjects as mental disorders, syndromes, intent, dangerousness, and child sex abuse victims either remained the same or actually increased in the first five years after that decision as compared to the five years prior to *Daubert*.[40] A third look at the case law, this time including cases since *Kumho Tire*, confirms that these tendencies have to a large extent remained unchanged, although it also suggests that courts are looking at social evidence more closely than they did before.[41]

Why Clinical Testimony Is Usually Left Alone

The first question one might ask in light of these facts is why diagnostic testimony and even much of the newfangled syndrome testimony have been exempted from *any* type of screening analysis. One rationale has already been suggested: many courts do not perceive behavioral testimony to be derived from "hard" or "physical" science and therefore see no need to subject it to special scrutiny. But that rationale is not very satisfying. Even if we can meaningfully determine when expert testimony is based on hard as opposed to soft science, nothing about that determination, by itself, indicates why such testimony should be given a free ride. As chapter 1 noted, it has been clear since *Kumho Tire* if it wasn't clear before that *all* expert testimony, whether based on science or on specialized or technical knowledge, must be evaluated for its reliability in those jurisdictions that follow *Daubert*.

Delving more deeply into the matter, judicial thinking about when such scrutiny is warranted seems to be affected by two other considerations, neatly summarized by the California Supreme Court in describing when it applies its version of the *Frye* test (which it adopted in *State v. Kelly*): "First, *Kelly-Frye* only applies to that limited class of expert testimony which is based, in whole or in part, on a technique, process, or theory which is new to science and, even more so, the law. . . . The second theme in cases applying *Kelly-Frye* is that the unproven technique or procedure appears in both name and description to provide some definitive truth which the expert need only accurately recognize and relay to the jury."[42] Applied in our context, this reasoning suggests that traditional psychological testimony is not subject to judicial scrutiny because it is . . . traditional and, more persuasively, because juries are not likely to consider it objective or infallible, but rather will naturally treat it with skepticism.

Cases that specifically deal with clinical opinion about culpability echo this reasoning. For instance, the first rationale is found in a 2003 Alaska Supreme Court decision refusing to apply screening analysis to diagnostic testimony: "Psychiatric testimony need not be subjected to analysis under the [*Daubert*] factors when the testimony is simply a diagnosis stemming from a typical psychiatric examination. A bare claim that psychiatric evidence is unreliable does not subject forensic psychiatry to a mini-trial in every case. We have repeatedly recognized the validity of independent psychological and psychiatric exams and forensic psychological and psychiatric exams in civil and criminal contexts."[43] This reasoning may be shallow, but it is not unusual. As we'll see later in this book, the Supreme Court has upheld the admissibility of concededly weak prediction testimony largely on the ground that a contrary holding "would be somewhat like . . . disinvent[ing] the wheel."[44] Courts rely on precedent. So a grandfathering theory of evidence law is not surprising.

The California Supreme Court's second rationale for refusing to look closely at traditional testimony—that juries know what to do with it—was the basis for the Supreme Court of Connecticut's decision finding battered woman syndrome testimony admissible:

> We have found the *Frye* test appropriate when the experimental,
> mechanical or theoretical nature of the scientific evidence had
> the "potential to mislead lay jurors awed by an aura of mystic
> infallibility surrounding scientific techniques, experts and the fancy
> devices employed." . . . [But] "where understanding of the method
> is accessible to the jury, and not dependent on familiarity with
> highly technical or obscure scientific theories, the expert's qualifi-
> cations, and the logical bases of his opinions and conclusions can
> be effectively challenged by cross-examination and rebuttal
> evidence."[45]

This rationale for relaxed admissibility criteria has more force and is endorsed, up to a point, later in this book. For now, we need merely note that it is the only one of the three excuses courts use for their relaxed approach to most clinical testimony—the other two being the "it's not hard science" and the stare decisis rationales—that has any persuasive value.

When Is Testimony Excluded?

Not all clinical testimony gets a pass from the courts. As noted earlier, testimony based on syndromes or that is otherwise novel is occasionally excluded. Given the critics' complaints, one would think that this exclusion results from an analysis of the testimony's reliability. In fact, however, this factor rarely plays a central role in the courts' calculus. Rather, excluding courts usually seem to be preoccupied with other concerns, some of which parallel the trends in nontraditional psychological testimony noted earlier. As a general matter, the more nomothetic, research-oriented, and nonmedical the testimony is, the more likely courts will exclude it.

As an example of the first two tendencies, consider testimony about the accuracy of eyewitness identification. As social science testimony goes, this type of opinion evidence is highly reliable, yet until recently courts often excluded it, and many courts still do.[46] Those that exclude often point to the fact that such testimony is not based on the facts of the case or contact with the eyewitness involved, but on prepublished research findings; in other words, it is social framework evidence par excellence. These words of a Massachusetts court capture the flavor of these decisions:

> [Expert testimony on eyewitness identification] in most cases deals with general principles, such as the fact that memories fade over time, that people under severe stress do not acquire information as well as alert persons not under stress, and that people tend unconsciously to resolve apparent inconsistencies between their memories and after-acquired facts. Obviously there are aspects of these general principles on which experts might make some contribution in particular cases. However, juries are not without a general understanding of these principles and, as the trial of this case demonstrates, they see the possible application of these principles in concrete circumstances. The jury [must] have the opportunity to assess the witnesses' credibility on the basis of what is presented at trial and not solely on general principles.[47]

Rape trauma syndrome evidence has sometimes been excluded on similar grounds. In the words of the Minnesota Supreme Court, "The jury must not decide this case on the basis of how most people react to rape or on whether [the victim's] reactions were the typical reactions of a person who has been a victim of rape. Rather, the jury must decide what happened in this case, and whether the elements of the alleged crime have been proved beyond a reasonable doubt."[48]

Examples of cases rejecting testimony that departs from an internalist account of behavior—the third tendency identified above—are found in cases involving opinions describing the effects on criminal defendants of poverty, television, and inner-city living. Compared to eyewitness testimony, the reliability of this type of testimony is relatively suspect, so one might think exclusion in these cases stems from that concern. But the decisions that refuse to admit this type of opinion evidence don't seem to focus on that point. Rather, judicial hostility stems from another source: these types of claims depart from the medical model to such a great extent that they conjure up fears of legal anarchy. After all, the judges in these cases seem to be saying, almost everyone who commits a crime is subject to some type of traumatizing condition; we cannot excuse them all!

Consider these comments from Judge McGowan, who wrote a portion of the majority opinion in *United States v. Alexander*, the leading "rotten social background/black rage" case:

> The tragic and senseless events giving rise to these appeals are a recurring byproduct of a society which, unable as yet to eliminate explosive racial tensions, appears equally paralyzed to deny easy

access to guns. Cultural infantilism of this kind inevitably exacts a high price, which in this instance was paid by the two young officers who were killed. The ultimate responsibility for their deaths reaches far beyond these [two African American defendants]. . . . As courts, however, we administer a system of justice which is limited in its reach. We deal only with those formally accused under laws which define criminal accountability narrowly.

Judge McGowan added that his court was upholding the trial court's instructions because they "remind the jury that the issue before them for decision is not one of the shortcomings of society generally, but rather that of appellant Murdock's criminal responsibility for the illegal acts of which he had earlier been found guilty."[49]

Of even greater interest, in light of his well-known willingness to broaden the scope of the insanity defense,[50] are the similar comments of Judge David Bazelon. In his dissenting opinion in *Alexander*, Judge Bazelon began by giving several reasons why the law should recognize a combination bad upbringing/black rage defense. He also conceded, however, that "it does not necessarily follow . . . that we should push the responsibility defense to its logical limits and abandon all the trappings of the medical or disease model. However illogical and disingenuous, that model arguably serves important purposes. Primarily, by offering a rationale for detention of persons who are found not guilty by reason of 'insanity,' it offers us shelter from a downpour of troublesome questions."[51]

The judges in *Alexander* are not alone in such sentiments. In *Zamora v. State*, involving the television intoxication defense, the appellate court made analogous observations. "In the concluding pages of defense counsel's lengthy brief the following language appears: 'In the case at bar, television was on trial . . . .' Such was simply not the case. . . . Television was not on trial; Ronny Zamora was on trial. . . . Stated simply, this was a murder trial, and it is to the trial judge's credit that he confined the testimony and evidence to the relevant issues."[52] In other words, these judges conclude, the criminal law's inquiry into accountability should focus on endogenous, not exogenous, causes.

Other cases excluding clinical evidence are not as explicit as these opinions but also seem to be based on fear that admission of particular evidence would push the doctrinal envelope too far. In this vein is a Wyoming Supreme Court case that purported to reject testimony about the battered child syndrome on *Frye* grounds but seemed to voice its real concern when it stated, "The notion that a victim of abuse is entitled to kill the abuser . . . is antithetical to the mores of modern civilized society."[53] The fear of legal anarchy can even extend to testimony focused on endogenous variables. Consider, for instance, *United States v. Lewellyn*, which rejected, on *Frye* grounds, expert opinion on the effects of pathological gambling.[53] The testimony in this case described internal compulsions, not external influences.

Moreover, the pathological gambling diagnosis had been ensconced in the *DSM* for four years and was thus presumptively "accepted."[54] Still, the court excluded the testimony. As Professor Bonnie has argued, the real motivation for this type of ruling is probably the concern that permitting acquittal in such cases would open the floodgates to traditionally disfavored volitional impairment claims.[55]

Clinical testimony can stretch procedural as well as substantive doctrine. This phenomenon occurs most commonly with psychiatrically based claims about whether a criminal act occurred and whether a witness is truthful or accurate. When judges resist these claims they do so in large part on the ground that the testimony is likely to "usurp" the role of the jury in determining credibility.[57] This type of language is a particularly common refrain in cases excluding eyewitness testimony. For instance, in *United States v. Kime*, the court excluded this type of testimony on the ground that it "intrude[d] into the jury's domain."[58]

One sees the same rationale in cases involving syndromes. For example, in excluding expert testimony about rape trauma syndrome alleging that the victim's post-offense symptoms were consistent with forceful intercourse, the Missouri Supreme Court stated, "The history of the exceptionally fine jury system in this state instructs us not to tamper with the jurors' decision process in such manner. . . . As applied here, [testimony concerning rape trauma syndrome] was inimical to the proper jury operation. In spite of the phenomenal and constant accomplishments of science, it does not seem fusty or anachronistic to preserve the integrity of that operation in a confrontation with scientific opinion."[59]

The court's protestations about fustiness notwithstanding, these types of holdings express the same precedent-adoring sentiment that we encountered in the cases that refuse to scrutinize diagnostic testimony. The difference here is that the precedent requires adherence to process (jury decision making) rather than to substance. In both cases, however, tradition trumps close analysis.

What about Reliability?

Perhaps the most interesting thing about the courts' approach to psychological evidence about culpability is how minimal a role reliability plays in determining admissibility. Recall first that the two reasons given by the California Supreme Court for exempting traditional testimony from special judicial scrutiny—precedent and the accessibility of the evidence[60]—have nothing to do with the evidence's reliability. Even more surprising, reliability does not seem to play much of a role in determining the admissibility of *non*traditional psychological testimony, even when it is subjected to one of the screening tests and is introduced on issues other than insanity. For instance, according to one review of rape trauma syndrome cases, although the courts are split as to whether testimony about the syndrome is "valid," "few have seriously evaluated the underlying scientific foundation for expert testimony based on RTS research."[61]

As a more general illustration of the judicial tendency to ignore reliability and focus instead on the types of factors discussed here, consider the way the courts have handled the different types of claims based on posttraumatic stress disorder (PTSD), that is, claims not just of rape victims but of Vietnam veterans, child sex abuse victims, and battered women. If reliability were the test, one might conjecture that, because the same basic diagnosis is at issue, the analysis of admissibility would be the same with respect to each. It is not, however. Vietnam veterans have had no problem introducing PTSD testimony.[62] In contrast, alleged rape victims have had some trouble doing so, and alleged child sex abuse victims have met much more judicial resistance. The differential treatment has to do with the substantive and procedural concerns identified above, not reliability analysis. Veterans use PTSD to support insanity claims, which courts will only dismiss if they seriously threaten doctrinal boundaries, whereas rape and abuse victims rely on PTSD to prove a criminal act occurred, or at least to bolster the victim's credibility, agendas which courts approach much more cautiously.[63]

Battered woman syndrome has the most interesting story in this regard. Women who introduced the syndrome in self-defense cases were rebuffed at first, but today not only do many jurisdictions judicially permit testimony about BWS, but a number actually guarantee its legitimacy through legislation.[64] The syndrome met initial resistance because it sometimes undermined the necessity requirement of traditional self-defense law; acquitting a woman for killing her batterer even when he was not attacking her at the time struck courts as antithetical to the "imminent threat" threshold of justification doctrine.[65] More recently, however, as Professor Mosteller has pointed out, the groundswell of support for battered women has led courts and legislatures, implicitly or explicitly,[66] to subjectify self-defense law in this type of case. BWS is now admissible not because it has magically become more reliable but because substantive law has been changed in response to political pressures, and thus the syndrome no longer pushes the doctrinal envelope.[67]

C. When Is Culpability Testimony Material?

Chapters 3 and 4, on the probative value factor, explore in detail the extent to which reliability *should* be an admissibility criterion and how it should be defined, and chapter 5 looks at the jury usurpation argument and related issues in discussing the helpfulness and prejudice factors. But the foregoing observations naturally lead at this point to a discussion of materiality, the first admissibility criterion in this book's proposed framework for analyzing admissibility issues. We have seen several examples of exclusionary decisions that purported to be using the screening tests but were actually based on doctrinal considerations. In these cases, the rules of evidence were merely placeholders, used as a smokescreen to hide a more pressing concern about substantive impact. At the other extreme, numerous courts at both the trial and appellate levels seem willing to admit almost any kind of testimony proffered by a mental health professional, without regard to its logical connection to the law of the jurisdiction. As James Q. Wilson has noted, many courts have ignored the distinction between judging a defendant, which involves considering "mental state only to the extent necessary to establish the existence of one or another of a small list of excusing or justifying defenses," and explaining the defendant's actions, which "searches for a full account of the factors—the motives, circumstances, and beliefs—that caused them."[68]

Neither approach is appropriate. Courts need to address the materiality issue head on. Doing so makes it less likely they will have to address reliability, helpfulness, and prejudice issues and more likely, in those cases where the evidence is material, that their analysis of those issues will be fully informed.

Immaterial Testimony That Some Courts Consider Material

The critics' demand for reliability has obscured what may be an even bigger failure on the part of some courts. No matter how reliable particular clinical testimony may be, it should be excluded if it is not pertinent under the relevant law. The point seems obvious, and many courts are quite aware of it,[69] but others ignore it, either because they become distracted by other evidentiary issues or because they simply don't understand the legal questions involved.

Two cases adequately illustrate this point. The first is the prosecution of Damian Williams and Henry Watson on twelve charges of aggravated mayhem, felony assault, and attempted murder.[70] Those charges arose out of the assault on Reginald Denny and seven others during the Los Angeles riots that followed the acquittal of the officers who beat Rodney King.[71] The lawyers in the Williams and Watson cases used a social scientist to support the argument, one that was largely successful,[72] that the defendants were caught up in the "group contagion" of anger and frustration following the King verdict, so much so that they did not possess the intent to harm.

The group contagion theory is not particularly well supported scientifically. But even assuming its reliability, the expert's testimony should still have been excluded on the ground that it was immaterial under the germane criminal law provisions. California law, like many states' laws, permits diminished capacity testimony only if offered to show the absence of "specific intent" (i.e., special or particularized intent).[73] Because both assault and mayhem are so-called general intent crimes in California,[74] the group contagion testimony is clearly immaterial on those charges. Attempted murder, in contrast, is a specific intent crime, requiring purpose to carry out a killing. Even here, however, testimony that Williams was "out of control" is not material; the mens rea for attempted murder does not require premeditation, only an intent to kill.[75] Killing out of "anger and frustration" is still intentional killing, even if done impulsively.

As a second, more common example of a situation where materiality analysis is crucial, consider *People v. Weinstein*,[76] in which the court permitted introduction of a brain scan of the defendant (using positron emission tomography, or PET) for the purpose of supporting an insanity defense. Under *Frye*, the court examined the extent to which professionals use the PET procedure and determined that it was reasonable for mental health professionals to rely on PET results. However, the court never focused on whether these results (which in this case showed an abnormal brain pattern) are material to M'Naghten analysis, which was New York's insanity test at the time. In fact, a good argument can be made that this evidence is not material to *any* defense based on cognitive impairment, whether it be lack of mens rea, the perception that self-defense is necessary, or M'Naghten's knowledge of wrongfulness test. Unless data exist showing that people with the defendant's brain abnormality act automatically, without forming intent or contemplating their actions, PET results are irrelevant to criminal responsibility.

The brain abnormality argument is similar to the argument defendants used to make about the XYY chromosomal abnormality. Although, in contrast to PET, this abnormality was at least shown to be correlated with heightened criminal propensity, it too is immaterial to criminal culpability. As many courts recognized, offenders with more maleness still intend to commit the crimes they commit and know that it is wrong to do so.[77] Even in a jurisdiction with a volitional prong to the insanity defense, XYY testimony is not material. That people with two Y chromosomes are more likely to commit a crime than people with only one does not mean the former are compelled to do so; at most, it means they have a stronger or more frequent urge to commit a crime than others. As Professor Michael Moore argues, because all behavior is caused by something—biology, environment, character, or situation—proof of causation alone cannot be proof of compulsion, nor can it support an excuse.[78] The consequence of this position is that, unless the causative agent renders one unable to control one's actions rationally, compulsion is not present.[79]

The same analysis can be directed at *any* psychological evidence that consists merely of a correlation between criminal activity and a certain trait (e.g., antisocial personality disorder, excess testosterone, low serotonin levels, or rotten social background). Nonetheless, not only courts, but many commentators seem to believe that evidence that simply describes a link between criminal behavior and an abnormality is material.[80] That approach disregards (and therefore undermines) the substantive criminal law.

One response to these observations, of course, is to advocate change in the substantive law. For instance, an insanity test that exculpates any crime that is the product of a mental disease (the so-called *Durham* test that at one time prevailed in the District of Columbia but today is the law only in New Hampshire)[81] might be sufficiently broad to permit brain scan and chromosomal testimony. But even that test requires a "mental disease or defect," which would have to be broadly defined to encompass these abnormalities. The fear of legal anarchy, discussed in connection with the rotten social background defense in *Alexander* case, makes widespread adoption of either change unlikely.

Sometimes, however, political and normative considerations trump that fear. Recall the law's approach to battered women testimony. Initially, courts typically held that psychological evidence about learned helplessness in battered women is material only in cases where the woman was imminently threatened by death or serious bodily harm at the hands of her victim. But many jurisdictions have abandoned this relatively objective approach and permitted acquittal on self-defense grounds, or at least a provocation defense, even when the perceived threats are more long term, and even when a person with average self-esteem and independence would have left the relationship.

This is not the place to elaborate on these difficult substantive issues. The important point for present purposes is that courts and legislatures need to think hard about the scope of the insanity defense, self-defense, and other defensive doctrines. They should not blithely allow admission of expert testimony simply because it comes from an expert.

Material Evidence That Some Courts Consider Immaterial

Just as some courts have been too willing to admit opinion evidence that is not material to accepted legal doctrine, other courts have been too eager to exclude, on lack of materiality grounds, expert testimony that is clearly material. The best example of this phenomenon is expert testimony about eyewitness miscues. Simply because information is general does not make it irrelevant to an individual situation. Certainly, testimony about weapons focus or cross-racial identifications is not useful in cases that don't involve weapons or cross-racial identifications. But assuming the expert evidence is linked to the characteristics of the crime, it should be considered pertinent. Many courts now recognize this point, not just with respect to eyewitness testimony but in connection with other types of social science testimony as well.[82] Indeed, some courts *limit* experts to nomothetic evidence and require that its application to the facts of the case be left up to the jury.[83] Although, as chapter 5 notes, there may be rare circumstances in which eyewitness testimony should be excluded because its general nature will lead to its misuse by the jury, it should usually be admitted over materiality objections.

Some courts have also too quickly dismissed clinical testimony about mens rea. Diminished capacity testimony may sometimes be unreliable and therefore inadmissible. But it is also often restricted in irrational ways. For instance, many jurisdictions limit diminished capacity testimony to murder cases (even though there are many other specific intent crimes), and several require proof that the defendant was suffering from a serious "mental disease or defect" (which in effect requires evidence of insanity for the testimony to be admissible).[84]

One of the latter cases was *United States v. Bright*,[85] where the defendant, who had tried to cash three checks made out to someone else that had been sent through the mail, was charged with violating a statute penalizing anyone who knowingly possesses stolen mail. Bright's defense was that she had not known the checks were stolen from the postal service; she testified that the checks had been given to her by a friend of her boyfriend and that she believed his statement that they were his, despite the fact that they were made out to a stranger. In support of this argument, she also sought to introduce the testimony of a psychologist, who would have testified that Bright had a passive-dependent personality disorder that made her particularly gullible to such statements because of a strong unconscious need to believe that men in her life would not take advantage of her.

In finding this testimony inadmissible, the court expressed some skepticism about its scientific basis (perhaps rightly so). It also noted (correctly) that Bright's mental condition, whatever it was, did not rise to the level of insanity. But it then combined that observation with the curious statement that the expert testimony was also inadmissible because it was not proffered to show that Bright lacked "the capacity to form a specific intent to commit the crime."[86] Apparently, the court wanted to establish a requirement that clinical testimony about mens rea must prove a mental condition that makes understanding an element of the crime impossible. But that is not the way the statute defines the crime. Rather, the crime with which Bright was charged required proof that, at the time of its commission, Bright knew that the checks were stolen from the mail. If she did not, she should not have been convicted, even if she was not insane and generally possessed the capacity to function in society. In holding as it did, the court was in essence allowing the prosecution to duck its obligation to prove the requisite mens rea (possessing mail known to be stolen) beyond a reasonable doubt.

The *Bright* court might have been primarily concerned about the reliability of the testimony. Those courts that limit diminished capacity testimony to murder cases might be worried that less serious crimes may not have an objectively defined lesser included offense for which a mentally impaired defendant can be convicted. Those are legitimate concerns. But they should be addressed directly (through exclusion on unreliability grounds and commitment statutes, respectively), not handled through suspect materiality rulings.

D. Conclusion

This brief survey of the cases shows that the law addressing the admissibility of clinical culpability testimony is in chaos. Courts consider a multiplicity of factors in making admissibility decisions, but not always the same ones, or with the same intensity. Two facts in particular should stand out from the foregoing analysis. First, as just discussed, many courts pay insufficient attention to the governing substantive law in determining the admissibility of clinical evidence about culpability. Second, as discussed earlier in the chapter, virtually all courts have avoided a close examination of its reliability. The next two chapters deal with the latter issue, which turns out to be highly complex.

3

The Case for Informed Speculation

Daubert is right: expert testimony should be reliable. Evidence that is unreliable has no probative value. Since 2000, of course, Rule 702 has explicitly recognized this point.

When the expert testimony is about criminal culpability, however, figuring out how reliability should be measured is no easy task. As section A of this chapter explains, the critics are accurate in their assessment that, when gauged "scientifically," the reliability of most clinical testimony about culpability is weak. Mental health professionals have a hard time even agreeing on simple diagnoses, much less on the motivations for crime. Most psychological theories about criminal behavior are untested, and most conclusions about criminal responsibility are, at best, informed speculation.

But that does not mean that expert testimony that is material to criminal responsibility issues should be inadmissible because it lacks probative value. I argue in this chapter that a failure to establish the scientific bona fides of past mental state testimony should not automatically result in exclusion, notwithstanding the teaching of *Daubert*. The first rationale for this position, presented in section B, is based on necessity. For legal, psychological, and practical reasons, defendants are often a poor source of information about their mental state at the time of the offense. Therefore, expert explications of that mental state should be permitted. Science-based expert testimony—that is, testimony based on research using controlled populations, adequate samples, and meaningful criterion variables—would be the best method of obtaining this explication. But past mental state simply cannot be studied with the same level of sophistication that external phenomena can be. Speculative clinical testimony, even if based only on experience and questionable research, is probably the best we can do for the foreseeable future.

A relaxed definition of reliability in assessing the admissibility of past mental state is also justifiable on jurisprudential grounds. In section C, I argue that the criminal defendant, the party most likely to use mental health professionals to support culpability claims, has a special entitlement to voice, stemming from both constitutional and procedural justice principles. That entitlement, I contend, should trump concerns about scientific reliability.

A. Clinical Testimony about Culpability: Simply Anecdata?

Daubert, it will be remembered, recognized a number of ways reliability can be gauged, including the scientific method, information on error rates, peer review, and the degree of general acceptance among the relevant experts. The *Daubert* Court appeared to place general acceptance at the bottom of the measurement hierarchy, and rightly so. The fact that professionals in the field routinely rely on particular theories or methodologies is useful information in determining admissibility, but it is no substitute for a straightforward assessment of accuracy, if such an assessment is possible. Thus, contrary to *Daubert*'s suggestion, the test developed in that case under Rule 702 is not always more "liberal" than the *Frye* test.

Indeed, in the behavioral science context, it is the latter test that is likely to produce more generous results. Testimony based on traditional psychiatric nosology is, almost by definition, generally accepted. If a particular diagnosis is in the American Psychiatric Association's *Diagnostic and Statistical Manual* it has survived considerable debate within the profession.[1] However, much of this diagnostic testimony is not very "reliable" in the usual meaning of that word. Whether that term is defined in its scientific sense to mean consistency of result or in the sense the Court appeared to use it, to mean a measure of accuracy or validity, behavioral science testimony, even of the traditional variety, usually does not fare well under a reliability standard.

Consider first studies of interrater reliability using the criteria found in the *DSM*. Although initial research using the third edition of that work, conducted in the laboratory, provided encouraging results, field research indicated that mental health professionals involved in everyday practice disagreed more than half the time even on major diagnostic categories such as schizophrenia and organic brain syndrome.[2] Diagnostic opinions concerning people who are not psychotic were even less reliable in the scientific sense.[3] The reliability of determinations about symptoms, such as whether a person is engaging in bizarre thought processes, was low as well.[4]

The advent of *DSM-IV* in 1994 and accompanying structured interview formats have clearly improved both diagnostic and symptom assessment.[5]

But even with the reduction in criterion variance produced by these new developments, agreement among trained clinicians can fall below 70 percent, and agreement among those who have not been specially trained is likely to be much lower.[6] If the question is simply whether a person is grossly impaired at the time of the offense (without reference to a specific diagnosis), agreement is much better,[7] but for reasons provided in chapter 5's discussion about the helpfulness factor, that type of assessment may not be of much assistance to legal fact finders.

Achieving diagnostic reliability is only half the battle in any event. As Grisso has noted, "The law does not presume that any psychiatric diagnostic condition is synonymous with legal incompetence [the term Grisso uses to refer to any legal doctrine, including insanity]."[8] To more directly address issues that are legally relevant at criminal trials, experts need to go beyond diagnosis and provide some insight into the reasons for criminal behavior. Unfortunately, dissonance among professionals is even more likely when they try to explain, rather than just describe, behavior, both because there are so many competing theories—genetic, Freudian, behavioral, social, and so on—and because even within a given theoretical framework there is considerable dispute. As Ronald Rychlak and Joseph Rychlak (a lawyer and a psychologist) have noted, "There are hundreds of 'mainstream' theories of human behavior" and, partly as a result, "psychiatry and psychology have poor records when it comes to theories relating to free will, personal choice, and self-determination."[9]

If reliability is low, validity is suspect as well, because a lack of agreement between two raters means that at least one of them is wrong. Even if reliability is high, however, validity may be poor; unanimity of opinion may hide the fact that all raters are wrong. Unfortunately, the validity of psychiatric opinion is hard to gauge. Diagnosis is merely a hypothetical construct; it lacks clear objective referents. Those studies that attempt to assess criterion validity (e.g., whether those who receive a particular diagnosis have the same traits) and construct or discriminant validity (whether a diagnosis avoids significant overlap with other diagnoses) have produced less than satisfying results. As Stephen Morse has said, "I think it is fair to conclude that most established syndromes, such as the disorders *DSM-IV* includes, have not been strongly validated. Validating syndromes is difficult; criterion validity data are often mixed, and discriminant validity is quite weak. These disappointing results are not surprising because understanding of the underlying causal mechanisms for most disorders eludes us and such understanding is the ultimate key to validity."[10] Even many symptoms—such as whether a person is depressed, anxious, or suffering from low self-esteem—are unverifiable in the same way a physical fact is, because the terms themselves are so amorphous and subjective; for instance, more than fourteen different modifiers of the term "depression" have appeared in the psychiatric literature.[11]

Attempts to explain the causes of behavior (e.g., unconscious conflicts, chemical imbalances, abuse as a child, relationship with parents) are even more speculative. Most opinion testimony of this type is based on untested theories, or theories that have been subjected only to the most preliminary scientific inquiry. Paul Meehl's highly critical comment twenty years ago is still true today: "Most so-called 'theories' in the soft areas of psychology . . . are scientifically unimpressive and technologically worthless."[12] In many of these situations, forensic clinicians can at best offer only *anecdata*: information obtained through experience in dealing with psychological problems, reading about case studies, and extrapolation from the theoretical speculations of others.

None of this is meant to suggest that scientific research about past mental state is impossible or should not be attempted. It does suggest that hard scientific evidence that directly addresses the issues raised by criminal defense doctrines is unlikely to be produced in the near future. As Meehl concludes, "It may be that the nature of the subject matter in most of personology and social psychology is inherently incapable of permitting theories with sufficient conceptual power (especially mathematical development) to yield the kinds of strong refuters expected by Popperians, Bayesians, and unphilosophical scientists in developed fields like chemistry."[13] More specific to the issues addressed in this chapter are the comments of Grisso, who has examined the scientific basis of forensic psychology in a number of areas. Singling out criminal responsibility assessments as a particularly primitive research domain, he concluded in 1996, "There is little reason to believe that past meager advances in performing evaluations for criminal responsibility will be augmented in the near future," both because the relevant "theoretical and operational definitions are difficult to identify" and because "we have not yet demonstrated our ability even to make . . . basic retrospective inferences [such as whether the defendant was under the influence of a mental disorder at the time of the offense] reliably and validly."[14]

Given these deficiencies in the behavioral sciences, much opinion testimony from psychologists and psychiatrists might be considered unreliable if that word is defined in a strict *Daubertian* sense. As Michael Graham put it, "The testability or falsifiability and potential error rate factors for appraising [social science evidence] will rarely be sufficiently present to meet the *Daubert* standard."[15] In any event, I will assume that such testimony is frequently of questionable, or at least not demonstrable, validity.

When the expert testimony concerns criminal responsibility, however, that fact should not always be a bar to admissibility. Whereas some sort of scientific validity test may be appropriate with respect to other types of expert opinion, *Daubert/Kumho* and other screening standards should be read to permit past mental state testimony even when it is not demonstrably reliable. The following sections explain why.

B. The Necessity Rationale

The necessity rationale is well-recognized in evidence law. For instance, some types of hearsay evidence, although less trustworthy than other evidence, are nonetheless admissible when the declarant is unavailable.[16] The necessity argument in this context is analogous. Past mental states, which are the basis for all culpability assessments, cannot be studied scientifically in the same way many other phenomena can be. Therefore, the necessity rationale dictates, defendants should be permitted to use nonscientific evidence to prove assertions about past mental state.

Scientific information about past mental state is hard to come by for three reasons. First, these states are not objective facts the existence of which can be proven in the same way the occurrence of an act can be proven. Second, even if that obstacle is overcome, obtaining useful empirical information about legally relevant past mental states is virtually impossible, and certainly much more difficult than studying the psychological correlates of actions. Third, any research that is produced will usually lack "fit," the word the Court used in *Daubert* to capture the gray area between materiality and probative value that deals with whether evidence that appears to be logically connected to a proposition is in fact linked closely enough to make it probative.[17] After expanding on these three reasons, this section ends with an explanation of why this state of affairs should lead not to exclusion but to a flexible assessment of probative value when expert testimony on past mental state is involved.

The Elusiveness of Past Mental States

The first assertion is well explicated by Professor Andrew Taslitz. Drawing on feminist literature and other sources,[18] Taslitz argues that we can never discover "objective truth" about past mental states in the same way we can know whether an event occurred. We can "know" such mental states only through acts of interpretation that inevitably differ depending on a host of factors, including the identity of the observer and the time at which the mental state is observed.[19] Thus, for instance, even the person whose mental state is in question, if asked to report what it was at a particular point in time (the type of report on which psychological evidence usually relies), engages in interpretation. As Taslitz notes, "Memory itself is an assertion, a self-report, which we play an active role in constructing. Our memories never involve solely historical truths, for we seek to create an account of the past consistent with a preconceived cognitive or moral scheme. Memory is thus at least partly a created narrative."[20]

The difficulty of ascertaining past mental state is exacerbated by the possibility that an actor may not "know" his or her mental state even at the time it is occurring. As Taslitz puts it, "We may be ambivalent, desiring and spurning simultaneously, leaving us confused; we may deceive ourselves out of fear, guilt, or self-protection."[21] This may be particularly true in criminal situations of the type normally the subject of clinical testimony, where motivations, thoughts, and urges are likely to be jumbled together rather than straightforward and logical.

When the fact finder is a third party rather than the subject, the truth about mental states becomes even more contingent. Triers of fact attempting to discern the individual's mental state add their own interpretive gloss to the evidence presented. As Taslitz states, "When jurors name a mental state as 'premeditation,' 'heat of passion,' or a 'belief in the imminent need to use deadly force in self defense,' they are crafting an interpretation that partly embodies their own assumptions, attitudes, and beliefs."[22]

In short, although ascertaining objective truth might be possible with respect to acts, *narrative thinking* dominates attempts to reconstruct mental state.[23] Any description of mental state is closer to a story than a depiction of an observable event. Science cannot tell us the truth about past mental states because science is meant to identify objective reality, not interpretations of reality. At most, science can help us decide whether acts and other types of more objectively discernable facts have occurred.

The Measurement Problem

Even if, in theory, particular past mental states can be said to "exist" in some objective sense, as a practical matter science will often not be up to the task of measuring them. The criminal law asks some very difficult questions: Did the defendant "know" or "appreciate" that his conduct at the time of the offense was wrong? Was he "compelled" to commit the criminal act? Did the defendant "premeditate" the crime? Was she aware of the risks her conduct posed? Did the defendant really feel that harm was imminent and that violence was the only way to prevent it? These questions have traditionally been answered by inferring mental state from the defendant's conduct and statements at the time of the offense. But left to their own devices, judges and juries are likely to assume that a person intends the consequences of his or her acts, knows that killing a person is wrong, and realizes that there are alternatives to killing a batterer. As chapter 5 develops in more detail, that is precisely why defense attorneys turn to mental health professionals: to help overcome those preconceptions.

So what can mental health professionals tell us, based on scientific study? For obvious reasons, crimes cannot be replicated in the lab, where variables such as degree of psychosis or the amount of precrime battering by the victim can be controlled for variance. Even if we could do so, accurate measurement or even approximation of degrees of awareness, fear, or compulsion is not possible. This latter point is not an assertion that perpetrators can't provide information about mental states or that we cannot gain access to them in some other fashion (that was the gist of the previous section). Rather, it is a recognition that we don't have a "degree-of-awareness meter" or an "urge gauge" that can measure the intensity of mental phenomena. The philosopher Alexander Rosenberg has noted that measuring "what a person believes by some distinct effect of the belief, in the way that a thermometer measures heat by its quite distinct effect . . . is impossible."[24] Similarly, the criminal law scholar Stephen Morse has pointed out that "there is no scientific measure of the strength of urges."[25] Yet that is precisely the information behavioral scientists need to answer the criminal law's questions.

This point about past mental state, and why it is different from assessments of conduct, can be illustrated more clearly through the work of Professors Thomas D. Lyon and Jonathan J. Koehler. Lyon and Koehler argue that the probative value of a given type of expert evidence can often be gauged by what they call the "relevance ratio."[26] The relevance ratio is simply the ratio between the proportion of cases in which a symptom is observed in the population of interest and the proportion of cases in which the same symptom is observed in the rest of the population. For instance, assume that 60 percent of abused children suffer from symptoms X, Y, and Z, and that 20 percent of children who are not abused suffer from symptoms X, Y, and Z. The relevance ratio in this case is 3:1 (60 percent/20 percent), meaning that proof that a child has these three symptoms has significant probative value on the issue of whether the child was abused.

Lyon and Koehler argue that the relevance ratio is "the most efficient way to think about evidentiary relevance."[27] Assuming that methodological problems do not render the information relied on invalid, this assessment seems to be on target; the ratio is an eminently sensible way of evaluating the probative value of evidence. If the subject population is no more likely than the general population to have the symptoms (i.e., the relevance ratio is around 1), then testimony to the contrary should not be considered a valid description of the relationship of the symptoms to the subject population. If the ratio is greater than 1, on the other hand, the evidence has some tendency to prove a fact at issue, the definition of relevance/probative value. In many types of expert testimony situations, then, relevance ratio analysis will be a useful way of conducting the reliability assessment demanded by *Daubert*, and this book will employ it as such.

Consider, however, the difficulty of gathering information necessary to calculate the relevance ratio where psychological evidence about past mental state is involved. For instance, when self-defense is asserted in a battered woman case, one would need to determine the proportion of battered women who kill their spouse believing they have no alternatives and the proportion of nonbattered women who kill their spouse believing they have no alternatives. Without any other information, the most plausible conclusion is that, of the two groups, the battered women are more likely to feel that they have no options. That kind of thinking, though, is not science; the scientific method would require large enough samples of both groups being compared and the development of reliable methods of obtaining the relevant information about them.

In conducting such research, one significant problem would be ensuring that no other variables taint the comparison; that is, the two groups should be similar in all significant ways except with respect to whether they were battered. This problem, however, confronts any attempt to use the relevance ratio.[28] A second problem, and one that is much more likely to afflict the study of past mental state phenomena, is measuring the dependent variable. Even assuming that past mental state is an objective fact rather than an interpretive story, how does one accurately tell whether a female killer believed she had no alternative way of avoiding serious physical harm at the time she killed? The researcher can, of course, ask the woman whether she felt that the killing was necessary. Even ignoring the possible inaccuracy of self-serving statements made about an event that may have occurred months ago, gauging the all-important variable—the intensity of the woman's belief in the necessity of her action—and then comparing it to the beliefs of other women is all but impossible. The same obstacles are likely to confront those who want to study the degree of legally relevant impairment associated with psychosis, personality disorder, genetic deficits, and other dysfunctions.

To put the point another way, even if research relevant to past mental state can be characterized as science, it is science that is so likely to be tainted by methodological flaws that, in effect, it is no different from interpretation and storytelling. In contrast, research conducted to assist in proof of acts would not need to determine the strength or existence of slippery phenomena like beliefs, emotions, or urges in the past. In the child abuse example given earlier, the task would be to locate abused and nonabused children and then catalogue their symptoms. This task would be challenging, but more of the symptoms will be objective (e.g., inability to sleep, fall-off in school work) and all will be discernable at the time of the evaluation. Thus cataloguing them would be much easier than ascertaining the intensity of past mental states, or whether they existed at all.

The Fit Problem

Some experimental designs can avoid the difficulties associated with pinning down a person's past mental state. Illustrating a sort of evidentiary Heisenberg principle, however, it is precisely because they avoid those difficulties that they inevitably suffer significantly in terms of fit, a problem that *Daubert* itself recognized.[29] For example, social scientists might examine whether people with certain types of conditions are more likely to commit crime than matched control groups, or whether battered women who kill their spouse are different in objectively measurable ways than battered women who leave, rather than kill, their spouse. Neither of these correlational studies necessarily requires assessment of past mental state. For that very reason, however, confirmatory findings are unlikely to be useful on past mental state issues. As already noted in the discussion of materiality, a finding that people with persecutory delusions, an extra Y chromosome, or a diagnosis of psychopathy commit more crime than a control group tells us very little about whether the former groups experience stronger urges or more cognitive impairment at the time of their offense; at best, such results tell us that their condition was a predisposing factor for crime, just as being a male or being poor is. A finding that battered women with the fewest job options or the greatest number of young children are more likely to kill their spouse says nothing about the extent to which the former group killed out of fear—which might form the basis for a self-defense claim—or instead out of anger or frustration.

Even when correlational studies do manage to address past mental state issues directly, their results are a weak fit. For instance, Steury and Choinski found in their sample of criminal defendants with serious mental illness that 22 percent of patient defendants and 14 percent of nonpatient defendants used "gratuitous" violence.[30] Similarly, Taylor found that 10 percent of psychotic individuals who committed a crime were "motiveless" compared to 6 percent of nonpsychotic individuals.[31] Leaving aside the difficulty of deciding when violence is gratuitous or motiveless (the measurement issue addressed earlier), these types of findings are almost useless as a way of determining mental state in an individual case, both because the percentage of patients who committed crime gratuitously or without motive is so small and because of the small differences found between the experimental and control groups. Thus, although an expert in a case involving a patient could say, based on the Steury and Choinski study, that patients are one and a half times as likely as nonpatients to engage in gratuitous violence, that and similar conclusions that could be drawn from the study are probably more misleading than helpful on issues like insanity or intent.

Analogue research is probably the most fruitful line of scientific inquiry into past mental state, but it too has significant problems. Such research might investigate, for instance, the extent to which people with psychosis feel "compelled" or are confused about reality in noncriminal situations, compared to a matched control group.[32] In theory, this type of research could provide valuable insights into how people with certain traits or experiences—mental illness, battering by one's spouse, abuse as a child—perceive and react to events, from which we might be willing to infer perceptions, beliefs, and feelings during a crime. Moreover, because researchers can collect information about mental states at the time they occur (something that is impossible in the typical crime situation), the memory problem is minimized.

The measurement problem discussed earlier still exists, however (*how* compelled or confused is the person?). More important, as with the correlational research, the usefulness of these studies may be compromised by the lack of fit. How people feel and behave in relatively mundane circumstances is unlikely to generalize well to the usually dramatic and often unique circumstances associated with criminal actions. Consider, for instance, these observations from Stephen Morse: "Even the craziest persons seem to behave quite normally or rationally a great deal of the time, especially if there is good reason to do so. On at least some occasions, including some instances when they are behaving crazily, crazy persons are clearly capable of playing by the usual rules. Nor do they always act on the basis of their crazy reasons."[33]

As should be clear from this brief discussion, the fit issue is actually better analyzed under the first and fourth components of admissibility analysis—materiality and prejudicial impact—than as an aspect of probative value. Although some of the actual and hypothesized studies just described might produce unreliable results, others may be relatively good at measuring what they purport to measure (e.g., correlations between crime and physiological symptoms or situational factors). The more significant problem is their weak logical relationship to past mental state culpability issues, and thus their potential for sending legal fact finders down the wrong path. More will be said about this problem in chapter 5.

Arguments against the Necessity Rationale

The necessity argument is that, given the pitiful progress of past mental state research, defendants should not be required to demonstrate the scientific validity of expert opinion they proffer on that topic. But of course, one could draw precisely the opposite conclusion. If one accepts the conclusions drawn above, jurisdictions that abide by *Daubert* have two choices with respect to past mental state evidence: they can either make accommodations for it (through an exception to *Daubert* or a flexible interpretation of it), or they can prohibit it. At least three reasons have been advanced for taking the latter approach, but none of them withstands analysis.

The first argument is that, without such a prohibition, there is no incentive even to attempt truly scientific investigation of past mental state.[34] Why go to the trouble of grappling with the methodological obstacles described above if judges are willing to admit more speculative opinion?

This argument assumes, of course, that true scientific research relevant to past mental state is feasible and that its results will be superior to clinical anecdata. This chapter has questioned both assumptions. Even granting them, however, the argument exaggerates the power of the courts and the gullibility of legal fact finders. First, the courts are seldom the only market for scientific research relevant to past mental state. For instance, vigorous study of battered women and of mentally ill people who are violent has occurred independently of any demands by the criminal defense bar and despite judicial acceptance of opinion evidence on those topics. And in those few instances where evidence of past mental state is custom-made for the courtroom, the skepticism of judges and juries provides a powerful inducement to base it on solid grounds. Rarely noted by those who bemoan junk testimony in criminal cases is the fact that legal decision makers are virtually never impressed by novel syndromes that have little basis in logic or the literature.[35] The pace of scientific inquiry into past mental state, to the extent such inquiry is possible, will depend on factors other than the courts' rulings on its admissibility.

A second possible argument for prohibiting opinion evidence about past mental state involves assuring adversarial equipoise. Given the fact that insanity, diminished capacity, and other past mental state doctrines are defenses, only the defendant is likely to present expert evidence of past mental state in his or her case in chief. In contrast, the type of behavioral science testimony the prosecution is most likely to offer in its case in chief consists of assertions that the defendant meets a criminal "profile" (e.g., a constellation of traits characteristic of an abusive parent or rapist). Because the latter evidence aims at proving the act element rather than the mental state element of the crime, its admissibility would not be relaxed on a necessity rationale. Yet that result might strike some as unfair, because it seems to favor the defense over the prosecution.

If one agrees with the previous assertions about the unique difficulties of researching past mental state, however, an imbalance in the admissibility thresholds for past mental state and profile evidence makes sense. The research necessary to construct a criminal profile does not rely on ascertaining amorphous mental states at the time of a crime, but rather links observable acts (e.g., rape) with other observable events or current mental states (e.g., abuse as a child, previous rapes by the offender, lack of remorse). In other words, it conforms to the typical scientific research model attempting to predict a given type of behavior. Thus, this type of behavioral information is eminently more scientifically testable and should not be evaluated under a relaxed admissibility standard, at least on necessity grounds.

It also should be noted that, in those rare instances when prosecutors rely on opinion evidence about past mental state in their case-in-chief, as they do, for instance, when proffering expert testimony about rape trauma syndrome to show that a victim did not consent to intercourse, the necessity rationale advanced here would apply to the prosecution as well. Furthermore, of course, if the defense relies on past mental state evidence, the prosecution should be permitted to rebut with the same type of evidence. As is true in other evidentiary contexts,[36] if the defendant opens the door, the prosecution should be able to enter as well.

Finally, when the defense relies on expert testimony to address something other than past mental state, it would not be exempted from a strict application of *Daubert*. Thus, for instance, if the defense wants to use an expert to show the defendant is a passive individual who is unlikely to commit assault, *Daubert* should apply with full force. The fulcrum of the necessity rationale is the type of testimony proffered, not the party proffering it.

The final argument in favor of rejecting the necessity rationale in connection with expert testimony about past mental state is simply that defendants do not *need* it to make their case; in other words, the necessity rationale does not really apply in this context. Advocates of this position point out that there are at least two other sources of information about past mental state. The first is lay testimony, primarily from the defendant himself or herself. The second is expert testimony that eschews opinion and is devoted solely to providing relevant psychological facts.

The most obvious source of information about past mental state is the defendant. Reliance on this source, however, is problematic for several reasons. First, the Fifth Amendment may prevent compelling the defendant to undergo evaluation or to testify.[37] Second, defendants asserting past mental state defenses often have difficulty communicating; although they must be competent to stand trial, their ability to recount their feelings and beliefs at the time of the offense will often be compromised, given the low threshold for competency.[38] Third, and most important, even fully competent defendants may not be aware of, or may be unwilling to admit to, crucial aspects of their past mental state. For instance, defendants may not suspect the effects of biological, childhood, and situational variables on their behavior, deny they have mental or relationship problems that in fact explain their behavior, or simply claim amnesia.[39] The best way to obtain all the relevant facts about past mental state is to rely on mental health professionals, who have special training in and skill at eliciting information from incompetent, reluctant, or oblivious subjects.

This latter ability suggests a second source of information about past mental state other than opinion testimony—expert description of relevant psychological facts. Psychological testimony, like any expert testimony, can be conceptualized in terms of multiple levels of inference, with each succeeding level incorporating a greater degree of generalization. Imagine, for instance, a case in which a forensic clinician conducts an interview of a defendant who is charged with assault and whose attorney is asserting an insanity defense, in part because of the defendant's bizarreness and in part because the victim of the assault swears he does not know the defendant and has no idea why he was attacked. During the interview, the defendant appears to think he is talking to people who in fact are not there, makes irrelevant and incomprehensible statements under his breath, and insists that the person he assaulted was an "archfiend" who was trying to hurt him. Based on this information, the clinician might infer (1) a particular symptomatology (the defendant was delusional at the time of the offense); (2) a diagnosis (the defendant was suffering from schizophrenia at the time of the offense); (3) the presence of legally relevant impairments (the defendant thought killing the victim was justified); and (4) an ultimate legal conclusion (the defendant was insane at the time of the offense). Clinical testimony today often includes all five levels of testimony (the facts plus the four levels of inference). However, one could argue, as Stephen Morse has,[40] that the defendant does not need this inferential testimony to lay out the case for insanity. The mental health professional's factual information about the defendant's behavior during the interview (together with any third-party observations) is probably crucial, but the rest of the expert's testimony—the opinion—might be considered surplusage.

Even in the simple example given here, however, consider how much more the defense could tell the judge and jury if allowed to use a seasoned forensic clinician. First, such an expert could provide information that bolsters the defendant's report about the offense. For instance, the expert might be able to tell the fact finder, based on his or her own experience and any analogue studies that exist, that people with schizophrenia often erroneously believe people want to hurt them and that they have difficulty attending to countervailing facts, thus combating concerns about malingering. The expert also could describe, again based on experience or a structured interview format, why he or she thinks the defendant is suffering from schizophrenia, a diagnosis necessary to make the experiential information and analogue studies relevant. Finally, the expert can conjecture, based on experience with mentally ill people, about the strength of the defendant's paranoia and the nature of his thought process at the time of the offense. This information—much of it anecdata that are idiopathic in nature—is speculative, but it is also plausible and not clearly wrong, given the vagaries of pinning down a person's past mental state.

A rigid interpretation of *Daubert*, however, might bar some or all of this testimony. The testimony that is based on experience and clinical intuition is not amenable to scientific verification, and the rest of the testimony is of questionable relevance. Admittedly, some of the expert's inferences could derive from hard data—the aforementioned analogue studies and diagnostic impressions based on structured interviews. But because most people with paranoid psychosis do not commit violent acts, the analogue studies will be a weak fit. And even standardized diagnoses can have high error rates or questionable pedigrees; as one court stated: "Based upon the procedure utilized to enter a proposed malady into the DSM-IV, there is some question as to whether some of the possible diagnoses listed in the DSM-IV could meet the admissibility requirements of [*Daubert*]."[41] Most important, testimony at level 4, about the degree of impairment at the time of the offense, will inevitably be unverifiable, and thus susceptible to a *Daubert* challenge.

Morse assures us that, if useful hard data cannot be obtained, a rich description of the defendant's behavior will be sufficient; because culpability is ultimately a normative decision, he argues, lay decision makers armed with the facts can arrive at a just conclusion, using their "common sense."[42] That phrase has a nice ring to it, but unfortunately, common sense can easily be tainted by superstition, fear, and popular misconceptions. Michael Perlin has documented the many common (erroneous) beliefs that laypeople have about mental illness: that it is often faked, that mental problems are not as severe as physical illnesses, and that defendants should "look crazy" if they really are insane.[43] As he notes, claims of insanity encounter "pervasive judicial hostility" unless the defendant shows "flagrant psychotic symptomatology," behaves like a "wild beast," or can demonstrate "organic roots" to his or her mental problems. Even in cases involving straightforward claims of serious mental illness, then, something more than a description of behavior is needed to counter the myths and temper the hostility that permeate deliberations on past mental state issues.

In other, less typical cases, an account limited to the bare facts may be even less edifying. My coauthors and I have described elsewhere a number of such cases:

> A man with no prior history of crime or mental illness who committed a gruesome sexual assault, during which he spoke in an unusual voice and referred to himself as a "Mexican stud" even though he was Caucasian. The expert provided a psychodynamic explanation for the rape, based on the defendant's relationship with his mother.[44]
>
> A man who claimed he killed his employer after he argued with him because "devils" in his head commanded him to do so. The expert opined that the defendant would have psychically disintegrated had he not committed the crime, an explanation that the trial judge stated was the only "reasonable" one for the crime (although he also stated, "Whether it was right or not, I don't know").[45]
>
> A woman who claimed that she did not realize a check she cashed was forged because she believed her boyfriend's statement that the check was legitimate (the *Bright* case described in chapter 2). The expert described the symptoms of the passive-dependent personality to bolster the defendant's supergullibility claim.
>
> A juvenile charged with breaking and entering and rape, whose expert presented plausible but speculative expert testimony at sentencing that his "impulse control may often be tenuous, at least partially because of his poor verbal skills and resulting inability to label feelings."[46]

Had these defendants been relegated to relying on their counterintuitive and self-serving claims about their mental state or an expert's repetition of the supporting facts without additional testimony as to why those claims might make clinical sense, they would have been prevented from providing a plausible, coherent interpretation of their conduct.

In all of these cases, hard data either did not exist or were only remotely relevant to the issue at hand. Even if such data had fit the facts, however, limiting defendants to such evidence would seriously undermine their ability to tell their own, personalized story. Meehl, a long-time advocate of scientific investigation, has nonetheless confessed that, when trying to explain behavior, "I would take Freud's clinical observations over most people's t tests [tests of statistical significance] any time."[47] This is a particularly dramatic admission, given the fact that Freud's conjectures on psychodynamics and the unconscious may well be one of the "best examples" of unfalsifiable theory.[48]

In short, criminal defendants need idiopathic, inferential, and speculative clinical testimony to relate their story. A rigid application of *Daubert* would deprive them of their ability to do so. The next section explains why this position is more than just a policy choice.

C. Voice and Appearance

The law, as laid down in *Daubert*, is that scientific validity is king. However, there are at least two principles, one firmly embedded in our jurisprudence and one an important utilitarian consideration, that suggest that deference to that goal should not always be our top priority as a normative matter. The first principle is the litigant's fundamental interest in having his or her full story told to the fact finder. The second is the litigant's and society's interest in a process that appears fair and just. Both of these principles have special implications in the context of criminal adjudications focused on the defendant's mental state at the time of the offense.

The Right to Voice

Ours is a society based on individualism and respect for diversity. We place supreme value on the dignity of human beings as individuals and on equality. Perhaps more than any other right, we treasure freedom of speech as a way of assuring that these principles are honored. Speech allows individuals to express their individuality and to promote their diverse points of view.

When the person who wishes to engage in such expression is a criminal defendant, special considerations arise. Not only are the First Amendment's protections triggered, but the Sixth Amendment's guarantees of the right to confront accusers and the right to present evidence are implicated as well.[49] Additionally, and of great importance in the present setting, the criminal defendant has a right to testify.

The 1987 U.S. Supreme Court decision that finally confirmed the constitutional basis of this right, *Rock v. Arkansas*, is instructive. After holding that the right to present evidence, the Due Process Clause, and the right to (decide whether to) remain silent all support a defendant's entitlement to take the stand, the Court in *Rock* had to determine whether an Arkansas statute barring testimony by a defendant who had been subjected to hypnosis was a permissible restriction on the right. Conceding that memories induced through hypnosis can be fabricated, a five-member majority nonetheless found that a per se rule such as Arkansas's is unconstitutional. The statute did not permit the trial court to take into account the reasons for undergoing hypnosis, the circumstances under which it took place, or any independent verification of the information it produced. Nor did it recognize that cross-examination, expert testimony, and cautionary instructions might counteract the inadequacies of posthypnotic testimony. A case-by-case approach is mandated, Justice Blackmun reasoned for the Court, unless the state can show "that hypnotically enhanced testimony is always so untrustworthy and so immune to the traditional means of evaluating credibility that it should disable a defendant from presenting her version of the events for which she is on trial."[50]

Rock's holding is a strong statement that defendants should be allowed to tell their story unless it is completely untrustworthy or so immune to the weapons of the adversarial process that its questionable nature is not likely to be exposed. Indeed, compared to the tests for expert psychological testimony discussed in Chapter 1, it may even surpass the 401/403 balancing test in laxness. However, *Rock* did not specifically deal with the admissibility of a defendant's story when it is told by an expert. Thus, when *Daubert* was decided six years later, one had to wonder how the two cases would be reconciled.

A partial answer to that question came in *United States v. Scheffer*, decided five years after *Daubert*. The defendant in *Scheffer*, charged with taking methamphetamines, wanted to introduce the results of a polygraph test that indicated a "nondeceptive" response when he denied drug use. In another close decision,[51] the Supreme Court upheld the trial court's rejection of the polygraph evidence. Justice Thomas explained, "There is simply no consensus that polygraph evidence is reliable. To this day, the scientific community remains extremely polarized about the reliability of polygraph techniques."[52] This language suggested that *Daubert* should trump *Rock* when a defendant wants to rely on suspect expert testimony.

Three other aspects of the opinion undercut that interpretation of *Scheffer*, however. First, as further justification for the ruling, Thomas made much of the assertion that polygraphs have an "aura of near infallibility." Jurors, said Thomas, may "give excessive weight to the opinions of the polygrapher, clothed as they are in scientific expertise."[53] Whatever the truth of this conclusion with respect to polygraph evidence,[54] clinical testimony about past mental state clearly does not possess the sirenic powers to which Thomas alludes. As noted earlier and explored more fully in chapter 5, jurors usually reject such evidence when offered by the defendant; at the least, it is more susceptible to rational assessment and dissection through cross-examination than the opinions of the polygrapher.

In the same passage, Thomas stressed that the polygraph expert is focused on credibility alone: "Unlike other expert witnesses who testify about factual matters outside the jurors' knowledge, such as analysis of fingerprints, ballistics, or DNA found at a crime scene, a polygraph expert can supply the jury only with another opinion, in addition to its own, about whether the witness was telling the truth." Echoing some of the lower court opinions discussed in chapter 2, he reminded that "a fundamental premise of our criminal system is that the jury is the lie detector."[55] Again, whatever one may think about psychological assessment of truth telling, psychological testimony interpreting past mental state, in an effort to evaluate culpability, does not raise the threat to the jury's lie detection duties that seemed to concern the *Scheffer* Court.

More important still is the way *Scheffer* distinguished *Rock*. Thomas quoted from *Rock* the statement that an accused ought to be allowed "to present his own version of events in his own words."[56] Rejection of the polygraph results in *Scheffer* did not violate this precept, Thomas stated, because the trial court "heard all the relevant details of the charged offense from the perspective of the accused." The defendant was not precluded from introducing "factual evidence" or "exercis[ing] his choice to convey his version of the facts"; rather, he was barred "merely from introducing expert opinion testimony to bolster his own credibility."[57] In contrast, expert testimony on past mental state presents facts, and inferences based on those facts, that not only support the defendant's story but may be the only source for it. Prohibiting such evidence would, in effect, prevent the defendant from giving "his own version of events in his own words."

Taken together, *Rock* (affirmatively) and *Scheffer* (by negative inference) reinforce the idea that psychological testimony, when presented on behalf of a criminal defendant seeking to mitigate culpability, deserves to be heard even if its validity cannot be proven scientifically. Indeed, these cases suggest that even *Frye*'s general acceptance test may not be required. Concluding otherwise would deprive the criminal defendant of the voice the Constitution guarantees.

The Importance of Appearance

Another reason for applying flexible evidentiary standards to psychological testimony proffered by criminal defendants is a utilitarian version of the voice argument: the goal of promoting a system that *appears* fair. This latter goal is important because societal respect for the criminal justice system helps ensure cooperation with the authorities and encourages obedience to the criminal law generally. As Tom Tyler has demonstrated, people obey the law not just out of fear of punishment but because they want to be law-abiding citizens.[58] From this premise, Robinson and Darley have argued that a substantial gap between community sentiment and the criminal law may reduce the latter's "moral credibility," and thus people's willingness to comply with it.[59] In short, to the extent the criminal justice system ignores the moral consensus of the laity, it reduces its power to command law-abiding behavior. On this view, preventing criminal defendants from telling the best story they can—which might be the impact of a ban on nonscientific psychological testimony—would detract from the system's legitimacy and its ability to exact compliance with the law.

The delegitimizing effects of exclusion are most easily imagined among those who are litigants in the system. The procedural justice literature has clearly established that a procedure that gives participants a full opportunity to present their version of the facts enhances perceptions of fairness, satisfaction with outcomes, and respect for the process.[60] Conversely, a procedure that does not do so is more likely to create antipathy toward the system among those it has frustrated, with the concomitant repercussions that Robinson and Darley hypothesize.

More speculative is the suggestion that denying criminal defendants the ability to tell their stories through experts would similarly affect the perceptions and behavior of the public at large. Many members of the public undoubtedly think that psychological testimony is mumbo jumbo, and a good percentage of this group probably are also hostile to the legal doctrines that give rise to it.[61] To such people, an individual who has done the crime should do the time, regardless of any exculpatory mental state; indeed, for them, a prohibition on psychological testimony might lead to more faith in the fairness of the system, not less.

Consider as a counterexample, however, testimony about battered woman syndrome. As recounted in chapter 2, a quarter-century ago most courts refused to hear such evidence because it suggested that women were justified in killing their batterer even when they were not in imminent danger at the time of the killing. Clearly, battered women were asking for a significant modification of traditional self-defense doctrine. Feminists and others, however, made persuasive arguments that the battered woman's reality was different from the ordinary person's. Just as important, the crusade against intrafamilial abuse became a cause célèbre. Today, not only do most courts admit testimony about battered woman syndrome, but many states require its admission by statute. Governors have commuted the sentences of battered women convicted for murder, and states have created clemency boards with the mission of making amends to such women.[62]

If the criminal justice system were suddenly to put a stop to testimony about the reasons battered woman kill their batterer on the ground that its basis has not been sufficiently tested scientifically, an uproar would surely follow. The perception, if not the reality, would be that battered women were being denied a vital means of telling their stories, at the same time other (male) defendants are allowed to tell theirs. To avoid such damage to the political viability of the system, one might conscientiously endorse continued admission of this syndrome testimony, despite its suspect nature.

Such a stance might also be justifiable in cases involving soft opinion testimony about the past mental state of those with mental retardation, serious mental illness, and at least some of the syndromes that have come along in the past several decades. A criminal justice system that routinely prevented criminal defendants from offering plausible stories based on theories that are accepted by the relevant professionals could well fall into disrepute. If so, once again an obsession with scientific validity would ill serve the ultimate goals of the system.

D. Conclusion

Daubert interpreted Federal Rule of Evidence 702, which mandates that expert opinion assist the trier of fact, to require proof of scientific validity or something akin to it. Assistance can come in many guises, however. When, as is usually true with past mental states, scientifically verified evidence is not forthcoming, experts might better be conceptualized as interpreters of ultimately unknowable mental states who help give the defendant the voice that the Constitution guarantees and that a criminal justice system seeking popular support demands.

At most, however, the foregoing discussion has established that a scientific validity test is not appropriate for clinical testimony on culpability when the testimony focuses on past mental state, as opposed to past conduct. I have yet to offer any substitute test. That is the task of the next chapter.

4

Redefining Probative Value

This chapter takes on the task of defining legally sufficient reliability when the expert testimony in question focuses on past mental state in a criminal proceeding. In those few instances when scientifically reliable information material to this issue is available, the expert should rely on it. If one agrees with the arguments in the previous chapter, however, the absence of such data, which is the normal state of affairs, should not automatically lead to exclusion. The question then becomes how probative value should be assessed when scientific reliability cannot be gauged.

Section A of this chapter argues that probative value of testimony that is not scientifically validated ought to depend on whether it demonstrates *generally accepted content validity*. Clinical testimony on past mental state should address those psycholegal factors that legal fact finders need to consider in arriving at conclusions about the particular issue in question. If it does, it should be admissible even if its accuracy cannot be demonstrated.

Sections B and C then discuss a method for assessing generally accepted content validity, borrowing from Professor Daniel Fishman's work on pragmatic psychology. Consistent with the gist of chapter 3, Fishman argues that, in resolving individual cases, idiopathic, textured clinical opinion is likely to be more useful to the legal system than generalized, positivist data. But he also suggests that individualized information in one case can be made useful in other cases as well, through the collection, in a computerized database accessible to forensic evaluators, of peer-reviewed forensic case reports that include legal outcome and follow-up data. In section B, I argue that this database could be the means of determining the psycholegal factors that the law considers useful in resolving particular culpability issues and that experts should therefore address. If the expert opinion attends to those factors, then the basis of the opinion would be considered valid. If it does not, it would be inadmissible.

Fishman's database proposal, while thus potentially quite useful, requires some significant fine-tuning. In section C, I explore some of the challenges to implementing the idea. These include obstacles to effective comparison of cases posed by the vagaries of language, the disparity in legal regimes and the difficulty of determining when a clinical opinion has been useful to the courts.

Section D discusses another aspect of probative value: the trustworthiness of the facts that underlie an opinion. Whereas most opinions about past mental state are inevitably speculative, the observations of behavior on which they are based generally should not be. The legal implementation of this idea is that clinicians who cannot demonstrate the reliability of hearsay or any other inadmissible information that informs their report should not be permitted to testify.

A. Generally Accepted Content Validity

Daubert has been widely interpreted to require scientific verification of the basis of an opinion's validity. But, as chapter 3 made clear, that verification will seldom be forthcoming for clinical opinion on past mental state. On the twin assumptions that such testimony should still be given a chance, but not without some demonstration that it avoids quackery, some other means of gauging reliability is needed. I propose the notion of generally accepted content validity.

Social scientists recognize several methods of evaluating validity, that is, the extent to which a test or assessment technique accurately measures what it purports to measure. These methods go by various names, but the three most common are criterion validity, construct validity, and content validity. Unfortunately, for reasons already alluded to in chapter 3, the first two types of validity are very hard to measure with respect to past mental state testimony.

For legal purposes, criterion validity would be preferable, because the courts need to know whether a particular criterion—that is, a particular act or mental state requirement—is met. For some types of culpability assessments, the criterion variable is fairly straightforward. In the child abuse example from chapter 3, the criterion is whether a particular child has been abused. If that fact is known, researchers can then ascertain which characteristics, such as sleeplessness or fear of the dark, correlate with abuse and use that information in future legal cases. As another example, the criterion in eyewitness experiments is accurate identification of the perpetrator. Experimenters studying eyewitness accuracy can arrange for a known individual to simulate crime in front of experimental eyewitnesses, varying any number of factors (with and without a weapon, same-race/different-race perpetrators) to determine those that affect the identification process. Because the researchers in these two situations know the criterion variable— who has been abused, who the perpetrator actually is—they can validly determine when and how frequently subjects are affected by the variations. They can then develop the information necessary to apply the relevance ratio described in chapter 3: which set of characteristics of a child differentiate those who are abused from those who are not; which aspects of a crime or a perpetrator disproportionately detract from eyewitness accuracy.

In contrast, any criterion chosen for evaluating past mental state determinations will be much more elastic. As long as the law talks about mental states using language such as "substantial inability to appreciate or conform," "premeditation," "recklessness," and a "belief that force was necessary" (rather than, say, in terms of IQ scores or psychosis), judgments about insanity, mens rea, and the like will not be easily reducible to objectively verifiable components in the same way abuse and eyewitness identifications are. That is because, in contrast to judgments about whether an act occurred, judgments about past mental state issues are best described as moral and normative, rather than scientific or positive. They are based on ideas of blameworthiness that come from many different sources, including religion and intuition. As one court stated, "Legal tests of criminal insanity are not and cannot be the result of scientific analysis or objective judgment. There is no objective standard by which such a judgment of an admittedly abnormal offender can be measured."[1] Thus, except at the margins, assessing the relative accuracy of such normative judgments is an oxymoronic exercise. Perhaps, as suggested in chapter 1, this problem should lead us to abandon the effort at making such judgments. Until we do, those looking for any scientific measure of ultimate accuracy are bound to be frustrated.

Accordingly, the only way the criterion validity of past mental state opinions can be measured is by studying the extent to which they are accepted by judges, juries, or panels of experts in mental health law, and then determining what factors (type of expert, length of evaluation, clinical tests used) correlate with those cases when the court/panel agrees with the expert. As Robert Simon has observed, *good* studies in this vein "are practically nonexistent."[2] Although the concordance rates between courts and clinicians in the studies that have been conducted tend to be high, that is very likely because the cases studied usually did not involve an adversarial process. And in the one study where this problem was avoided, the experts were court-appointed and therefore likely to be given more credence by the fact finder.[3] In any event, even well-done studies of this sort would tell us only whether legal fact finders agreed with the ultimate opinion of the clinician (which chapter 5 argues clinicians should not be offering in any event), not whether the underlying inferences are accepted by the legal decision maker.

In theory, construct validity, which is the usual method of evaluating measures aimed at gauging abstract concepts, would be more useful in analyzing past mental state opinions, which are, as should be clear by now, the ultimate hypothetical constructs. Construct validation compares the outcome of the assessment with the outcome of another assessment that is thought to bear some relationship to it. To use an example from Julian Simon and Paul Burstein's book on social science methods, one might test the construct validity of a "happiness scale" by comparing the outcomes from that scale to "other putative aspects of happiness, such as health, social status, stable family situation, and so on."[4]

The problem in our context is figuring out a meaningful comparison phenomenon for opinions on past mental state. In the insanity setting, perhaps we could look at how often opinions that support an insanity defense involve diagnoses of serious mental disorder, such as psychosis, since insanity is supposed to represent serious dysfunction. But the fact that many non-psychotic people are found insane undermines the usefulness of that check.[5] Even more discouraging, as with the criterion validity studies, this methodology would not give us a very fine-tuned assessment of what makes for good or bad evaluations and opinions.

In the end, it may be that the best we can hope for in evaluating expert testimony on past mental state is content validity. Content validity is "the least satisfactory but most commonly used procedure in social science."[6] It exists if the content of the assessment *looks like* it addresses the relevant issues. Thus, an opinion about insanity that did not address whether the defendant had a serious mental disorder at the time of the offense or whether the disorder caused significant cognitive or volitional impairment would not have content validity.

Because virtually any clinician with a minimum amount of forensic training could write a report that passes this test, a requirement of content validity may not be much of a restriction on such testimony. But it is possible the concept could be made much more robust by defining the requisite content in more detail, based on what is consistent with good standard practice. Combining evidentiary and social science terminology, this inquiry could be dubbed an assessment of *generally accepted content validity*. The next two sections explore how one might determine whether an evaluation's content is generally accepted for legal purposes.

B. The Insights of Pragmatic Psychology

In his book *The Case for Pragmatic Psychology*,[7] Professor Daniel Fishman argues, consistent with my observations in chapter 3, that human behavior can best be studied on a case-by-case basis, rather than through grand research designs. To facilitate access to this idiopathic information by other clinicians and the court system, he has suggested that model forensic case reports be collected in a computerized database. This section explores these ideas in more detail. It then shows how they might help operationalize generally accepted content validity, and how the latter concept might, in turn, resolve the tension between *Daubert*'s demand for reliability and *Rock*'s requirement that criminal defendants be permitted to present *any* assessable evidence that can help present their version of events.

Pragmatic Forensic Psychology

Pragmatic psychology, as envisioned by Fishman, attempts to bridge the gap between a number of oppositions: the statistical and the clinical, the positivist and the constructivist, the objective and the subjective, nomothetic data and idiopathic anecdata, and even psychology and psychiatry. In *The Case for Pragmatic Psychology*, Fishman discusses the "culture wars" that have pitted those behavioral scientists, often researchers, bent on discovering universal laws governing human behavior against those mental health professionals, often practitioners, who believe or intuit that all knowledge is contextual and thus is often not reducible to scientific principles. He proposes that clinicians adopt a third approach which recognizes that both empirical procedures and interpretations of individual behavior (at least those that are systematic and methodologically rigorous) can produce information that is useful to those who seek guidance from psychology. As Fishman emphasizes, to a pragmatist usefulness is the ultimate purpose of knowledge.

Much of *The Case for Pragmatic Psychology* is devoted to laying out the history of how we have studied human behavior. Fishman begins with the development of positivism, the belief that there are laws governing human behavior and that those laws can be discovered through the application of scientific methodology. He then describes the postmodern reaction to positivism, consisting of a number of movements, hermeneutics being perhaps the most conspicuous, which coalesce around the assumption that there is no objectively knowable reality and that our view of the world is inevitably socially constructed, given our different perspectives and organizing capacities. Finally, he looks at the pragmatist compromise, which is less nihilist than some versions of social constructivism but also less enamored of the scientific enterprise than is classic positivism. For the pragmatist, "the positivist search to discover general 'laws of nature' is . . . doomed." Although "the process of natural science inquiry—which encourages disciplined openness to new experiences and empirical data—is one of the best techniques for deriving pragmatically useful information," "pragmatic knowledge is more resonant with ethnography, geography, ecology, and history than with the models for positivism: mathematics, physics, and chemistry." On the other hand, in contrast to the hermeneutic paradigm, "the primary goal of research [for a pragmatist] is not knowledge for its own sake, but to improve the lives of particular individuals, groups, communities, and societies within specific historical and cultural contexts."[8]

Fishman's book then fleshes out the implications of these tenets for clinical treatment. Given pragmatism's emphasis on usefulness, "a pragmatic psychological project starts with a specific practical problem to be solved." Thus, the unit of analysis in a pragmatic enterprise is a single case, or perhaps a pair of cases, not a sample across a given population of the type prevalent in positivist research. Consonant with the latter approach (and in tension with a purely hermeneutic one), a pragmatic clinician does use quantitative methods to help predict and measure behavior, as well as to gauge interrater reliability and the success of a given intervention between cases. However, the primary goal of the pragmatic evaluator/researcher is to obtain as many perspectives as possible on the client's or clients' problem, rather than to narrow the variables, as positivists do in an effort to keep the measures and relationships manageable.[9] The ultimate emphasis for a pragmatic researcher is on thick description of the process and outcome so that future researchers and practitioners can compare more precisely their case or cases with those currently subject to study. Only in this way, Fishman asserts, can contextual variables be taken into account.

In other work, Fishman contends that the pragmatic approach can be useful in forensic work as well. His innovative proposal in this regard is the aforementioned computerized database, which would contain peer-reviewed forensic reports. Thus, for example, he envisions that cases in which an abuse excuse is asserted can be written up in detail and, subject to peer review, entered into the database, together with the case outcome, all of which would then be readily accessible to other forensic practitioners involved in similar cases.[10]

Although Fishman does not provide much detail beyond this brief description, elaboration of the idea is not difficult. Expert panels could create the database, which could appear both in hard-copy journals and on Internet vehicles akin to Westlaw, Lexis, and Medline. The computer versions could be categorized by legal subject matter and made conducive to Boolean and other types of searches that would enable practitioners to find cases most similar to their own. Once found, these case studies could provide illustrations of the types of inquiries, instruments, tests, and analytical processes that experienced forensic clinicians have developed in evaluating various legal issues and that have proven useful and persuasive to the courts.

Of course, academicians would also have access to this database. They would find it very useful for detecting patterns that might generate research hypotheses. They could also use it to fine-tune structured interview formats and other instruments that would assist practitioners and courts in identifying and addressing legally relevant psychological factors.

How Pragmatic Forensic Psychology Might Meet the Daubert Challenge

As noted at the end of section A of this chapter, the challenge in assessing generally accepted content validity is determining whether particular content

is generally accepted. That is where Fishman's program for pragmatic forensic psychology comes in. A computerized database of cases that includes
legal dispositions could well be the predominant source for such information. Each report should indicate the standards or tests used by the law for
the particular case in question and the psychological variables that the legal
system and experienced clinicians believe correspond to them. The latter
factors might often be research-based but, in a pragmatic regime, they would
not need to be; assuming the legal client finds the speculation useful, these
factors should be considered part of the culpability construct.

Assume, for instance, that a defendant charged with murder is asserting
an insanity defense and a psychologist is ordered to evaluate his mental state
at the time of the offense. The psychologist carries out a thorough evaluation and concludes that the defendant was suffering from posttraumatic
stress syndrome as a result of fighting in the Iraq war. She testifies at trial
and the jury finds the defendant insane. The psychologist's report, her testimony, and the jury's verdict could all be submitted to a board of forensic
experts. The board might decide that this packet of information should go
in the database because it represents a well-organized effort to document the
current psychological effects of the war, rule out malingering and other
diagnoses, and explain how the posttraumatic stress affected the defendant's
cognition and volition at the time of the offense. The report might include
statistical information about, for instance, the prevalence of PTSD among
war veterans but, for reasons related in chapter 3, this type of data will
seldom be useful in making individualized culpability determinations, except to the extent it may bolster a claim that the defendant had PTSD.[11] The
more important information will be the sources consulted, the questions
asked, the instruments and psychological tests used (e.g., the SIRS, a well-
constructed instrument designed to detect malingering),[12] and the reasoning
that led to the evaluator's conclusions.

This evaluation report could provide several lessons for future evaluators. First, of course, it would provide an illustration of how the *DSM*'s
PTSD criteria apply in a criminal case. Second, it may identify several post-
trauma behaviors that are indicative of people with PTSD who commit
crime. Third, it could provide a list of potential sources of information—
research-based and anecdata—in such cases. Fourth, it should indicate what
kinds of psychological tests, if any, are relevant in such an investigation.
Ideally it would also identify the clinical factors the legal fact finder considered relevant to its finding of insanity.

Evaluators who found the report useful and other evaluators with
similar cases might subsequently submit their own evaluation reports, which
could lead to fine-tuning of the first evaluator's scheme. Over time, a
consensus might develop as to how PTSD-based insanity claims should be
assessed, aided perhaps by researchers with access to the database who could
test interrater reliability. Analogous to the "structured professional judgment" approach taken in prediction cases (to be discussed in chapter 6), one

or more generally accepted evaluation formats for this type of case might emerge.

The role of such a format in determining admissibility would be straightforward. If future evaluators faced with potential PTSD cases failed to consider the various clinical factors it incorporates—the diagnostic criteria, their forensic implications, sources of information, testing information—the admissibility of their opinion would be called into doubt, depending on the degree of failure and whether reasonable alternatives were used. Ultimately, a clinician who wanted to testify about PTSD-induced insanity but who paid little heed to various factors that case law (in both the legal and pragmatic psychology sense of the term) has identified as significant to that inquiry would be prohibited from taking the stand. In this sense, at least, *Daubert*'s demand for verification that an expert's opinion be reliable *can* be implemented in the culpability context.

This generally accepted content validity test for probative value is more relaxed than a strict *Daubert* reliability standard and explicitly adopts a *Frye*-oriented approach. Any evaluation by a qualified professional that is based on a well-established structured interview instrument would suffice. However, as case studies revealed more about the factors that courts and clinicians consider relevant, the interview formats would become more sophisticated. Initial efforts along these lines have already been made.[13] They should develop into the templates courts use in determining whether a valid opinion is being offered.

Legal precedent for this approach to expert clinical testimony exists. In Florida, the rules of criminal procedure break down the competency to proceed concept into six factors (e.g., capacity to appreciate the charges, capacity to relay pertinent information to the attorney).[14] The Florida Supreme Court has held that competency reports must, at a minimum, address these six factors, and that any judicial finding about competency based on a report that does not do so is reversible error.[15]

The same type of rule could exist in culpability cases. Over time, this requirement that expert reports and testimony demonstrate generally accepted content validity should significantly improve forensic practice. In chapter 3, I argued that exclusion of *all* nonscientific testimony on past mental state is not necessary to encourage good research. But exclusion of testimony that does not follow accepted practice in terms of content and scope *is* necessary to differentiate good practitioners from bad and to provide an incentive to be good.

C. Problems of Implementation

Because it can help scientize the evidentiary evaluation of nonscientific opinions about past mental state, Fishman's suggestion that we develop a database of peer-reviewed forensic case studies is an idea well worth pursuing. But the project assumes that a repository of case studies can be developed and that its existence will make possible valid and useful comparisons across cases. That assumption is subject to serious challenge. The case-based system proposed by Fishman will confront many implementation problems, some of them significant. The following discussion identifies some of these problems, as well as possible responses to some of them.

Legal Concerns Raised by Construction of the Database

How is the database of the type envisioned by Fishman created? Every day in this country forensic practitioners produce hundreds of reports concerning criminal responsibility. The authors of these reports should be encouraged to submit the work products they consider excellent, together with the reports of opposing experts, information about legal disposition, and other relevant follow-up information, to a group of peer reviewers. As noted earlier, the latter could be formed from experts on existing forensic board organizations and editors of forensic journals, who would select the most useful submissions for the database. The result would be an ever-growing body of model case studies.

This system raises at least three immediate legal quandaries, however. The most significant potential obstacle to the system is posed by confidentiality law. Although many clinical reports and legal dispositions are matters of public record, any mechanism that makes them accessible on a nationwide basis, especially if it involves use of the Internet, magnifies their exposure and therefore exacerbates privacy concerns.[16] Unfortunately, the two most obvious remedies for this problem—sanitization of reports and limiting access to them—undermines the central purpose of the database, which is to provide detailed descriptions of all potentially relevant variables in each case (which could include commonly sanitized facts such as age and location) to every practitioner who conducts similar evaluations. An associated legal concern is whether the informed consent of the subject must be obtained before the report is submitted for inclusion into the database.[17] Still another legal problem concerns copyright law;[18] forensic clinicians who develop good model reports may well assert a proprietary interest in their work product. None of these issues is resolved here; perhaps others can do so.[19]

Clinical Inconsistency

To be useful, a comparative case study system must use concepts that can be reliably (consistently) applied. It is not clear that language is up to the task. Human behavior is very difficult to describe in a reliable fashion, as chapter 3 made clear. Recall, for instance, the study that found that at least fourteen different modifiers of the term "depression" have appeared in the psychiatric literature.[20] These problems are most obviously troublesome for those conducting positivist research, which tries to apply terms such as these to large samples. But they afflict the pragmatic psychologist as well. Even if a practitioner is convinced his client is depressed, behaving bizarrely, or suffering from schizophrenia, he cannot be confident that case studies in the database that use the same terms are similar enough to make accurate comparisons.

Structured interview formats that produce relatively consistent investigative procedures can help with this problem. But many structured interviews rely on vague terminology as well. For instance, the Brief Psychiatric Rating Scale (BPRS), used in a number of research projects,[21] requires ratings of symptoms such as "anxiety" (defined as "worry, fear, or over-concern for present or future"), "conceptual disorganization" (defined as the "degree to which the thought processes are confused, disconnected, or disorganized"), and "excitement" (defined as "heightened emotional tone, agitation, increased reactivity")—concepts hardly susceptible to consistent quantification on the seven-point scale the BPRS provides.

A more aggressive solution is to break down the diagnoses and the symptoms into more detailed behavioral observations. That is not a simple task, however. Consider an actual forensic report produced by Dr. Philip H. Witt, which in many respects is quite exemplary. It states that the juvenile subject of the report (H.H.) exhibited "no signs" of "hallucinations or delusional thinking" or of "thought disorder," that her conflicts with other teenagers were "normal," and that she "expressed remorse" about the victim. The report also states that H.H.'s mood is "chronically dysphoric," that she "lacks energy," and that she has "feelings of worthlessness," "little appetite," and "disturbed sleep," but that she does not experience "suicidal ideation."[22] This list barely touches on the ambiguous terminology used in his report. One might respond that these types of words and phrases are self-explanatory, or at least that it will be obvious to the experienced clinician what is meant by them. But, as Witt reports, the opposing doctor in the case found little evidence of depression and at the same time opined that there was evidence of paranoid personality disorder and dissociative disorder.[23] These conclusions are significantly different from Witt's (both intrinsically and in terms of their legal implications) and leave one hungering for reports of even more specific behavioral observations.

That solution has its own problems, however. At some point, thick description produces diminishing returns. Carrying hermeneutic logic to its ultimate conclusion, even a videotape of every encounter between subject and clinician would be insufficient to convey the factual and interpretive nuances of each case. Yet extremely long and detailed case studies are unlikely to help the typical forensic practitioner, who may conduct several evaluations a week. The tension between usefulness in the pragmatic sense and usefulness measured in accessibility terms will not be easily resolved.

The Opaqueness of Legal Dispositions

For the pragmatic psychologist, Fishman states, the primary measure of any psychological endeavor is its success at meeting the goals of its clients or "stakeholders."[24] In the forensic context, making that measurement would seem to require not just access to the clinical reports in a given case, but also, at the least, a description of the legal consumer's reaction to them. Most important, the case file should detail the extent to which the legal fact finder found the information in the report relevant and helpful. Inclusion of the case's outcome (e.g., the ultimate verdict, opinion, sentence, or disposition) might also provide an indication of a particular expert formulation's impact in the legal arena.

In the culpability context, however, this type of direct feedback about the utility of a report or testimony is extremely rare. Insanity defense and other mental state defenses are often tried to juries, which virtually never provide reasons for their decisions. Even many bench trials do not result in a formal opinion. Most important, a huge proportion of criminal cases, including those involving past mental state issues, are resolved without ever going to trial in the first place,[25] so here too the reasons for the outcome are opaque. In such cases, the most one can determine is whether particular reports or testimony supported the prevailing side. But drawing the further conclusion that the clinical data influenced the result would usually be inappropriate, given the numerous variables that can affect legal decision making.

Furthermore, because of the law's variability, even a well-documented verdict is of questionable usefulness as an indicator of how the law views particular types of findings. America's federalist system of government often produces a multitude of approaches to every legal issue; with respect to insanity, for instance, there are as many as five formulations extant in the forty-five states that recognize the defense.[26] More fundamentally, even juries and judges applying identical legal provisions to identical facts can easily arrive at divergent conclusions; a different judge or jury, sitting in the same jurisdiction and interpreting the same law, might come to the opposite conclusion. Although the appellate structure may correct some of these inconsistencies, the fortuity of appeal, the double jeopardy doctrine, and various other obstacles prevent such reliability-enhancing features from occurring on a routine basis.[27] In short, the behavioral sciences are not the only human endeavor plagued by inconsistency.

This discussion exposes the difficulties inherent in Fishman's hope that a pragmatic system of case studies will help answer normative legal questions. He states, for example, that "one way to help decide appropriate and inappropriate instances of the 'abuse excuse' for criminal responsibility would be to provide a range of specific, systematic case examples that are arrayed along a continuum, from much more clearly exempt from responsibility because of external factors to much less clearly exempt."[28] The jury system does not provide fine-tuned assessments of criminal responsibility, and even if it did, differences in legal provisions and decision makers would make creation of such a continuum, at least one based on legal decisions, an almost futile effort.

The good news is that case studies do not have to fulfill this role in order to be useful. Even if they will not provide much help in telling us which people should be found responsible and not responsible, they can help forensic practitioners and legal decision makers zero in on the factors relevant to responsibility assessments (thereby enhancing assessment of content validity). Furthermore, to the extent that such a system encourages judges and other legal decision makers to provide reasons for their decisions and feedback about the usefulness of clinical information, it will improve the legal system as well as the forensic evaluation process.

The Conservatism of the Common Law Method

Assume that the foregoing implementation problems are overcome sufficiently to give us some confidence that the case studies can provide both reliable evidence of psychological variables and a good sense of which variables the law considers relevant in a given type of case. On this assumption, as Fishman recognizes,[29] the pragmatic case study system begins to resemble the common law method of adjudication. The case studies function as *precedent*, providing evaluators and lawyers with valuable insights based on past experience and research that can either be "persuasive" or "distinguished," depending on the precise variables at issue. Inductive reasoning, rather than positivist, deductive analysis, characterizes both the pragmatic endeavor and the common law.

The incrementalist approach of the common law method has benefits, including the preservation and accretion of wisdom and the avoidance of costs associated with rapid change. Consider, however, the critique of Christopher Langdell's case study method,[30] a well-known pedagogical analogue to the common law developed in the late nineteenth century and still used today in many law school classrooms:

> A central implication of Langdell's case method was that, in the study of law, one need not venture beyond appellate judicial opinions. If, as Langdell postulated, law is a self-contained science, with the law library as its "laboratory" and cases as its "specimens," one need only study those appellate decisions. But, according to Richard Cosgrove: "For all the emphasis on law as science, Langdell's declarations had the curious result of limiting the field of legal inquiry rather than expanding it. . . . The Langdellian account of law implied a closed, logical legal system where theoretical questions, if not exactly ruled out, never occupied a central position."[31]

The same conservatism can afflict pragmatic psychology. Indeed, pragmatism writ large has been attacked on the ground that, given its focus on whatever brings the community together, it may "devolve into an apology for the prevailing ideology."[32] If the case study approach is to reflect what psychology has to offer, evaluators and peer reviewers must work diligently to avoid empirical and analytical inertia and educate the judiciary on scientific progress.

The Difficulty of Gauging Usefulness

Thus far, this chapter has adopted a fairly narrow definition of *usefulness*—the ultimate pragmatic concern—because it has assumed that the only client of the forensic evaluator is the legal decision maker. There are many other potential stakeholders in the forensic process, of course, ranging from the subject of the evaluation to the community at large.

In discussing the usefulness inquiry, Fishman describes two types of "performance indicators": those that measure process and those that measure outcome. The former gauges "how well a system is working internally," and the latter looks at "how well the system is accomplishing its goals in the outside world."[33] As elaborated above, the peer review process and the legal decision maker can provide fairly good feedback on how well the clinical and legal evaluation process works internally. But outcome data about effects in the outside world are much more difficult to obtain.

This is so even when the effects are objectively observable, as when an evaluator makes a prediction about conduct, if only because of the time needed to determine if the prediction is borne out and the need to separate out confounding variables. When measuring the effects of testimony regarding past mental state, the task is virtually impossible, for reasons already noted. For instance, insanity is what a given jury in a given case tells us it is and thus is extremely variable.[34] Although this observation conforms with a social constructivist view of the world, it also means that outcome indicators—was the verdict "correct"?—are hard to conceptualize.

This does not mean, of course, that usefulness cannot be measured at all in these types of situations. We can still assess the generally accepted content validity of an opinion, a process indicator. In other words, in many forensic situations, outcome indicators and process indicators will collapse into an assessment of whether the legal system has engaged in a meaningful decision-making procedure.[35] The pragmatic case study system can assist significantly in that endeavor.

D. Probative Value and Data Collection

As the amended Rule 702 recognizes, to be admissible, testimony must be based not only on sound constructs but on "sufficient facts or data." The database described earlier should help immensely in identifying the types of facts and data that should be collected in a particular type of case. Courts can use it to ascertain whether a given expert's informational basis is sufficient.

Curiously, however, Rule 702 does *not* require that the expert's facts and data be "reliable," in contrast to its treatment of principles and methods, which must be "reliable" and "reliably applied." Instead, the amended Rule 703 continues to allow experts to rely on facts that are not otherwise admissible in evidence if it is "reasonable" to do so. This rule has been far too laxly applied in the forensic setting. For instance, clinical opinions based on the hearsay statements of a government agent, a codefendant, and the reports of nonclinical staff have all been ruled admissible under Rule 703,[36] despite the fact that these declarants were not in court to be cross-examined about their "testimony."

These types of decisions are generally based on one of three grounds. The first is that experts can be trusted to make adequate credibility assessments of third parties, because those assessments are so important to their everyday practice. As the Advisory Committee Note to Federal Rule of Evidence 703 explained, "The physician makes life-and-death decisions in reliance upon [third-party information]. His validation, expertly performed and subject to cross-examination, ought to suffice for judicial purposes." Second, it is contended, the third-party information is not actually hearsay because it is not being admitted for the truth of the matter asserted. Instead, as one court put it, the data are admitted "for the limited and independent purpose" of enabling the jury to scrutinize the expert's reasoning.[37] Third, some authorities have justified experts' use of hearsay on the grounds that requiring the proponent of the evidence to bring all relevant third parties into court would be inefficient.[38]

None of these justifications is satisfactory. First, whatever may be true about physicians who make "life-or-death decisions," mental health professionals conducting forensic evaluations seldom operate in analogous high-stakes settings, and they usually deal with significantly less objective facts. Second, regardless of how a court might formally characterize experts' descriptions of out-of-court statements, the jury is likely to consider them for their independent content, not just as a subsidiary component of the expert's opinion. And although producing the source of every third-party statement may prove unnecessarily burdensome, requiring the testimony of sources for *important* third-party statements (e.g., those that incriminate a criminal defendant) is unlikely to involve many witnesses, and most of those are probably closely related to one of the parties. The bottom line is that mental health professionals are not necessarily any better at evaluating the credibility of witnesses or documents than are laypeople,[39] and thus cannot be counted on to do so accurately.

Apparently, the drafters of Rule 703 thought they had fixed this problem with the second part of the rule, which states, "Facts or data that are otherwise inadmissible shall not be disclosed to the jury by the proponent of the opinion or inference unless the court determines that their probative value in assisting the jury to evaluate the expert's opinion *substantially* outweighs their prejudicial effect." This language is meant to keep misleading information underlying an opinion from the jury. But it only makes matters worse, in two ways. First, it tells the expert that an opinion can be based on relatively unreliable evidence, as long as the judge can be convinced that reliance on the evidence is "reasonable." Second, it prevents the expert who relies on inadmissible evidence from explaining the full basis of the opinion; even information that is crucial (a statement from a third party, results of a sodium amytal interview) will not be heard by the fact finder and will not be subject to cross-examination unless it is highly reliable. Instead of banning the opinion, or admitting it but requiring the expert to reveal all of his or her sources so that their reliability can be examined in open court, Rule 703 allows introduction of a questionable opinion without allowing its basis to be questioned; in essence, it trusts experts, but not the jury, to judge credibility. That turns accepted legal doctrine on its head and is hardly a prescription for reliable testimony.

All of this may soon change in the right direction, in criminal cases at least, because of the U.S. Supreme Court's new approach to the so-called Confrontation Clause found in the Sixth Amendment. The Confrontation Clause states that a criminal accused shall have the right "to be confronted with the witnesses against him." In *Crawford v. Washington*,[40] decided in 2004, the Court substantially modified its previous approach to the Clause by holding that this language prohibits the government from introducing in a criminal trial out-of-court statements that are "testimonial," unless the maker of the statements is unavailable and the defendant had a prior opportunity to cross-examine the declarant. The Court did not clearly define "testimony," although it did state that this concept included a declaration to a government agent "made for the purpose of establishing or proving some fact."[41] A New York court has since held that third-party statements solicited by a mental health professional during a forensic evaluation and relied on at trial by the state are testimonial as that word was used in *Crawford*.[42] This holding, which appears to be a correct application of *Crawford*, could have major repercussions for forensic clinicians supporting the government's position in a criminal case. If they solicit information from a third party and intend to rely on that information at trial, the government must either (1) ensure that the third party testifies, (2) show that the third party is unavailable and that the defendant had an opportunity to cross-examine him or her at some earlier proceeding, or (3) obtain a waiver of confrontation rights.

Even if *Crawford* does not require it, as part of their assessment of probative value courts should insist on identification of all sources of information and on assurances that the information is reliable. Generally, the latter requirement should mean that the basis of the expert's opinion must be independently admissible. If it is not, but a plausible argument can be made that it still has probative value, the opinion can be admitted, but the entire underlying basis for it should be introduced as well. As discussed further in chapter 5, any concern that the jury will misuse the inadmissible information is usually exaggerated when the proceeding is an adversarial one.

E. Conclusion

A requirement that expert testimony about past mental state demonstrate generally accepted content validity would be beneficial both clinically and legally. Clinically, it would accelerate the movement toward "best practice" evaluation procedures and opinion formation and increase the legal usefulness of the forensic product, because courts would begin insisting that clinical experts address all psycholegal factors that past case law considers relevant, as well as make sure that the facts underlying opinions are admissible or at least of proven reliability. Structured interview formats, designed to focus evaluators on the variables that legal tests make relevant, would become increasingly important.

The legal benefit of equating the probative value inquiry with an assessment of generally accepted content validity is its reconciliation of truthseeking and fairness concerns. A focus on content validity would allow courts in *Daubert* jurisdictions to demand at least some form of reliability verification even of testimony that is not easily subject to traditional scientific testing. At the same time, it would avoid routine exclusion of expert testimony on past mental state proffered by the defense, which ensures preservation of the defendant's constitutional right to tell an effective story about the crime.

5

Beyond Relevance

This chapter discusses application of the final two components of admissibility analysis—helpfulness and prejudicial impact—to clinical testimony about criminal culpability. To a large extent, these factors are the converse of one another: evidence that is helpful will probably not be unfairly prejudicial, and evidence that is likely to be misleading is not likely to assist the fact finder. Further, as *Daubert* recognized, helpfulness is closely linked to materiality and probative value, which are thus also inversely related to prejudicial impact.

Despite the intertwining of these factors, they do focus on identifiably independent considerations, which are teased out in this chapter. In section A, I discuss how the helpfulness inquiry can be analogized to the social science concept of incremental validity, which suggests that even material and probative evidence is not helpful if it does not provide specialized knowledge that improves the accuracy of decisions made by judges and juries. Not surprisingly, this idea is more problematic when applied to past mental state testimony as opposed to testimony about conduct. In the former setting, incremental validity may be measurable only through a determination of whether the expert testimony enhances the *factors* that the legal decision maker considers and, in the absence of research on that point, whether the testimony challenges typical lay preconceptions about culpability.

Section B applies the helpfulness factor to the form, rather than the substance, of clinical testimony. In particular, I address the "ultimate issue" issue: whether clinicians should be permitted to declare an opinion on a legal issue the fact finder is obliged to resolve, such as the defendant's sanity.

I conclude that testimony on the ultimate issue, even if material and probative, is beyond the expert's expertise, but that testimony just short of it should probably be permitted, as long as the proceeding in which it is delivered is adversarial in nature.

The latter stipulation leads into section C's discussion of the prejudicial impact factor. Many critics of clinical culpability testimony assume that juries and judges are too easily influenced by speculative "soft" testimony. Research on jury decision making suggests otherwise, especially when the adversarial process is working to expose flaws in the theoretical or factual basis of the testimony. But there are some situations, particularly when the prosecution wants to use clinical testimony that plays to the fact finder's preconceptions about culpability, where careful judicial scrutiny might be necessary.

Section D deals with a special subcategory of prejudicial impact: the impact of clinical testimony on society at large. Some defense theories send messages not just about the defendant but about people of the defendant's race or gender. Professor Anthony Alfieri has argued that such testimony should be excluded, even if it is material, probative, and helpful, when it might accentuate negative stereotypes. In this section I raise several objections to this argument.

A. Helpfulness

If expert evidence is material and probative, isn't it also helpful? Sometimes the answer to that question is no. Some information may be so obvious, or so easily accessible through common sense, that experts are not needed to relay it to the jury. In other words, the information may not come from a body of knowledge and experience that only qualified professionals—in this case, psychiatrists, psychologists, and social workers—have accumulated.[1] That is why Rule 702 requires not only that expert testimony be reliable but that it be based on "scientific, technical or specialized knowledge" that can "assist" the fact finder.

On its face, clinical testimony about culpability is often helpful in this way, as the examples in chapter 4 should have demonstrated. But *Daubert*'s emphasis on verification suggests that something more than this type of anecdata is required to ensure admissibility. Here I suggest two more concrete methods of evaluating the helpfulness of culpability testimony, the first based on social science concepts, the second on legal ones.

Factor-Based Incremental Validity

If some sort of research were necessary to prove that culpability testimony is helpful, what might it look like? A starting point in answering this question is the concept of incremental validity, a type of validity that, in contrast to the three validity measures discussed in chapter 4, depends on whether the information *improves* accuracy rather than on accuracy per se.[2] Applied in our context, incremental validity would require proof that proffered expert evidence enhances the accuracy of the decision maker on culpability issues, an approach that is consistent with Rule 702's injunction that expert testimony assist the fact finder.

The first thing to note about incremental validity is that it may sometimes fail to correlate with other types of validity. Consider two examples. Testimony about the factors that detract from eyewitness credibility, among the most accurate types of social science testimony, may nonetheless have low incremental validity if it tends to make jurors believe, contrary to fact, that few eyewitnesses are right when they identify the perpetrator of a crime. In contrast, testimony about dangerousness, even if associated with very high error rates, may have good incremental validity if it improves fact finders' ability to differentiate between those who will recidivate and those who will not. Even relatively weak expert testimony can have incremental validity if the issue it addresses is one that is difficult for anyone to get right.

A second and, for our purposes, more important aspect of the incremental validity concept is that it can help generate testable hypotheses. For instance, in the two settings just mentioned, scientists could test the above assertions about incremental validity through laboratory and field research comparing expert-informed and uninformed juries. If the informed and uninformed juries routinely agree in their conclusions about the accuracy of eyewitnesses or the dangerousness of offenders, the expert testimony would have no incremental validity. Consistent differences between the two groups, on the other hand, would confirm or disconfirm the hypothesis that experts assist the fact finder depending on whether the expert testimony pushed the fact finder in the correct direction.

When the expert testimony is about past mental state, however, application of the incremental validity concept would have to be modified, for reasons that the reader by now should be able to conjecture. Ideally, we could look at the accuracy of past mental state verdicts from expert-informed juries and from noninformed juries. As chapter 4 pointed out, however, compared to scenarios involving eyewitness identifications and predictions, both of which have relatively objective criterion variables, clear criteria for determining the validity of a decision about past mental state do not exist. A panel of legal authorities may be able to tell us whether a given expert opinion about insanity is consonant with their views on culpability (and thus judge ultimate criterion validity), but it would find much harder second-guessing the *accuracy* of a jury decision that someone is sane or insane (which is what is required for incremental validity), precisely because juries are supposed to be the ultimate decision maker in this area.

A compromise method of evaluating helpfulness, which ties in with the generally accepted content validity notion espoused in chapter 4, is to assess what could be called *factor-based incremental validity*. To determine this type of validity, experimenters would attempt to ascertain the factors or variables that a jury informed by an expert considers in making decisions about past mental state (perhaps from the forensic database described in that chapter) and then compare those to the variables considered by a jury left to its own devices. If, compared to the uninformed jury, the informed jury considers more variables that the law considers material to the past mental state issue in question, then the factor-based incremental validity of such evidence has been established. This type of research, which has been carried out in other forensic areas,[3] is much more feasible than studies aimed at demonstrating whether experts improve the accuracy of legal decisions about culpability.

The concept of factor-based incremental validity is in some ways analogous to the idea of moral progress described by Michael Shapiro.[4] Conceding that the assertions of moral philosophy cannot be proven, he argues against skeptics who think that moral progress is therefore impossible by pointing to the incremental usefulness of the new ways of thinking about old problems that moral theorists generate. As he puts it, "Even if experts and non-experts are equal at the penultimate decision point, the skills of non-experts may nevertheless be aided by the experts' moral analyses."[5]

Ultimately, Shapiro concludes, "The ideas of knowledge, expertise, and progress in moral inquiry do not and cannot rest on a belief in an objective moral reality that always provides firm and certain answers."[6] Analogously, there are no firm and certain answers about the normative past mental state questions the law asks. But research of the type suggested above is likely to show that experts are able to provide laypeople with perspectives about culpability that they otherwise would not have, and that, in itself, could be said to add to the validity of the decisions they make.

Counterintuitiveness

To date, there is no research on whether past mental state testimony has factor-based incremental validity. In the meantime, a rougher test of helpfulness, derived from the law itself, can be suggested. Stated most simply, testimony about acts or mental states that is meant to rebut presumptions, overcome statements or innuendo from the opposing side, or in some other way provide counterintuitive or corrective information should be considered helpful. A few examples of each of these three situations should suffice to make the point.

The criminal law presumes sanity and permits an inference that one intends the natural and probable consequences of one's acts.[7] These legal rules are based in part on normative and procedural considerations,[8] but rely primarily on empirical assumptions that are probably right: most criminal defendants are sane and most do intend the natural and probable consequences of their acts. More important, these assumptions are undoubtedly shared by most people, including the majority of jurors and judges. Thus, any past mental state evidence offered to the contrary ought to be considered helpful. Specifically, probative testimony tending to support an insanity, provocation, or lack of mens rea defense ought to be considered helpful because it rebuts legal and lay preconceptions about mental state.

In other situations, it is a party, rather than the law itself, that relies on commonly held assumptions. For instance, when self-defense is the issue in a battered woman case, the prosecution might make much of the defendant's failure to leave a battering husband despite several apparent opportunities to do so.[9] In a child abuse or rape case, the defense might emphasize the victim's failure to report the alleged offense immediately after it "supposedly" occurred.[10] In these situations as well, probative psychological evidence about BWS, CSAAS, and RTS, respectively, would be helpful because it would disabuse jurors of the notions that most battered spouses leave their batterer and that abused and raped victims usually report the assault right after it happens. Even courts that are generally resistant to syndrome testimony often permit it as rebuttal evidence in such cases.[11]

Finally, there are situations in which no explicit statements about behavior or mental state are made by either the law or the parties, yet psychological evidence can be helpful because it provides counterintuitive information. Determining when such a situation exists can be difficult. Ideally, empirical information indicating people's preconceptions about various issues would be available; in some areas, such research has been carried out.[12] But that kind of information often does not exist, and in certain types of cases might in any event be misleading, because stereotypes change and may differ between jurisdictions or even juries. When in doubt, if the other evidentiary prerequisites are met, the court should err on the side of admissibility.

Consider psychological evidence that the defendant has a "passive" character, proffered to show that the defendant did not commit the act charged. Because it does not involve proof of mental state, it would first have to pass a *Daubert*-relevance ratio test of probative value (rather than the less onerous generally accepted content validity test). If it gets past this threshold, however, it should be considered helpful as well, because most jurors are likely to assume that those who are charged committed the act. Although this assumption may seem to run afoul of the presumption of innocence,[13] that presumption, unlike the presumption of sanity or the inference regarding intent, is not supported empirically (most people charged are guilty) and is probably not believed by most laypeople. By the same token, unless offered in rebuttal of such evidence, proof that a person is *not* passive should not be admissible, because it would merely reinforce the widespread assumption that a person charged with a crime committed that crime. Such an outcome is consistent with the traditional character evidence rule barring proof of propensity by the prosecution unless the defense "opens the door."[14]

Psychological evidence about the credibility or accuracy of a witness can be analyzed in the same way. Because most people probably assume that, with the exception of criminal defendants, most witnesses who are put under oath and testify under threat of perjury will try to tell the truth, testimony suggesting otherwise would be helpful, whereas testimony supporting truthfulness would not be, unless offered in rebuttal.[15] The more significant hurdle for this type of testimony is whether it is probative. Testimony about credibility or eyewitness accuracy usually concerns whether an act, rather than a mental state, occurred, and thus, under the framework advanced in chapters 3 and 4, would have to meet the *Daubert*-relevance ratio test.

An even more difficult case involves psychological testimony about so-called repressed memories, designed to bolster or attack testimony from an alleged abuse victim about incidents often decades old. Although jurors probably assume that witnesses tell the truth, they might also assume that an account of something so long ago, the memory of which was just recently discovered, is not likely to be accurate. Accordingly, evidence about the repressed memory phenomenon might be considered helpful regardless of which side seeks to offer it; however, its ultimate admissibility would be analyzed under the *Daubert*-relevance ratio test because it too depends on whether an act occurred.[16]

The implications of these observations for the defense and the prosecution are parallel to those produced by this book's conclusions about the probative value inquiry. In the absence of empirical evidence showing a lack of incremental validity, most clinical testimony about culpability proffered by the defense should be considered helpful. In contrast, most clinical testimony about culpability proffered by the prosecution, at least in its case in chief, will not be helpful, but rather will merely reinforce lay preconceptions about sanity, intent, and guilt generally. However, rebuttal evidence proffered by the prosecution is helpful, because it assists the jury in considering defense evidence evenhandedly.

B. The Ultimate Issue Issue

The form as well as the substance of expert testimony should be helpful. All would agree that experts should explain jargon and avoid unnecessary technicalities. More controversial is the principle, found in Federal Rule of Evidence 704, that mental health professionals should not address the "ultimate issues" of whether a criminal defendant "did or did not have the mental state or condition constituting an element of the crime charged or of a defense thereto," a provision that is particularly noteworthy because clinical testimony is the only type of expert testimony singled out in this way in the Federal Rules. Many commentators, a good portion of them academicians, agree with Rule 704 that courts should prohibit any language in clinical testimony or reports that embraces the ultimate legal issue.[17] However, many other forensic specialists, the vast majority of them practicing lawyers and clinicians, just as firmly believe such opinions should be permitted.[18] After canvassing the arguments of both sides, I suggest that the setting in which the expert opinion is presented should determine the extent to which we should be concerned about the ultimate issue issue and opinion testimony generally.

The Debate

For reasons that will become clear, at the outset it is important to differentiate between testimony concerning the *ultimate* issue and testimony using *penultimate* language. An ultimate conclusion directly addresses the dispositive legal issue, that is, whether a person is or is not incompetent, insane, or guilty. In contrast, a penultimate conclusion does not reach this level of generalization but speaks only to the relevant legal test. For example, in the insanity setting, a penultimate opinion would be testimony that, under the American Law Institute test for insanity, a person accused of crime does (or does not) lack substantial capacity to understand the wrongfulness of his or her act or to conform his or her behavior to the requirements of the law as a result of mental disease or defect.[19]

Many academicians, as well as the American Bar Association, the American Psychiatric Association, Congress (in Rule 704), and a small but growing number of states,[20] would prohibit testimony using ultimate issue language. A substantial portion of these would also bar testimony using penultimate language. There are two rationales for this position.

Most fundamentally, it is argued, such testimony is not properly the province of the mental health professional. As Rule 702 states, a witness may offer an opinion only on those subjects concerning which he or she is "an expert by knowledge, skill, experience, training, or education." Reaching the ultimate legal conclusion on, or applying the legal tests for, insanity and other past mental state issues calls for a legal-moral determination, not a psychiatric one. In addition to the information provided by the clinician, the fact finder deciding whether someone is insane might be influenced by the seriousness of the crime, the identity of the defendant, and, most important, an intuitive sense as to the types of impairment that should be grounds for an excuse.

Certainly mental health professionals are capable of making moral judgments. But making such judgments is not their field of *expertise*. Mental health professionals are not trained, as are judges, nor institutionally qualified, as are juries, to reach legal or moral conclusions; they may have studied the relevant legal tests, but they are no more experts on the law than lawyers who have studied the most recent medical texts are experts in the behavioral sciences. Thus, so the argument goes, they should refrain from addressing the ultimate issue in their capacity as experts. Indeed, doing otherwise would violate ethical, as well as legal, rules.[21]

The second argument by those who advocate a ban on ultimate and penultimate issue testimony is the concern that if such testimony is allowed it will have undue influence on the fact finder, which might even be led to abdicate its decision-making duties. Out of inertia or a misunderstanding of its role, the fact finder might rely on the expert's opinion about the legal conclusion instead of independently assessing the many factors that go into legal decision making. This danger is exacerbated if the willingness of the expert to provide an ultimate conclusion and the eagerness of judges and juries to hear it minimize efforts to examine the basis of the conclusion; the opinion on the ultimate issue may come to assume disproportionate weight relative to the underlying facts in the mind or minds of the fact finder because the facts are not developed or are not properly emphasized.

The responses to these arguments are numerous. First is the contention that, at least with respect to the penultimate, legal test language, the terms involved are within the professional lexicon of the clinician. A person's ability to "appreciate" the wrongfulness of certain acts is a concept that may have clinical content. Merely because it may also have legal significance does not mean that, by using this language in a legal proceeding, the mental health professional is no longer testifying on the basis of specialized knowledge. In its commentary on the ultimate issue issue, the American Bar Association recognizes this point.[22] Although it would unconditionally bar truly ultimate legal conclusions by mental health professionals, the ABA would permit expert testimony using penultimate, or legal test, language that also has clinical connotations. However, it does make one major caveat to this position. If the legal test language has been given a specific meaning by statute or appellate decision, then the ABA recommends it should not be used by the clinician, because it has assumed a particular legal signification.

The second argument against an ultimate issue ban is that, even if certain language does take mental health professionals beyond the boundaries of their expertise, opinions that they may legitimately voice will often be such close approximations of the legal test that one might as well allow ultimate issue testimony. For example, a ban on ultimate and penultimate testimony would not prevent a mental health professional in an insanity trial from stating that he or she believed the defendant's "impulse control was severely impaired at the time of the offense." This statement is remarkably similar to the second prong of the ALI test for insanity, which asks whether the defendant possessed "substantial capacity to conform his or her behavior to the requirements of the law." Yet it is based on the clinician's specialized knowledge and is therefore proper expert testimony. And if such a statement can be made by the expert, then barring testimony that uses the actual test language will accomplish little. Prohibiting paraphrasing of the test is not a solution. This step would not only exclude legitimate expert testimony but be futile as well, given the ingenuity of both lawyers and mental health professionals.

Moreover, it can be argued, any tendency toward expert dominance and failure of the fact finder to consider the factual bases of the expert's opinion can be counteracted through vigorous cross-examination, rebuttal experts, and instructions to the effect that the opinion is just that and nothing more. To ensure that the fact finder does not think of the witness as an expert on legal as well as psychological matters, clinicians can preface their opinions with the observation that what they are about to say is based on their interpretation of the legal test and is not meant to be dispositive of the issue. Empirical research suggests that under these conditions ultimate or penultimate testimony does not change jurors' final determination.[23]

In addition to these essentially negative arguments in favor of ultimate issue testimony is a positive one. Such testimony can help organize and clarify the expert's evidence for the fact finder. Without a conclusion, the fact finder might have difficulty discerning the clinician's position and thus might not be able to make sense of the testimony. Conversely, the fact finder might guess the clinician's position, given the content of the testimony or the identity of the party who called the expert, but believe that, because the expert is not straightforwardly stating a conclusion, he or she is trying to hide something; prohibiting ultimate issue testimony might therefore unfairly detract from the credibility of the rest of the testimony. Indeed, the available research strongly indicates that judges, lawyers, and juries all want ultimate issue testimony from the expert.[24]

Reconciling the Opposing Views

There are plausible aspects to both points of view. Those who wish to bar ultimate issue testimony seem to have a particularly strong argument when the testimony is truly ultimate. Terms such as "insanity," "premeditation," "specific intent," and "self-defense" are solely legal. They are not phrases that a mental health professional would use in everyday practice; they have no clinical content. Thus, their use would not only gloss over the ultimately moral nature of the determination at issue but also violate the notion that expert testimony be based on specialized knowledge.

On the other hand, the legal tests often contain language that is meaningful to mental health professionals in their expert role. My view, contrary to the ABA's,[25] is that so long as a term has clinical content, the fact that it has been given specific legal meaning as well should not prevent it from being used by the clinician. For instance, a decision by an appellate court defining "appreciate" in the insanity test to mean "emotional understanding" should not preclude mental health professionals at insanity trials from using the word "appreciate," as long as they make clear to the fact finder what they mean by the term. Barring such testimony would merely lead to paraphrasing, perhaps (ironically) referring to "emotional understanding" in place of the prohibited "appreciate," and probably confuse the fact finder.

The conclusion that a blanket ban on legal test language with clinical content is inappropriate does not mean it should be permissible in every type of legal proceeding, however. Such language should be allowed only if the protections against undue influence described earlier—cross-examination, rebuttal evidence, and cautionary instructions (when a jury is involved)—are actively utilized. When they are not—when lawyers either are not present or are passive—the likelihood that the fact finder will fail to assess the factual basis of the expert opinion or adequately consider nonclinical/moral factors increases dramatically. Instead, there is a great temptation to accept unquestioningly what appears to be the bottom line: the expert's opinion on the ultimate issue. Studies showing an extremely high correlation between judicial decision making and clinical opinion in legal contexts that are not normally adversarial bear this out.[26] Granted, any failure to abide by the adversarial tenets of the system is the fault of lawyers and judges, not clinicians. But we should not allow clinicians to exacerbate this failure by sanctioning their presentation of conclusory testimony in such proceedings.

In a full-blown insanity trial, it can usually be assumed that procedural protections against expert dominance will be present. Cross-examination, rebuttal witnesses, and instructions are all commonplace at such a trial. But the majority of proceedings in which forensic issues are decided are far from adversarial. And even most insanity findings are the result of plea bargains that receive only minimal attention from a judge.[27] Permitting ultimate and penultimate language in such proceedings is suspect.

Indeed, in a nonadversarial setting, *any* kind of conclusory language, not just ultimate or penultimate testimony, is more likely to assume undue importance. Thus, an argument can be made that in such a setting much of what is currently accepted as expert testimony should be significantly curtailed. To understand this point, recall the example from chapter 3 describing five levels of clinical inference:

1. Behavioral observations (the defendant talks to people who are not there and claims the victim was an "archfiend").
2. Inferences or symptoms (the defendant was hallucinating or delusional at the time of the offense).
3. Diagnosis (the defendant was suffering from schizophrenia at the time of the offense).
4. Application of the clinical information to the legal issue (the defendant did not believe that his or her act was wrong because he or she felt justified in carrying it out).
5. Application of the clinical information to the ultimate legal issue (the defendant was insane).

Most practitioners would permit testimony at all five levels. The American Bar Association would bar testimony at the fifth level but permit testimony at the fourth level so long as there is no supervening legal interpretation of the legal test. Many academicians would bar opinions at the fourth and fifth levels, whereas the federal courts, operating under the prohibition in Rule 704(b), have vacillated between that position and the ABA's.[28] With a few exceptions, everyone would allow testimony through the third level.

One of the exceptions is Stephen Morse, who, as noted in chapter 3, would bar testimony on any level other than the first.[29] His rationale for such a prohibition is that, at any of the subsequent levels, mental health professionals do not possess specialized knowledge sufficient to assist the fact finder in making legal judgments and therefore are not qualified to offer opinions on such subjects. Given my take on probative value and helpfulness, I obviously disagree with that conclusion. But I agree with Morse that inferences beyond the first level are relatively more speculative. And when the legal proceeding at which the clinician's testimony or report is considered is nonadversarial in nature, such speculative clinical testimony, because it will go unchallenged, is decidedly more likely to lead to invalid decisions. Especially risky is untested testimony that is directly relevant to the legal issue (levels 4 and 5), and therefore is most likely to influence the legal fact finder. Unless we can be reasonably sure that the fact finder will ask for and pay attention to information at all levels of inference rather than merely the most conclusory ones, the latter type of testimony should not be allowed given its suspect and at the same time alluring nature.

In the end, the ultimate issue debate is a subtext in the larger debate on the value of clinical testimony. In evidentiary language, it concerns whether inferential testimony is helpful to the fact finder. In my view, the worth of such testimony is largely a function of how it is presented. The more "ultimate" such testimony becomes, the more energetic we should be in subjecting it to adversarial testing. Conversely, if such testing, including cross-examination of the expert's data and the submission of rebuttal evidence, is present, opinion testimony that is based on specialized knowledge should be not only accepted but welcomed as helpful to the fact finder. More is said about the nature of this legal, as opposed to scientific, testing in the next section.

C. Prejudice

If clinical testimony about culpability is material, probative, and helpful, as defined in the foregoing discussion, it should rarely be excluded. In other words, nonultimate culpability testimony should usually be admissible if it (1) is logically related to a culpability issue, (2) meets the relevance ratio test (when about past conduct) or the generally accepted content validity test (when about past mental state), and (3) is incrementally valid or counterintuitive and subject to adversarial testing. The critics who argue otherwise often seem to focus on the fourth component of admissibility analysis, prejudicial impact. They believe that clinical testimony ought to be excluded because of its potential for overwhelming the legal decision maker.

That position is wrong both legally and empirically. The rules of evidence express a preference for admitting probative evidence. Federal Rule of Evidence 403 states that relevant evidence may be excluded only "if its probative value is *substantially* outweighed by the danger of unfair prejudice, confusion of the issues, or misleading the jury, or by considerations of undue delay, waste of time, or needless presentation of cumulative evidence." The critics of expert culpability testimony appear to reverse the balancing analysis found in this rule. They would require its exclusion unless its probative value substantially outweighs the danger of prejudice.

In any event, clinical culpability evidence that is material, probative, and helpful is not likely to pose any of the dangers listed in Rule 403 (wasting time, confusing the jury, or misleading it). Given its importance in criminal cases, such testimony will rarely be a waste of time unless it is redundant. And, compared to other types of expert evidence, it is unlikely to befuddle the average jury; testimony about human behavior, even when put in psychiatric terminology or expressed in terms of syndromes and relevance ratios, is far more understandable than discussions of physics, DNA analysis, and economic principles.[30] Finally, for much the same reason, psychological testimony is relatively unlikely to carry undue weight, as most laypeople understand that psychological evidence is more fallible than testimony based on the hard sciences. A metareview of jury research in nonscientific cases summarized the findings this way: "It is clear that expert testimony is not accepted in a mindless fashion by gullible jurors awed by flashy credentials. Rather, expert testimony is scrutinized as intensively as the testimony of any other witness and even viewed somewhat cynically."[31] More directly on point is the well-known fact that past mental state defenses rarely succeed in front of juries, and the findings of Neil Vidmar and Regina Schuller that jurors do not treat expert testimony on battered woman syndrome, rape trauma syndrome, and eyewitness reliability with an unwarranted aura of accuracy.[32]

A few recurring scenarios might conceivably pose a Rule 403 risk, however. Not surprisingly, these scenarios occur when evidence is weak in materiality, probative value, or helpfulness. Yet even in these situations, the availability of corrective measures usually supports a decision in favor of admissibility. These two points are explored below.

Prejudicial Impact Scenarios

The scenario most likely to trigger Rule 403 concerns is when the clinical culpability testimony is weakly material. Consider again the abuse example in chapter 3, where it was posited that the expert offers testimony that a child with symptoms X, Y, and Z is three times more likely than a child who does not have those symptoms to have been abused. Given the relevance ratio of 3:1, and assuming it is based on methodologically sound research, this testimony is highly reliable with respect to its distinction between abused and nonabused children. But it may still be of limited materiality in an abuse case. The testimony not only does not prove that a child with those symptoms was abused, it probably does not even suggest that the child was *likely* to have been abused, given the low base rate for abuse in the general population. Even assuming that 10 percent of all children are abused (likely to be an overestimate of the base rate) and that 60 percent of these abused children have symptoms X, Y, and Z in any group of a hundred children, fewer abused children (60 percent of 10, or 6) than nonabused children (20 percent—one-third the rate of abused children—of 90, or 18) will exhibit those symptoms. Yet jurors may nonetheless consider the evidence to be strong proof of abuse.

As suggested earlier in this chapter, the same thing might happen with eyewitness testimony. Assume an expert is willing to testify that a person who witnesses a crime involving a gun is three times more likely than a person who witnesses a weaponless crime to misidentify the perpetrator. That testimony does not, of course, mean that an eyewitness in an armed robbery case is wrong, or even likely to be wrong, in identifying the defendant as the perpetrator. Yet jurors, impressed by the probative value of that evidence (which, given the strong research on the subject, is very high), might nonetheless rely on the testimony in disbelieving any such eyewitness. At least, that is a result some courts have admitted they fear.[33]

This type of problem is likely to occur frequently with social framework–type evidence, where an almost inverse relationship between probative value and materiality (or fit) may exist. In such situations, courts may need to evaluate the impact of the psychological evidence not only by itself but also in conjunction with other evidence. The evidence of abuse described above is most vulnerable to objection when no other evidence corroborating that proposition exists. Similarly, a judge is more likely to exclude generalized testimony about eyewitnesses if it is the entire defense case and involves only one or two potentially witness-distorting factors than when the defense also has a colorable alibi claim and the crime involved multiple perception-reducing features, such as high-stress, a weapon, cross-racial identification, and poor lighting.[34]

Psychological evidence that is clearly material but has only minimal probative value might occasionally require similarly delicate balancing. Imagine evidence of past mental state that is based on a new theory that has yet to find its way into the forensic database, or suppose that syndrome evidence tending to show an act occurred exhibits a barely positive relevance ratio. These types of evidence might be excluded, despite passing the official threshold test for probative value, because of their potentially untoward impact on the jury.[35] Unlike judges who have heard many cases involving expert evidence, juries do not have a comparison sample. Although jurors are not incapable of understanding that theories are arcane or that a given relevance ratio is weak, they may sometimes have trouble putting that information in context or gauging its relative accuracy.

Finally, testimony that is material and has probative value might be excluded because its helpfulness is suspect. As suggested earlier, this is most likely to occur with expert evidence that merely bolsters strong preconceptions. For instance, evidence that a person charged with rape fits a "rapist profile" reinforces the assumption of guilt and should be excluded as prejudicial.[36] Of course, such evidence should also be excluded as inadmissible character evidence, as unhelpful, and perhaps also because it lacks probative value. Some wily prosecutors, however, may be able to evade the character evidence prohibition by characterizing the testimony as proof of intent or motive,[37] and might also be able to make a colorable argument that any probative scientific evidence adds to the jury's knowledge. Even if they can, they should not be able to get past the Rule 403 hurdle.

Correctives

Despite the concerns just described, exclusion on unfair prejudice grounds should be rare, at least in situations involving weak materiality or probative value. In these two situations, a functioning adversarial system furnishes a significant corrective to prejudice risks. Through cross-examination and rebuttal experts, lawyers should be able to expose the attenuated materiality of statistical evidence or the relative implausibility of a theory (the effect of the third type of prejudicial testimony—the type that bolsters preconceptions—is harder to dispel through adversarial means, for reasons that are discussed at length in chapter 7).

Some authorities view the assertion that lawyers can reveal the flaws in clinical culpability testimony to be overly optimistic. In *State v. Cressey*, for instance, the court stated, "An expert using [the typical clinical multisource methodology] may candidly acknowledge any inconsistencies or potential shortcomings in the individual pieces of evidence she presents, but can easily dismiss the critique by saying that her evaluation relies on no one symptom or indicator and that her conclusions still hold true in light of all the other available factors and her expertise in the field. In such a case, the expert's conclusions are as impenetrable as they are unverifiable."[38]

This is not an accurate description of how a good adversarial process should work, however. An expert who states that his or her opinion relies on no single source but then is unable to defend *any* of those sources under cross-examination is not getting away with an "impenetrable" opinion and is very likely to be perceived as incredible, whether or not the opinion is ultimately "verifiable."

Conversely, the usually minimal risk that psychiatric theories, relevance ratios, and ultimate issue testimony will overwhelm the jury's capacity to think for itself may increase significantly if they are not subject to challenge. As one study concluded, "Nonadversarial expert testimony causes less systematic processing of...expert testimony."[39] Accordingly, Rule 403 should also require some consideration of whether clinical evidence will be subject to adequate adversarial testing. Of course, that assessment can be difficult before trial takes place. Judges normally cannot foresee the adequacy of a lawyer's preparation or his or her skill during trial. Even if they could, a rule that evidence should be excluded because the opposing side is too incompetent to combat it is paradoxical to say the least.

Some steps designed to enhance adversariness are possible, however. Judges can conduct hearings in limine to get a sense of whether evidence will be effectively explored; if it appears the evidence will not be, they can appoint their own expert to flesh out the issues.[40] Indeed, under the authority of Federal Rule of Evidence 706, the court might routinely appoint "expert experts" who can point out the weaknesses (and strengths) of evaluation procedures and research methodologies.[41] Additionally, as recommended by the American Bar Association, the jury can be authorized to ask questions as a way of making up for attorney oversights, and briefs on the scientific issues can be provided to the jury as well.[42] Ethical rules, governing both mental health professionals and attorneys, can be enforced more vigorously against incompetent, lazy, or pretentious professionals.[43] In short, the judicial system can develop effective ways of ensuring that the fact finder is not presented a one-sided or confused picture of the evidence.

One might argue that if good adversarial presentation of the evidence could be guaranteed through these or other methods, then courts should welcome even psychiatric opinions that have little or no demonstrable probative value; after all, the reasoning might go, the weaknesses of such opinions can be uncovered by the process. Adversariness that clarifies rather than obfuscates cannot be guaranteed on a routine basis, however, and even if it could be, knowingly giving the fact finder information that lacks any indicia of reliability is antithetical to the ideal of a system that purports to do justice. Thus, although a well-functioning adversarial process does allow courts to be more flexible in their admission of evidence than they would otherwise be, it should not nullify the threshold materiality, probative value, and helpfulness requirements.

D. Prejudice to Third Parties

A separate attack on clinical testimony about past mental state comes from feminists and critical scholars, who view it as potentially stigmatizing and denigrating to women and minority groups. For instance, the battered women syndrome's focus on "learned helplessness" has been castigated as demeaning to women.[44] The black rage and rotten social background defenses have similarly been said to pathologize African Americans.

Professor Alfieri is one of the strongest critics in this vein, and his work has attracted considerable attention. He argues not only that such defenses, in particular race-based defenses, should be prohibited under most circumstances, but that defense attorneys should be sanctioned for raising them because of the negative messages they send.[45] As a backup position, Alfieri proposes that sanctions be imposed on defense attorneys who do not make diligent efforts to dissuade their clients from raising these types of defenses.[46]

Alfieri is essentially arguing that prejudice should be defined with the community, as well as the individual litigants, in mind. In some cases, such an approach might make sense. For instance, where the race- or gender-based defense argument is only tenuously material or reliable, or its harm to the community will be palpable, an antidefense ruling might be appropriate. But that type of showing will rarely be forthcoming. In the usual case, the impact of a race- or gender-based argument is unknowable; indeed, it is quite possible that Alfieri's approach is more damaging to his overriding agenda of improving societal relations than the current regime. Because Alfieri focuses on race-based defenses I will as well, although much of what is said here is relevant to gender-based defenses and other claims that might be seen as stigmatizing to various groups in society.

The Argument against Race-Based Defenses

Alfieri's articles use a number of cases as a springboard for arguing that defense attorneys have an ethical obligation to avoid certain types of race-based defenses. The one I describe here was briefly mentioned in chapter 2: the prosecution of Damian Williams and Henry Watson on twelve charges of aggravated mayhem, felony assault, robbery, and attempted murder. Those charges arose out of the beating of Reginald Denny and seven others during the Los Angeles riots that followed the acquittal of the officers who beat Rodney King, much of it caught on videotape by news cameras.[47] The lawyers in the Williams and Watson cases argued, largely successfully,[48] that the defendants were caught up in the "group contagion" of anger and frustration following the King verdict, so much so that they did not possess the intent to kill or even an intent to cause severe harm.

Despite the success of this argument, Alfieri criticizes it for labeling young black males as "ignorant," "unsophisticated," and "out of control," all characteristics the attorneys attributed to Williams or Watson and, by implication, the other rioters as a group.[49] Although neither the lawyers nor their witnesses suggested that only blacks are prone to mob violence, Alfieri asserts that this "deviance narrative constructs racial identity in terms of bestiality or pathology [and] . . . portrays young black males as deviant objects controlled by bestial instincts or pathological impulses." Further, he contends, this type of argument causes significant harm to black individuals and black communities by undermining their self-image and reinforcing the biases of the dominant white society.[50]

As a corrective to this perceived problem, Alfieri argues that lawyers should forgo "racial[ly] deviant narratives" unless necessary "to subvert an excessive and discriminatory prosecution." Alternatively, as a "weak" prescription, defense attorneys should explicitly deliberate with the client about the potential for racial injury that such a narrative would cause and attempt to dissuade the client from such a course. At the same time, Alfieri would apparently permit lawyers to suggest and raise "defiance narratives," that is, narratives that depict crime committed by African Americans as a rebellion against an oppressive system rather than as a deviant act. These prescriptions are all based on Alfieri's primary aim of avoiding "narratives or stories that construct racial identity in terms of individual, group, or community deviance."[51] Shorn of the verbiage, Alfieri appears to be saying that neither clients nor attorneys can be trusted to make the right (race-conscious) decision, so that authority should be taken away from them and replaced with a rule that requires the attorney to forgo race-based defenses, at least those that focus on deviance.

An Evidentiary Analysis of Race-Based Defenses

Alfieri pays little attention to the types of evidence rules that concern this book. He should have done so. The admissibility analysis that I have proposed can adequately accommodate Alfieri's concerns without upending the system in the way he envisions. In particular, it permits consideration of the impact that given testimony will have on groups outside the frame of the adjudication (although I will argue that Alfieri grossly exaggerates the harm that race-based defenses pose).

Using the Williams and Watson case as an example, the first issue under the four-part analysis proposed in this book is determining whether a group contagion/diminished capacity theory is material to mayhem, aggravated mayhem, and attempted murder charges. Chapter 2 has already explained why the expert testimony in that case could well have been excluded at this threshold stage. Diminished capacity, which focuses on lack of intent, is not a defense for general intent crimes such as mayhem, and in any event is generally not proven simply by evidence of impulsivity, which is the gist of the group contagion defense.

If that is so, Alfieri's aim of avoiding a race-based defense in the Williams case would be achieved without resorting to ethical sanctions against defense attorneys or paternalistic prohibitions on the nature of defendants' defensive claims. Materiality analysis might also lead to exclusion of rotten social background arguments and some of the other defenses that Alfieri abhors, for reasons explored in chapter 2. Whether such defenses *should* be considered immaterial is another question. Contrary to Alfieri's apparent assumption, the black community might seek to change criminal liability rules to accommodate racialized arguments, just as feminists have brought about analogous change in connection with criminal defenses in prosecutions of battered women who kill their batterer.[52] Again, this book is not the place to develop substantive criminal law doctrine. But at the least it can be said that, contrary to Alfieri's prescription, the political process and judges, not defense attorneys operating in isolation, should determine which arguments are material and which are not.

Assuming that the materiality hurdle can be overcome, the next two evidentiary considerations are probative value and helpfulness, analysis of which I combine here for brevity's sake. The group contagion testimony in the Williams case was presented by a social worker, not a psychiatrist or psychologist, which may mean the expert was not really an expert on the behavioral dynamics of mob violence.[53] Reinforcing that view is the fact that the witness did not appear to rely on any published research describing mob violence or its effect on the mental states of individuals who are in a mob. Nonetheless, the expert felt able to state that at "the height of the contagious feeling . . . especially in those situations where there is frenzy or a lot of anger . . . one is governed by . . . a lot of impulsive behavior, a lot of impulsive action where there isn't much thinking prior to acting."[54] That conclusion, while plausible, is not based on the scientific method and could well fall short in the eyes of a court adhering to the spirit of *Daubert*.[55] If that test is applied rigidly, once again neutral evidentiary principles will accomplish Alfieri's goal of excluding racialized defenses, without reference to potential racial harm.

If, however, my approach to past mental state testimony is adopted, a relaxed definition of probative value would apply and this testimony might be considered sufficiently reliable if the defense can demonstrate that other mental health professionals consider its content plausible and that it is based on specialized experience, theory, or research. These race-based arguments can also be truly helpful to the fact finder, which otherwise might succumb to preconceptions about criminal behavior, and in particular criminal behavior by blacks. By providing technical and often counterintuitive explanations for this behavior—based on mob dynamics, environmental influences, rage at white society and so on—these arguments can educate a jury toward a more nuanced decision on culpability issues. If one accepts these propositions about the probative value and helpfulness inquiries, and assuming race-based arguments are material, their admissibility may then ultimately depend on the final evidentiary inquiry: the extent to which they will have a prejudicial impact.

An Expanded View of Prejudice

Under Rule 403, "unfair prejudice" appears to be defined solely with reference to the parties in the dispute and considers only the effect of given evidence on the decision maker.[56] Thus, the claim that a particular trial argument will harm nonlitigants (e.g., blacks) in the eyes of third parties outside the trial setting (e.g., the rest of society), which is the type of claim Alfieri is making, does not fit neatly into the traditional prejudice inquiry. But there are many evidentiary analogues to his type of reasoning, even when the litigant whose case will be undermined by concern about third-party interests is a criminal defendant. For instance, exclusion of a witness's testimony based on privilege law, such as the privilege against self-incrimination and the physician-patient privilege, can easily harm defense efforts to obtain relevant, exculpatory evidence. It is nonetheless permissible, as a means of protecting the constitutional and privacy rights of third parties.[57] The same justification underlies rape shield laws, which render inadmissible possibly relevant evidence about past sexual acts of alleged rape victims, both to protect the privacy of rape complainants and to encourage reporting of rapes and thereby enhance public safety.[58] Admittedly, these evidentiary rules are not generally considered to be implementations of the prejudice concept. But they are based on a desire to protect the interests of people other than the litigants and can require case-by-case analysis of whether those interests outweigh the defendant's in a particular case.[59] It is thus not untenable even from a traditional perspective to construe the term "prejudice" to encompass harm to third parties, including the offender's racial community, which concerns Alfieri.

The problem is how to measure this type of prejudice. While Alfieri is convinced that racialized defenses do irreparable harm to society as a whole, and particularly to minority ethnic groups, that stance is subject to serious question. First, even on Alfieri's own terms, differentiating between prejudicial and nonprejudicial defenses is impossible in many cases. Second, if we are to speculate, Alfieri could well be wrong about the negative impact of the typical racialized defense on the black community. Contrary to his claims, many of these defenses are likely to have no such effect or even a positive one on race relations.

The differentiation difficulty permeates Alfieri's entire project. As noted earlier, Alfieri wants to avoid "deviance" narratives but is willing to countenance "defiance" narratives. As he readily admits, however, these two types of narratives often "intersect,"[60] and probably unalterably so. Take the "black rage" claim. Examples of individuals who might raise such a defense range from Williams, who proffered a group contagion defense, to Colin Ferguson, whose attorneys, before he fired them, wanted to argue that he killed six people on the Long Island Railway because he was driven into psychosis by an oppressive white society.[61] One could also include in this category Benjamin Murdock, who contended that his violent reaction to being called a "dirty nigger bastard" by a white Marine, whom he subsequently shot and killed, was due in part to his upbringing in a racist society and his "rotten social background."[62] Each of these individuals could be called "deviant." However, each could also be called "defiant," because each rebelled, albeit in a particularly violent fashion, against racism.[63] The deviance and defiance labels, at least as defined by Alfieri, place virtually no constraints on the defense attorney's strategic (or ethical) decisions or the judge's evidentiary choices.

The deeper question that Alfieri and the expanded prejudice inquiry raise concerns the type of message these types of arguments—whether denominated as deviant or defiant—send to the public about African Americans. One possibility, of course, is that any message sent is not received. This side of the O. J. Simpson case, the public, as compared to scholars and the press, is probably apathetic about the details of these trials. For instance, it is unlikely that most people know Williams asserted a group contagion defense, even if they remember that he escaped conviction on his most serious charges.

If the message is received, what is it? One way to answer that question is to consider the message sent by a regime that *rejects* race-based defenses, as Alfieri's would. Note first that Alfieri would not permit such a defense even if the defendant wants to pursue it. A policy that disregards the expressed desires of black criminal defendants on the ground they do not really know what is good for them or their community is deeply denigrating to both individual clients and to blacks generally. As far as the client is concerned, ignoring his or her current choice about an important strategy is likely to be much more psychologically debilitating than arguing that a past choice was influenced by situational variables such as social background or rage at white society.[64] As for impact on the community, minimization of the choices black defendants make has the added disadvantage of being unequally applied; presumably, attorneys will still assert diminished capacity and like defenses for white clients, so that it will appear as if attorneys believe that only African-American clients are confused about the issues in such cases.

Even more damaging to his position is the imagery of Alfieri's illustrative trials had the racialized defense not been raised. Without the group contagion defense, Williams would have looked like the stereotypical psychopath so routinely depicted by Hollywood. Simply watching, without explanation, the videotape of Williams repeatedly clubbing Denny with a brick is likely to trigger the specter of soulless evil and feed into preexisting fears of young black males. Thus, as Professor Margulies has stated, "Unless one believes that the King verdict was not a sign of subordination, or that Damian Williams and his co-defendants would have pulled Reginald Denny from his truck on any sunny Los Angeles day," excluding the expert testimony "would have been unjust."[65]

Even testimony that consists solely of a description of how poverty and a violent, racist upbringing can condition random murderous responses such as Ferguson's and Murdock's is likely to do more good than harm. Margulies joins Alfieri here in expressing concern about such testimony's mechanistic explanation of human behavior and its potential for besmirching all ghetto males, as well as its detrimental impact on the efforts of those churches, families, and individuals who try to overcome the rottenness in inner-city communities.[66] Yet such testimony also helps explain criminal behavior in terms other than those that invoke badness or evil; it reminds us that behavior is as much situational as it is attributable to a deliberate human reasoning process,[67] thereby creating in the public audience empathy where there might otherwise have been hate. Such testimony might also occasion a "There, but for the grace of God, go I" response; it could suggest that the sickness resides in society, not the defendant or the black community. In other words, those types of messages could improve, rather than diminish, race relations. In contrast, the absence of such testimony can accentuate negative stereotyping. Deprived of testimony explaining the effects of being called a "nigger," for instance, African American defendants in Murdock's situation may well be viewed as trigger-happy subhumans, rather than people who understandably are enraged by that emblem of oppression.

In short, cases where fear of third-party prejudice might outweigh defendants' right to tell their story, on their own or with the help of experts, will be rare. A possible example of one such case, involving a white rather than a black defendant, is the prosecution of Bernhard Goetz. Charged with the attempted murder of four black youths who had accosted him without a weapon on a subway full of people, he avoided conviction of any serious offense by arguing that he honestly and reasonably thought his victims were about to kill or seriously injure him.[68] Assume that the law of self-defense is subjectified sufficiently to make material his central assertion, that is, that people with Goetz's prior history (he had been mugged before) might reasonably act as he did.[69] That assumption allows direct confrontation of the prejudice issue. Goetz's argument not only depicts all young inner-city black males as potentially deadly assailants, but also sends the message that, when confronted by one or more of them, use of deadly force is excusable, if not justifiable. That type of third-party prejudice to innocent actors is on its face much more tangible than any of the negative effects that Alfieri mentions. Perhaps in this unusual type of case, the concern about injury to African Americans outweighs the defendant's Sixth Amendment right to present evidence. Even then, I would want some proof that a Goetz-type argument has the hypothesized effect of encouraging others to believe it is open season on aggressive inner-city African Americans.

Another example in the same vein comes from the case of Daimian Osby, an African American whose lawyer claimed his client killed another African American youth due to an overwhelming fear of black urban youth. Osby was convicted on retrial after the trial judge excluded the testimony of both of the defense's experts—a psychologist and a race relations expert—which was meant to support the attorney's argument that Osby suffered from "urban survival syndrome."[70] That result might make sense not only because the "syndrome" was essentially the creation of the defense attorney (and therefore lacking in probative value), but also because it fed rather than contradicted preconceptions about inner-city blacks (and therefore was both unlikely to be helpful and likely to exacerbate stereotypes that might lead to greater violence).

E. Conclusion

In the work briefly referenced just above, Professor Margulies writes about four perspectives scholars have taken when considering the admissibility of social science evidence that rests in whole or in part on identity issues such as race, gender, or sexual orientation.[71] *Responsibility theorists* insist on keeping exceptions to the general presumption of criminal accountability narrowly defined, and thus tend to view identity defenses with suspicion. *Empiricists* also are uncomfortable with such defenses because of their speculative nature. *Critical defense advocates*, on the other hand, generally endorse these defenses because they enlighten others about the effects a stratified society has on relatively powerless groups. Finally, *feminists*, although sympathetic to racialized and similar arguments, are sensitive to their potential for exoticizing or pathologizing the groups they purport to describe. In Margulies's scheme, Alfieri falls somewhere between the third and fourth groups.

What is interesting about Margulies's taxonomy for present purposes is how it parallels traditional evidentiary analysis. Responsibility theorists are most interested in the materiality question because they focus on the scope of substantive criminal law doctrines such as insanity and diminished capacity. Empiricists look most closely at the probative value inquiry because scientific accuracy is their main concern. Critical scholars are more attuned to the helpfulness issue because they want judges and juries, who often come from the mainstream, to understand the nuances of minority group politics. Feminists are most involved with assessing prejudicial impact (under the expanded definition adopted in this chapter) because they want to avoid unfairly or harmfully characterizing these groups.

These parallels also emphasize the main point of this part of the book. The determination of whether clinical culpability testimony should be admitted depends on a number of factors. Professor Alfieri is right to emphasize race consciousness as an important variable, but wrong to give it dispositive impact. Similarly, empiricists are wrong to make probative value the sole focus of admissibility analysis. That analysis must take into account considerations relating to the substantive law, the defendant's right to voice, and fact finder preconceptions, as well as what is known empirically about culpability assessments and stereotyping. If the courts look closely at the materiality and prejudicial impact of expert testimony, they can mediate conflict over the normative messages clinical claims send about offenders and their cohorts. If they are attentive to relevance ratios, generally accepted content validity, factor-based incremental validity, and counterintuitiveness, they can meaningfully address the tension between *Daubert*'s reliability requirement and psychological queries that are not susceptible to statistical analysis.

Part II

DANGEROUSNESS

6

The Current State of the Science
and the Law

We now move from culpability assessments focused on past mental state to dangerousness determinations that seek to predict future behavior. In non-capital sentencing proceedings, the latter determinations often are based entirely on lay judgments, usually made by probation officers and judges. But in numerous other settings—capital sentencing, police power civil commitment, sexual predator hearings—mental health professionals are almost always involved in assisting the decision makers who predict antisocial conduct.

As chapter 1 recounted, a number of commentators believe this practice should stop or be severely circumscribed. At one time, the official organs of the professions voiced similar views. In 1974, the American Psychiatric Association stated, "Psychiatric expertise in the prediction of 'dangerousness' is not established."[1] Four years later, the American Psychological Association came to much the same conclusion, asserting that "the validity of psychological predictions of violent behavior, at least in . . . sentencing and release situations . . . , is extremely poor, so poor that one could oppose their use on the strictly empirical grounds that psychologists are not professionally competent to make such judgments."[2]

The courts have paid no attention to such assertions, however. In 1983, despite amicus briefs from both APAs incorporating statements like those just quoted, as well as John Monahan's 1981 conclusion that two out of three long-term predictions of violence are wrong,[3] the Supreme Court upheld the admissibility of prediction testimony from mental health professionals in *death penalty* proceedings. That holding, in *Barefoot v. Estelle*,[4] still stands. If offenders may be executed based on prediction testimony, presumably sex offenders and mentally ill people subject to commitment may be confined on such opinion evidence as well.

Barefoot, however, announced only the constitutional minimum; evidentiary rules can demand more of experts, as *Frye* and *Daubert* do. Using the same four-part evidentiary framework applied to culpability assessments in Part I, I take an intermediate position between complete exclusion and unquestioned acceptance of expert testimony on dangerousness. Traditional clinical testimony regarding a person's future behavior, though material and probative, is so prejudicial (and thus ultimately unhelpful) that in most settings it should be admissible only if the person first seeks to use clinical testimony to show that he or she is not dangerous. If the person eschews such testimony, then the state should be limited to proving dangerousness using appropriately normed actuarial instruments or structured interview instruments that are tied to explicit probability estimates.

This chapter is the first of two making the case for this approach. Section A of this chapter describes the state of prediction science by explaining the differences among the three primary prediction methodologies—clinical, actuarial, and structured professional judgment—and then evaluating their relative reliability. Section B examines the relevant evidentiary case law, which for the most part has not differentiated among prediction methodologies, and in any event has usually permitted any type of prediction testimony, regardless of its basis. The chapter ends, in section C, with an analysis of the materiality of prediction testimony, in particular the extent to which materiality is undermined by nomothetic (group-based) prediction or prediction based on characteristics over which the person has little or no control.

Throughout the two chapters in this part of the book, the discussion focuses on expert assessments of dangerousness to others (as opposed to dangerousness to self) in four types of proceedings: civil commitment hearings, criminal commitment hearings (commitment and release hearings for sexual predators and those acquitted by reason of insanity), noncapital sentencing hearings, and capital sentencing hearings. Much of what is said here may also apply to other settings.[5] Limiting the discussion to these four types of proceedings, however, keeps it within manageable boundaries and at the same time allows closer examination of those contexts in which expert assessments of dangerousness are most frequently requested and the type of predictions that have been most thoroughly researched.

Even within these parameters, the term "dangerousness" can take on a number of different meanings. For example, in capital sentencing, the term usually refers solely to one's propensity to cause serious bodily injury to another.[6] In the civil and criminal commitment contexts, in contrast, it might also refer to the likelihood that a person will cause damage to property, and can even encompass emotional harm.[7] In civil commitment, the focus is on one's potential for injurious behavior in the immediate future, whereas in the other three contexts long-term dangerousness is the primary consideration. Finally, the precise likelihood of harm required to justify the intervention may differ depending on the type of intervention. For instance, aggravators in death penalty cases usually must be proven beyond a reasonable doubt, whereas civil commitment is permissible on the lesser clear and convincing evidence standard.[8]

The implications of these and other distinctions are emphasized where appropriate. In particular, differences between civil commitment and the other three settings may call for relaxation of the limitations on prediction testimony that I propose. Nevertheless, many of the points made in the following pages are applicable to all four contexts, despite their differences. As one consequence of this assumption, this book uses the term "dangerousness" or, as a synonym, "violence proneness," without further explanation, trusting the reader to recognize that these terms are subject to variations in definition and proof requirements.

A. The Science of Prediction

Mental health professionals use a number of different prediction techniques. Research evaluating the accuracy of these techniques suggests that clinicians are not as poor at prognostication as critics suggest, although it also leaves no doubt that expert prediction is far from perfect. The following discussion describes the various prediction methodologies and their strengths and flaws, including their relative accuracy.

Prediction Methodologies

Until the late 1980s, almost all expert testimony regarding dangerousness was *clinical* in nature. That is, it relied on whatever information the individual clinician deemed pertinent. In the past twenty years, more structured approaches to prediction have been developed. An *actuarial* approach relies, as insurance actuaries do, on a finite number of preidentified variables that statistically correlate to risk and that produce a definitive probability or probability range of risk. A third prediction methodology, known as *adjusted actuarial assessment*, begins with an actuarial assessment that the professional then adjusts, based on individualized factors not considered in the actuarial formula. A final prediction method, called *structured professional judgment* or *guided clinical assessment*, relies, like the actuarial approach, on an evaluation of a finite number of predefined factors that have been associated with risk, but neither the factors nor the final conclusions about risk are mathematically obtained.[9]

An exemplary illustration of the clinical approach to prediction, back in the days when it was king, is found in a study conducted by Harry Kozol and his associates. Each prediction in the study was based on independent examinations by five clinicians, a battery of psychological tests, and "a meticulous reconstruction of the life history [of the subject] elicited from multiple sources."[10] A second example of clinical prediction, but one that sits at the other end of the spectrum, comes from the case of *Estelle v. Smith*, in which James Grigson, a psychiatrist in Texas, purported to be able to deliver an opinion on competency to stand trial, insanity, and dangerousness based solely on a ninety-minute interview with Smith.[11]

The types of information underlying clinical predictions vary immensely, from examiner to examiner and case to case. Of particular importance to Kozol and his associates were "details in the description of the [triggering crime]."[12] In addition, they attempted to ascertain the extent to which the individual

> harbors anger, hostility, and resentment; enjoys witnessing or inflicting suffering; lacks altruistic and compassionate concern for others; sees himself as a victim rather than as an aggressor; resents or rejects authority; is primarily concerned with his own satisfaction and with the relief of his own discomfort; is intolerant of frustration or delay of satisfaction; lacks control of his own impulses; has immature attitudes toward social responsibility; lacks insight into his own psychological structure; and distorts his perception of reality in accordance with his own wishes and needs.[13]

This detailed focus on themes or commonalities in the examinee's behavior in order to identify risk or protective factors is sometimes called *anamnestic assessment*.[14] Dr. Grigson again provides a contrast. In *Barefoot*, another case in which he was the prosecution's key witness, he stated that there was a "one hundred percent and absolute" chance that Barefoot would commit acts of criminal violence, despite never having interviewed him; rather Grigson's testimony was in response to a hypothetical question describing Barefoot's four nonviolent offenses, his arrest on charges of statutory rape and unlawful restraint of a child, his escape from prison after that arrest, and the events surrounding the capital murder (which admittedly were horrific).[15]

Actuarial prediction is much more structured than clinical prediction. Probably the most prominent actuarial prediction device is the Violence Risk Appraisal Guide (VRAG).[16] The VRAG focuses on twelve empirically derived and relatively narrow variables—no other information is considered in making the assessment—and its goal is to produce a score that indicates a particular probability of recidivism. Thus, a score of 0 through 6 on the VRAG is associated with at least a 35 percent probability of "violent recidivism" within seven years, and a score of 21 through 27 is associated with a 76 percent risk of such recidivism over that period.[17] A key variable on the VRAG is the individual's score on the Psychopathy Checklist–Revised (described in more detail below); all by itself, a rating of 35 or more on this measure results in 12 points on the VRAG, which indicates a recidivism risk of 44 percent (whereas, for example, a rating of 0–4 on the PCL-R results in

−5 points on the VRAG, associated with a 17 percent risk). The eleven other variables and their relationship to risk are (1) elementary school misconduct (with "severe" disciplinary or attendance problems warranting 5 points); (2 and 3) *DSM* diagnosis (broken into two variables, with a diagnosis of personality disorder garnering 3 points and a diagnosis of schizophrenia −3 points); (4) age at time of triggering offense (26 or under: 2 points); (5) absence of one or both parents before sixteen, other than through death (3 points); (6) failure on conditional release (3 points); (7) nonviolent offense score (3 points if there are either more than two minor offenses or one serious offense, such as robbery, felony theft, or fraud); (8) marital status (1 point if never married); (9) victim injury (counterintuitively, 2 points if none, −2 points if death); (10) history of alcohol abuse (e.g., 2 points if the person is a long-term alcoholic and alcohol was involved in the triggering offense); and (11) victim gender (−1 point if female, 1 point if male).

Another actuarial approach, initially known as the multiple iterative classification tree (ICT) and now called Classification of Violence Risk (COVR), requires the examiner to analyze risk using what amounts to risk flow charts.[18] For instance, under one classification tree the evaluator first determines whether the person demonstrates low or high psychopathy. If low, the evaluator then determines whether the individual has been arrested only a few times or many times: if the former, the evaluator then looks at recent violence; if the latter, the examiner ascertains whether the individual abuses drugs or alcohol. If the individual instead demonstrates strong psychopathic tendencies, the evaluator first determines whether the individual suffered serious abuse as a child; if yes, then inquiry into substance abuse occurs. At each step, a particular answer is associated with a particular recidivism probability.

Other actuarial devices focus specifically on sex offenders. For instance, the Minnesota Sex Offender Screening Tool relies on sixteen variables (for front-end commitments) or 21 variables (if the offender is being considered for release).[19] In addition to scoring points for convictions and arrests and other items similar to those on the VRAG, this instrument requires the examiner to look at the age of the victim, the length of sexual offending history, and employment history. Living up to its name, the Rapid Risk Assessment for Sexual Offense Recidivism (RRASOR) relies on only four variables (prior sex offenses, age at release, victim gender, and relationship to victim).[20] Each of these instruments also produces a score that is associated with a particular risk of recidivism.

In an *adjusted* actuarial approach, the examiner would use one of these devices as a baseline, but then raise or lower the risk prediction based on other considerations, typically those known to relate to offending. For instance, an examiner administering the VRAG might lower the probability of recidivism if he or she knows the offender has done well in treatment or is about to get married. Or the risk level might be raised if the individual has made threats or has stated that, if released, he or she will join a gang.[21]

One of the best examples of the final methodology—structured professional judgment—is the HCR-20 violence risk assessment scheme, which consists of twenty items relating to three categories of information: historical, clinical, and risk management.[22] The history scale contains ten items: previous violence, age at first violent incident, relationship instability, employment problems, substance use problems, major mental illness, psychopathy, early maladjustment, personality disorder, and prior supervision failure. The five items on the clinical scale are lack of insight, negative attitudes, active symptoms of major mental illness, impulsivity, and unresponsiveness to treatment. The five risk management scale items are unfeasibility of plans, exposure to destabilizers, lack of personal support, noncompliance with remediation attempts, and stress. Examiners rate each item on a scale of 0 to 2, making 40 the maximum possible score. Although this scheme resembles the actuarial devices described earlier, there is no algorithm that statistically correlates a given score with a risk probability. Rather, the examiner arrives at risk ratings of low, moderate, or high based on his or her clinical assessment of the various items in the protocol.

Of course, the scores obtained using the HCR-20 can be and have been correlated with risk. For instance, a follow-up study of patients who were evaluated using this instrument found that whereas only 11 percent of those who scored in the 0–14 range committed or threatened to commit a physically violent act during a two-year period, 35 percent of those who scored over 26 did so, and 75 percent of those who received the highest scores did so.[23] When combined with such studies, the HCR-20 is not very different from an actuarial device. But a distinction still exists: whereas actuarial devices like the VRAG were developed empirically (through studies as to which items statistically differentiated violent and nonviolent offenders), the items on the HCR-20 came from observational and theoretical research as to the likely correlates of risk.

The same can be said for the PCL-R, which consists of twenty factors scored on a 0–2 scale, designed to identify the extent to which an individual is psychopathic.[24] As with the HCR-20, the items on the PCL-R were developed through clinical observation rather than mechanistically. Further, the ultimate score obtained indicates degree of psychopathy, not risk potential. But, as noted in the discussion about the VRAG, additional research has found that the instrument is also a good predictor of violence, with a score of greater than 30 (on a 40-point scale) indicating a strong propensity for violence.[25]

Comparing Actuarial and Clinical Prediction

Because both the research reported below and my proposed approach to prediction testimony make distinctions between these various methodologies, a closer look at them will be useful. Each methodology has advantages and disadvantages.

One advantage of both the actuarial and structured judgment techniques is that the manner in which they combine variables is more reliable (i.e., capable of being replicated) than the way clinical opinions are formed.[26] Each of these two approaches transparently designates the specific factors the predictor must consider. Compared to actuarial prediction, the structured clinical approach gives the examiner more flexibility as to how much weight to be assigned to each predictor, but it still focuses the examiner on the listed predictors and, at least with the HCR-20, requires reference to a specified scale (0–2). An unstructured clinical prediction, in contrast, "must ultimately be based upon an overall subjective impression which is based upon an understanding of the interrelatedness of many facts."[27] Because "subjective impressions" may differ from clinician to clinician, and even from case to case for the same clinician, each clinical prediction will probably be based on a different constellation of factors, some of which may be irrelevant or based on erroneous stereotypes and prejudices.[28]

Furthermore, as indicated earlier, the probability of violent behavior obtained through actuarial and structured approaches can be more explicit than that reached through the clinical process. Because it is not standardized, a clinical evaluation of dangerousness cannot be reliably compared to other predictions. At best, the evaluator can give the court information about his or her own accuracy rate (which is rarely available) and the accuracy rate of other clinicians who make predictions (which is not particularly helpful in assessing this evaluator's work). As a consequence of this paucity of data, honest clinical evaluators asked to state the violence proneness of a particular individual can at best rate subjects as high or low risk, and in doing so have only their experience to back them up. In contrast, the VRAG and similar devices definitively state the probability of reoffending within a certain time period.

An actuarial prediction does have at least two drawbacks, however. First, actuarial information is not presently available for some of the populations likely to be evaluated. For instance, minimal data exist about the reoffending rates of insanity acquittees and offenders sentenced to death. A purely clinical prediction does not rely on such information. An actuarial prediction, in contrast, depends on some type of follow-up data for the relevant population or one related to it, as do structured approaches to the extent their results are tied to specific recidivism probabilities.

A more telling criticism associated with actuarial prediction is that it cannot help neglecting pertinent characteristics of the individual evaluated.[29] An actuarial prediction may give us the most explicit information we can obtain about sex offenders who committed their first sex offense before age twenty-six against a female victim. But it tells us nothing about the extent to which other factors that were not included in the instrument (and not researched by its developers)[30] might increase or decrease the potential for reoffending. It is in discovering these idiosyncratic characteristics that the clinical process provides information, however imprecise, that an actuarial prediction cannot. Thus, leading researchers in the area have stated that "actuarial instruments...are best viewed as 'tools' for clinical assessment.... This reliance on clinical judgment—aided by an empirical understanding of risk factors for violence and their interactions—reflects, and in our view should reflect, the standard of care at this juncture in the field's development."[31]

One final difference between the methodologies, but one that is not as great as some have suggested, has to do with the types of variables consulted. Actuarial instruments tend to be more objective than more clinical approaches, in the sense that they rely heavily on "hard" variables that are relatively easy to ascertain, such as prior convictions and age. But it should also be apparent from the above descriptions that actuarial devices can incorporate more subjective, soft variables as well. The VRAG's reliance on the PCL-R illustrates the point. The latter instrument requires assessment of the individual's glibness, grandiosity, need for stimulation, penchant for pathological lying, manipulativeness, lack of remorse, affect, callousness, and similar variables, in addition to delving into specific types of antisocial conduct.[32] Although the scoring criteria for these variables are fairly tightly defined and can be reliably scored by trained examiners,[33] they do not eliminate the subjectivity of the prediction process.

The Validity of Prediction Methodologies

In the three previous chapters, it was asserted that measuring the accuracy of culpability assessments is impossible because of the protean, socially constructed nature of culpability concepts such as insanity, extreme mental distress, and necessity. Happily, assessing the validity of predictions of dangerousness is not as treacherous an enterprise; the criterion variable in this setting, subsequent antisocial conduct, is relatively clear. At the same time, the difficulties of gauging the validity of a given prediction are not trivial. Most important, those predicted to be at high risk are generally confined or at least treated, making ambiguous the relevance of any subsequent failure to offend to assessment of the prediction's accuracy. Even if release of the purportedly dangerous person occurs for some reason, following up on a particular prediction to ascertain whether it is accurate can be very difficult; conviction and arrest records may seriously underreport crime,[34] and self-reports about incriminating acts are obviously problematic as well. Thus, any research evaluating predictive validity is likely to underestimate it.

Even with these caveats, early research on dangerousness predictions was not encouraging. The initial studies measured validity in terms of false positives (the proportion predicted to be violent who were not) and false negatives (the proportion predicted to be nonviolent who were not). These studies reported false-positive rates of anywhere from 40 to 90 percent, with the usual finding somewhere in the 60 to 70 percent range.[35] That led to Monahan's conclusion in 1981 that the best clinical prediction methods produce erroneous predictions of dangerousness two out of three times.[36]

In light of more recent studies that try to correct for the methodological difficulties mentioned above, the typical false-positive rate for expert predictions should probably be revised downward to around 50 percent. For instance, a study of the COVR showed that 49 percent of those predicted to be high risk committed at least one violent act within twenty weeks.[37] More recent studies, using both clinical and actuarial methodologies, produce similar or even somewhat better results.[38] As early as 1984, only one year after *Barefoot* and only three years after his one-out-of-three statement, Monahan conceded that even clinical predictions of violence might be correct one out of two times.[39]

The false-positive rate is only part of the story, however. The accuracy of expert predictions can be fully understood only if base rates of recidivism are taken into account. If, for instance, the base rate for violence among the population studied (say, serial sex offenders) is 50 percent, then a 50 percent false-positive rate would be no better than chance selection. Those carrying out the prediction would do just as well simply randomly assigning, with no evaluation, every second individual to the dangerous category. On the other hand, a false-positive rate of 50 percent is quite impressive if only one out of a hundred people in the relevant population commit crime during the follow-up period; under these circumstances, a correct prediction of violence one out of two times would be fifty times better than chance.[40]

In recognition of this interplay between accuracy and base rates, researchers developed a second way of measuring predictive validity. The receiver operating characteristic curve represents the true-positive rate (sensitivity) as a function of the false-positive rate (specificity). The area under the curve (AUC) produced by this function provides a measure of accuracy as it relates to base rates. If the AUC value is .50, the predictive power of the methodology is no better than chance, whereas an AUC value of 1.0 represents perfect accuracy and a value of 0 means complete inaccuracy. An AUC value of .75 for a given prediction methodology indicates a 75 percent chance that a recidivist will receive a higher risk rating than a nonrecidivist.[41]

Douglas Mossman reanalyzed fifty-eight early studies (from 1972 to 1991) and found that, despite their often high false-positive rates, forty-seven of them demonstrated prediction accuracy "significantly better than chance," with an average AUC value of .67 for clinical prediction and of .71 for actuarial prediction made on a cross-validation group.[42] Representative AUC values for modern actuarial devices are generally as good or better: .76 to .80 for the VRAG, .70 for the COVR, and .71 for the RRASOR.[43] Studies of the HCR-20 have found AUC values ranging from .69 to .89, depending on the population studied, and research on the PCL-R has obtained a value of around .72.[44] These findings obviously do not indicate a high degree of accuracy, but they do demonstrate that professional predictions are much better than chance selection.

A separate validity issue is whether adjusting an actuarial prediction using additional, nonactuarialized factors improves the ultimate prediction. Some commentators have stated that "actuarial methods are too good and clinical judgment too poor to risk contaminating the former with the latter."[45] But others point to research indicating that "considering current clinical conditions (especially regarding the presence of heightened anger or violent fantasies) can be an important contribution to assessments of dangerousness."[46]

B. The Courts' Nonchalance toward Prediction Testimony

Until very recently, none of these nuances affected judicial analysis of prediction testimony. As noted earlier, the Supreme Court's decision in *Barefoot* refused to put constitutional limitations on such testimony, at least as long as it is presented in an adversarial proceeding. Justice White's majority opinion gave two reasons for this stance. First, the Court characterized the suggestion that clinical prediction testimony be prohibited in death penalty proceedings as "somewhat like asking us to disinvent the wheel," given the multiple contexts in which dangerousness predictions have always been permitted, by laypersons and experts alike.[47] This unquestioning reliance on precedent represents legal reasoning at its most primitive, but it is quite common in the evidentiary setting, as chapter 2 pointed out. The second reason given by the Court provides a more substantial, if still highly debatable, rationale: "We are unconvinced . . . that the adversary process cannot be trusted to sort out the reliable from the unreliable evidence and opinion about future dangerousness, particularly when the convicted felon has the opportunity to present his own side of the case."

The Court has not revisited the *Barefoot* issue since *Daubert* was decided, so we do not know if the latter decision's emphasis on reliability would affect the Court's constitutional analysis. But it is unlikely to do so. *Daubert, Frye,* and similar cases interpret the rules of evidence, not the Constitution. The Court is cautious about using the Constitution to mandate evidentiary practices that must be followed by every jurisdiction in the country. Instead, the Court usually sets a low constitutional floor, above which courts and legislatures are free to experiment.[49]

To date, only a handful of courts and no legislatures have exercised this freedom, even when the context is the death penalty. In the 1998 decision of *Nenno v. State,* for instance, the Texas Court of Criminal Appeals concluded that any defect in clinical prediction testimony introduced in a capital proceeding "affects the weight of the evidence rather than its admissibility."[50] Four years later, the Fifth Circuit Court of Appeals found this position so clearly supported by precedent that it was willing to characterize any objection to such testimony as "frivolous" (a particularly strong statement given the fact that the testimony at issue was offered by the infamous

Dr. Grigson).[51] Testimony based on actuarial and structured professional judgments is also routinely admitted in death penalty cases.[52]

If prediction testimony is admissible to support an execution, it presumably should be admissible in any case. A survey of the case law largely confirms this surmise. A review of sexual predator cases conducted in 2002 found virtually no appellate decisions upholding challenges to expert prediction testimony, and decisions since then have continued that trend.[53] A 2003 survey of civil commitment cases likewise concluded, "Judicial opinion, split on virtually every other form of behavioral or psychic expertise, has so far unanimously accepted predictive expertise in civil commitments."[54]

There are signs of judicial discontent, but they have been scattered and uninfluential. In his dissent in *Barefoot*, Justice Harry Blackmun argued that, given the inaccuracy of clinical prediction testimony and its potential for overinfluencing the jury, courts should hear only "lay testimony, frankly based on statistical factors with demonstrated correlations to violent behavior."[55] Judge Emilio Garza, countering his colleagues on the Fifth Circuit, made the same argument seventeen years later, and bolstered it with the assertion that, because it is so often wrong, expert prediction testimony "fails" *Daubert*.[56] A federal district court judge echoed the latter view in 2004, albeit in dictum.[57] And in the past decade a smattering of state courts have forthrightly concluded that some types of prediction testimony are inadmissible.[58]

Also noteworthy is the fact that most of the state court decisions that excluded prediction testimony took aim at the *actuarial* method, while continuing to permit clinical opinion, despite its lesser accuracy. That result should not be surprising to readers of earlier chapters in this book; similar to judicial treatment of culpability testimony, these courts exempt traditional, idiopathic expert opinion from screening rules but are willing to subject newer, more scientific-looking testimony to *Daubert* or *Frye* analysis. In contrast, at least one court has concluded that clinical prediction testimony is so unreliable it must be excluded; the force of this decision was undercut, however, by that court's subsequent willingness to allow clinical opinion as long as it is combined with actuarial findings.[59]

In short, the courts have paid virtually no attention to the critics' plea that expert prediction testimony be barred or severely limited. No court has pronounced a complete ban on expert prediction testimony. In those very few cases where exclusion has occurred, it usually involved actuarial-based testimony, not more suspect clinical testimony. The rest of Part II of this book analyzes this state of affairs, using the four-part framework developed in chapter 1 and beginning with materiality.

C. Materiality

If dangerousness is at issue—as it often is at sentencing, and always is in criminal and civil commitment proceedings—the materiality of prediction testimony would seem to be a foregone conclusion. The issue is not that simple, however. Especially when, as is true for actuarial prediction, the basis for the prediction is transparent, three types of questions can be raised: Is prediction that is based on studies of groups ever applicable to a given individual? Assuming so, is the particular prediction methodology used applicable to this particular individual? Assuming so, is the prediction nonetheless immaterial because it relies on factors that are not legally cognizable (such as race)?

Nomothetic Prediction Data

Justice Coyne of the Minnesota Supreme Court succinctly raised the first issue in his dissenting opinion *In re Linehan*: "Not only are . . . statistics concerning the violent behavior of others irrelevant, but it seems to me wrong to confine any person on the basis not of that person's own prior conduct but on the basis of statistical evidence regarding the behavior of other people."[60] Assume that a person convicted of a sex offense, call him John, receives a score of 21 on the VRAG. The most accurate characterization of this score is that John shares a number of traits with a group of individuals, 76 percent of whom are known to have engaged in violent recidivism. Justice Coyne's position is that this information is immaterial in a proceeding to determine whether John is dangerous because it speaks of other people, not John.

Mental health professionals have long expressed similar concerns, with the psychologist Gordon Allport making the following statement more than sixty years ago: "A fatal non sequitur occurs in the reasoning that if 80% of the delinquents who come from broken homes are recidivists, then this delinquent from a broken home has an 80% chance of becoming a recidivist. The truth of the matter is that this delinquent has either 100% certainty of becoming a repeater or 100% certainty of going straight."[61]

Neither of these objections render group-based predictions legally immaterial, however. First, Justice Coyne mischaracterizes the nature of prediction testimony, because a prediction based on research examining the behavior of others can still be directly linked to the individual who is the subject of the prediction. It is *John's* age, prior record, marital status, psychopathic personality traits, and so on that place him in the 76 percent recidivism category. Moreover, these types of characteristics are all logically related to recidivism, allowing us, as John Monahan has pointed out, to make "the inferential leap from membership in a class that has in the past been violent to the prediction that this member of the same class will in the future be violent."[62] Although it is true, as Allport's comment notes, that any given individual either will or will not offend, it is not incoherent to say that the VRAG score means there is a 76 percent chance that John will recidivate. This type of statement is no different in kind from an assertion that John probably committed a criminal act in the past (even though he either did or did not) or a prediction, based on a clinical interview, that he is highly likely to reoffend, a type of statement that mental health professionals make all the time.[63]

This latter comparison suggests another reason why prediction testimony cannot be considered immaterial simply because it is nomothetic in nature. Such a position would prohibit not only actuarial prediction testimony, but clinical prediction testimony as well, and indeed would bar virtually any type of testimony from mental health professionals and other experts because such testimony is inherently based on inferences drawn from others (recall in this regard chapter 3's discussion of culpability testimony). While clinicians look at individual patterns, they do not do so in a vacuum. Rather, they make comparisons—sometimes implicit, sometimes explicit—between these patterns and the patterns of other individuals or groups of individuals that they know about through experience, training, or education.[64] In this regard, most clinical predictions differ from actuarial ones only in the sense that the link between past groups and present individuals is not statistically correlated.

Nomothetic Prediction and Individual Cases

A willingness to permit reliance on predictions based on nomothetic information does not necessarily mean that such predictions will be material in every case. Much depends on the underlying data's generalizability. Sometimes the group statistics are not applicable to the individual who is the subject of the prediction (the norming problem). Even if they are, they may not address the question the law wants answered (the criterion variable problem). Finally, even if the group data do answer the legal question, the prediction may provide misleading information about the individual in question (the lack-of-individualization problem). All of these points about what *Daubert* called the "fit" issue can be illustrated by John's case, which was introduced above.

Recall that John's score on the VRAG is a 21 and that this score supposedly indicates a 76 percent chance of reoffending. But note that the VRAG was normed on a group of offenders released from a maximum security psychiatric hospital in northern Ontario, Canada, in the 1970s, most of whom were white. What if John is an African American sex offender in the United States at the present time? The applicability of the VRAG data to his case is open to serious question. In fact, the VRAG's AUC value when cross-validated on sex offenders is only .60.[65] One commentator has suggested that the norming problem is "vast and potentially insurmountable" and that without finely tuned cross-validation, "absolute risk predictions based upon [actuarial instruments] are meaningless."[66]

Second, in determining who in their sample population engaged in "violent recidivism," researchers for the VRAG included not only those who committed felonies but those who engaged in two or more simple assaults.[67] As a result, the risk ratios reported by the developers of VRAG do not refer to the probability of *serious* violence. That fact substantially reduces the materiality of the VRAG score for capital sentencing and other contexts in which the legal inquiry is usually focused on precisely that issue. Consider, for instance, how a jury should interpret John's VRAG score of 21, even assuming it is appropriately normed, if the question to be addressed is whether John exhibits a "propensity to commit murder which will probably constitute a continuing threat to society" (an aggravating factor under Idaho's death penalty statute), or a "probability that the defendant would commit criminal acts of violence that would constitute a continuing threat to society" (an aggravating factor under Texas's capital statute).[68]

Finally, as noted earlier, actuarial devices consider only a limited number of variables. John's score on the VRAG does not take into account whether he is undergoing treatment, is about to get married, has recently lost functioning in one or more limbs, or has found religion. The proponents of the VRAG argue that, based on their data, these factors are irrelevant.[69] But their samples were certainly not large enough to encompass statistically significant numbers of every type of treatment or religious conversion experience, or every type of individual's reaction to these sorts of events.[70] Unless data exist demonstrating that these factors do not lower the score of people like John, reliance solely on the actuarial information might be considered immaterial.

These are all worthy concerns, but none should lead to wholesale exclusion of prediction testimony. Difficulties concerning norming, criterion variables, and lack of individualization can all be brought to the attention of the fact finder. The subject of the prediction can also be given wide latitude to question the generalizability of the research underlying the actuarial prediction, and to suggest why that prediction may be off base in his or her case. With these precautions, any weakness in the materiality of prediction testimony can usually be exposed.

Sometimes, however, these difficulties, in combination or alone, will be so significant that they should go to admissibility and not weight. Further discussion of when that might occur is best left to analysis of the prejudice factor in chapter 7.

Illegitimate Bases for Prediction

The materiality of a prediction may be threatened not only by the factors it does not consider, but also by the variables it does. At one time, race was considered a good predictor.[71] And the gender and age of the perpetrator play crucial roles in many prediction methodologies, explicitly when the prediction is actuarial and implicitly when it is clinical. Yet in many areas of the law, differentiating between individuals on the basis of race, gender, and age often runs afoul of antidiscrimination principles, in large part because these are immutable characteristics that usually have very little to do with any legitimate purpose.[72]

Some commentators have gone further, suggesting that *any* characteristic of an individual over which he or she has little or no control—diagnosis, personality traits, abuse as a child—should be anathema as a basis for a prediction. In the course of arguing that actuarial prediction should be barred from the sentencing setting, Daniel Goodman put this point as follows: "It is a fundamental orthodoxy of our criminal justice system that the punishment should fit the crime and the individual, not the statistical history of the class of persons to which the defendant belongs. To allow a criminal defendant's sentence to be determined to any degree by his unchosen membership in a given [group] denies the very premise of self-determination upon which our criminal justice system is built. It raises the threat that defendants will be sentenced not only on the basis of their personal merit or conduct, but on the basis of their 'status.' "[73] Others have echoed this view, with John Monahan recently arguing that "past criminal behavior is the only scientifically valid risk factor for violence that unambiguously implicates blameworthiness, and therefore the only one that should enter the jurisprudential calculus in criminal sentencing."[74] If these prescriptions are followed, then both actuarial and clinical prediction would be immaterial at capital and noncapital sentencing proceedings to the extent that their predicate ventures beyond criminal history.

A first response to this argument is that even suspect classifications such as race and gender are constitutionally permissible when they significantly further a compelling government interest.[75] The identification of dangerous individuals is a very important government interest, and gender and age, at least, are extremely useful in making that determination. (Race, on the other hand, is not a particularly good predictor, and reliance on it for prediction purposes should probably be barred in any event, because of the societal and symbolic repercussions such reliance would occasion.)[76]

Second, and more important, when the government relies on prediction to enhance a sentence based on dangerousness, it is not pursuing punishment based on blameworthiness and retribution, but rather is interested in prevention based on assessment of risk, a completely different enterprise. When the government is engaged solely in assessing blameworthiness for past conduct, as is the case at trial, then Goodman and Monahan are right that prediction should play no role. But at sentencing proceedings in those states that view the goal to be a mix of retributive and other objectives, blameworthiness is not the only issue. For instance, retributive considerations might be considered relevant only in setting the outer limit of the sentence, with its precise length in a given case dependent on an evaluation of dangerousness and rehabilitative potential.[77] In such instances, limiting the basis of any prediction made to factors that indicate blameworthiness (such as prior crimes) is *inconsistent* with the purpose of punishment.

What Goodman and Monahan are really saying is that dangerousness is not a legitimate basis for a sentence. That is a defensible position.[78] But if one accepts the substantive law as a given, as this book does, and if the relevant law permits sentences to be based on dangerousness, as is the case in many states,[79] it does not undermine the criminal justice system's "premise of self-determination" (a premise that has already been honored at trial) to permit predictions based on immutable or quasi-immutable factors. Furthermore, as a practical matter, it is hardly protective of the individual's interests to make prediction a sentencing issue and then deny the fact finder the best means of making the prediction.

Monahan himself acknowledges the force of these points in concluding that, *outside* the criminal setting, any prediction factor (other than race) is material. Because blameworthiness is "irrelevant to imposing civil hospitalization," for instance, Monahan would allow all risk factors to be considered in that arena, which for him includes civil commitment and, to the extent it is not punishment in disguise, sexual predator commitment.[80] Again, for me the issue is easy, given governing law. In both commitment settings, blameworthiness is *clearly* not at issue as far as the Supreme Court is concerned.[81] Thus, the principle of self-determination that the law seeks to implement when blameworthiness is an issue is not threatened by reliance on immutable or difficult-to-change risk factors in commitment proceedings.

D. Conclusion

The common wisdom that expert predictions about violence risk are wrong more often than they are right is probably not true. Although such predictions are likely to be wrong a substantial percentage of the time, they are not as inaccurate as once thought, and improved prediction techniques have significantly reduced false-positive rates (which in any event are usually inflated by methodological problems). Furthermore, virtually all prediction methodologies—clinical, actuarial, and structured judgment—produce results well above chance levels, with the latter two methodologies demonstrating the best AUC values.

All three types of prediction necessarily rely on comparisons to the conduct of other individuals, and usually also rely on characteristics over which the subject individual has little or no control (although clinical prediction is better than the other two at hiding both facts). If the law insists on making predictions about offending, then these attributes of prediction should not be disqualifying. Expert prediction testimony that relies on nonracial characteristics of the individual is not irrelevant to the prediction task simply because it is nomothetic in nature or relies on unchangeable characteristics.

These observations do not, of course, end analysis of expert prediction testimony's admissibility. Still to be considered are the probative value, helpfulness, and prejudicial impact of such testimony. The information about error rates and predictive factors introduced in this chapter plays a significant role in each of these inquiries.

7

Are There Experts on Dangerousness?

The previous chapter demonstrated that prediction testimony, whether based on actuarial data, clinical interviews, or something in between, will often be material to commitment and sentencing proceedings. In the first two sections of this chapter, I argue that prediction testimony is also usually probative and helpful, despite its relatively low accuracy rate. It is probative whenever it is derived from a methodology that produces predictions that are better than chance, and it is helpful whenever it is based on the literature about violence risk and avoids ultimate issue language.

Those conclusions establish a presumption in favor of admitting prediction testimony. However, the fourth component of evidentiary analysis, which looks at potential prejudicial impact, requires significant limitations on this type of testimony, at least outside the civil commitment context. Section C of this chapter asserts that when the *government* wants to use expert testimony in its case in chief during sentencing or criminal commitment proceedings, it should be limited to evidence that is linked to a specific, empirically derived probability of recidivism. In other words, the government should be able to introduce only prediction testimony that is based on actuarial instruments or on structured professional judgments that are empirically correlated with specific probability assessments, unless the subject of the prediction decides to rely on softer prediction testimony. When offered by the government in its case in chief, testimony that is not linked to specific risk probabilities is too subject to misinterpretation and misuse, and thus whatever probative value it has is substantially outweighed by its prejudicial impact.

In contrast, when proffered by the subject of the prediction (the criminal offender or the respondent in a commitment proceeding), the prejudicial impact of probative prediction testimony is likely to be slight, given the natural inclination of fact finders to assume that those subject to sentencing and commitment are dangerous. Thus, the subject should be permitted to introduce clinical prediction testimony whenever he or she sees fit. Only if the subject decides to do so should the government be able to use softer prediction testimony as a method of responding.

The fourth part of the chapter spells out how this subject-first regime would work in practice. Where material, empirically derived probability estimates do not exist, the government would have to rely on lay testimony (presumably regarding past conduct), unless the subject of the prediction opens the door to use of clinical prediction testimony. That door would be opened when the offender/respondent uses clinical testimony to contradict claims that he or she is dangerous, volitionally impaired, or untreatable, but not when the defense expert focuses solely on culpability issues in a sentencing proceeding. This regime allows the government to prove dangerousness in the most accurate, least confounding manner, while permitting the offender/respondent to attack the state's attempt at preventive detention on the ground that the numbers do not accurately reflect his or her violence potential.

The final part of the chapter briefly describes why the foregoing analysis may not be applicable to emergency civil commitment. Simply put, short-term clinical predictions of danger of the type at issue in civil commitment hearings are probably more accurate than the long-term predictions required in other settings. Even if they are not, practical reasons might dictate continued reliance on clinical prediction in this one setting.

A. The Probative Value of Prediction Testimony

Prediction testimony may not be very accurate in an absolute sense, but it is sufficiently accurate to meet the law's test of probativeness, whether that term is defined in the traditional manner or in a *Daubertian* sense. A separate, but closely related, issue is whether prediction testimony, even if probative, can ever be enough to satisfy the relevant standard of proof. Although not technically an admissibility issue, a negative answer to this question could result in exclusion as well, so it is considered here.

The Evidentiary Threshold

Under Federal Rule of Evidence 401, evidence is probative if it has "any tendency to make the existence of any fact that is of consequence to the determination of the action more probable or less probable than it would be without the evidence." Expert prediction testimony, even if clinical in nature, virtually always satisfies this test when dangerousness is the fact to be determined. As explained in the previous chapter, most expert prediction methodologies produce predictions that exceed chance or random selection. Thus, assuming no objection on materiality grounds, a prediction using these methodologies makes a correct resolution of the dangerousness issue more probable than if no evidence were produced.

As noted in chapter 1, critics of prediction testimony have been fond of comparing it (unfavorably) to coin flipping, apparently on the assumption that the best possible false-positive rate for such testimony is 50 percent. Even accepting that assumption, the discussion in the previous chapter should make clear why the coin-flipping analogy does not work. Experts who are wrong more than one out of two times are only outdone by a coin toss when the base rate for violence is 50 percent or more. Yet the base rate for violence in the groups subject to prediction is seldom that high. As the AUC values reported in chapter 6 suggest, today experts can correctly identify those who will be violent at an accuracy rate, ranging from 45 to 75 percent, that is considerably higher than the base rate for violence within the prediction group, usually in the 15 to 35 percent range. Thus, the coin-flipping analogy is specious and misleading.

Nor is expert prediction testimony so unreliable that exclusion is required under *Daubert*, despite that decision's focus on error rates. The main thrust of that decision is not that expert testimony should be admitted only when it is provably accurate (a rule that would require exclusion of virtually all expert testimony), but rather that its basis should be subjected to some sort of verification process, preferably scientific in nature, so that it reflects "the knowledge and experience of [the relevant] discipline."[1] And, in contrast to culpability testimony, that verification process has been carried out with prediction testimony. Even if such testing produces false-positive and false-negative rates well *above* 50 percent, material prediction testimony derived from a methodology that does better than chance should be admitted, as long as the relevant error rates are also provided to the fact finder.

Others have similarly contended that *Daubert* cannot sensibly be construed to require accuracy, but rather should be read to require only good information about the *degree* of accuracy. For instance, Michael Saks, long an advocate for rigorous interpretation of *Daubert*, nonetheless has counseled against excluding expert evidence simply because "the witnesses practicing in that field assert erroneous conclusions with some regularity." As long as the fact finder is "informed about the likelihood of error in the opinions, and the court [is] satisfied that the factfinder is capable of properly adjusting the weight to be given to the evidence," Saks would permit such testimony.[2]

Daubert additionally suggests that courts look at whether the methodology employed by the expert is generally accepted among those in the relevant field, which is, of course, also the inquiry required by the *Frye* test applicable in most of the jurisdictions that have not adopted *Daubert*. This definition of probative value may, at first glance, appear to pose more of a problem for prediction testimony. As noted in chapter 6, even though clinical prediction testimony has been the mainstay of sentencing and commitment hearings for some time, the relevant official organizations have expressed considerable concern about its dependability, as have many adherents of the actuarial approach to prediction. Nor has the latter methodology always escaped criticism under *Frye*: at least one court has excluded actuarial prediction testimony because only a small proportion of the relevant profession is familiar with it.[3]

The fact remains that both methods of prediction are routinely used by large segments of the mental health profession, in practice and in court. The general acceptance notion cannot meaningfully be employed as a means of determining whether prediction evidence, writ large, should be banned. Rather, it is best used as a tool for ferreting out good and bad methods of obtaining such evidence, consistent with Rule 703's requirement that the facts or data forming the basis for expert testimony be "of a type reasonably relied upon by experts in the particular field." Recall from chapter 6 the contrast between the clinical prediction process employed by Dr. Kozol and his associates and that of Dr. Grigson. If the facts on which a clinical opinion is based are obtained during a short interview with no reference to third-party sources, or are taken entirely from a hypothetical question, as was true of Grigson's testimony in *Smith* and *Barefoot*, respectively, they should not be deemed "of a type reasonably relied upon by experts in the field." Such procedures do not, on their face and according to most mental health professionals, afford adequate protection against inaccuracy.[4] Similarly, there are accepted and unacceptable ways of using actuarial instruments and structured professional judgment.

An analysis of prediction testimony's probative value, then, reduces to two simple prescriptions. First, a court should permit a mental health professional to testify on the dangerousness issue only if it is established that he or she has followed generally accepted assessment procedures that attempt to insure a high degree of reliability, in both the social science and legal sense of the word. Second, if the testimony is admitted, error rate information must be provided the fact finder, either through the expert or some other means. If these conditions are met, the testimony should be considered sufficiently probative.

Evidentiary Sufficiency

Conceptually separate from, but practically related to, the probative value issue is the claim that prediction experts do not possess the ability to answer the prediction questions the law asks. As noted in chapter 6, in capital sentencing cases dangerousness must be proven beyond a reasonable doubt, a standard of proof that is also required by many sexual predator statutes. In all other commitment contexts, the Supreme Court has required that dangerousness be proven by at least clear and convincing evidence.[5] If one adopts the standard quantification of "proof beyond a reasonable doubt" as a 90 to 95 percent degree of certainty and of "clear and convincing proof" as a 75 percent degree of confidence (distinguishing both from the lower "preponderance of the evidence" standard used in civil cases, which is traditionally equated with a 51 percent level of certainty), prediction experts cannot, so the argument goes, satisfy the relevant standard of proof, given their 50+ percent false-positive rate. If that is true, the argument continues, there is no point in having them testify in the first place.[6]

A first response to this argument is that it confuses the admissibility issue with the sufficiency issue. As a leading evidence treatise states, "Whether the entire body of one party's evidence is sufficient to go to the jury is one question. Whether a particular item of evidence is relevant to the case is quite another. . . . Thus, the common objection that the inference for which the fact is offered 'does not necessarily follow' is untenable. It poses a standard of conclusiveness that very few single items of circumstantial evidence ever could meet. A brick is not a wall."[7]

One might note, however, that in a substantial majority of sentencing and commitment cases the expert prediction testimony *is* the entire body of evidence. In such cases, the testimony is both the brick and the wall. Then shouldn't the sufficiency and admissibility inquiries be merged?

If so, two other responses, one empirical and one legal, are possible. First, at least when the standard of proof is clear and convincing evidence, expert prediction testimony meets the sufficiency threshold if, rather than looking at false-positive and false-negative rates alone, we focus on their relationship to base rates. Specifically, expert prediction testimony might be considered clear and convincing proof any time the AUC value for the methodology in question is .75 or higher. Recall that such a value means that, given two randomly selected individuals, one drawn from the population of people who reoffend and the other drawn from the population of people who do not, there is a 75 percent chance that the methodology at issue will designate the violent individual a higher risk than the nonviolent individual.

The legal response to the sufficiency problem is to define "dangerousness" in such a way that error rates are minimized. For instance, many state commitment laws provide that a person is dangerous when he or she is "likely" or "substantially likely" to harm another.[8] If the word "likely" is equated with a 51 percent probability, then proving beyond a reasonable doubt that a person is dangerous under this definition would require only a 46 percent likelihood (.90 × .51) that the person will harm another. Even clinical prediction testimony can produce such proof of a "definite maybe," as Monahan and Wexler described this way of combining the standard of proof with the legal standard of dangerousness.[9] Other legal responses to the sufficiency problem include requiring a heightened standard of proof only for the relevant risk factors (e.g., two prior crimes, abuse as a child), or for the person's particular risk level (whether it be high, moderate, or low).[10]

All of these ploys may strike some readers as sleights of hand. The tension between society's urge to confine those who will harm others and its inability to identify precisely who these people are is not easily resolved. At bottom the lack-of-sufficiency argument is an attack on dangerousness as a legal criterion, not an argument about admissibility. Elsewhere I have contended that, in many settings, lowering the standard of proof when dangerousness is the issue is normatively justifiable and consistent with our current criminal justice jurisprudence.[11] But one can also sensibly conclude that, given the myriad proof problems, dangerousness should be eliminated as a ground for liberty deprivation. For purposes of this book, the substantive point is simply recognized and left at large.

B. The Helpfulness of Prediction Testimony

In chapter 5, I argued that expert testimony about culpability is helpful when it provides the judge and the jury with relevant information they may not otherwise have considered or, if such factor-based incremental validity has not been demonstrated, when the testimony provides information that is likely to challenge preconceptions about past mental states. In theory, such indirect approaches to evaluating helpfulness, necessitated by the untestable nature of culpability decisions, can be avoided in gauging the helpfulness of prediction testimony, given our ability to measure the accuracy of a prediction. A test of incremental validity in the prediction context would simply compare the accuracy of predictions made by experts with the accuracy of predictions made by judges and juries unassisted by experts.

To date, no such direct comparison has been made. However, several commentators have speculated that, given the inaccuracy of prediction experts, laypeople could do just as well, at least when compared to decisions using the clinical methodology for prediction.[12] More concretely, an analysis of the earliest studies on prediction efficacy concluded that "a nonclinician furnished with knowledge of past behavior may outperform a mental health professional relying solely on information garnered from a clinical interview."[13]

If these observations are borne out, *clinical* prediction testimony might not be sufficiently helpful to be admissible. In the meantime, however, common sense suggests that, under certain conditions, such testimony can be very useful to laypeople who have no experience with prediction. Just as culpability testimony can attune judges and juries to mitigating mental states they would not otherwise have considered, clinical prediction testimony can apprise them of potential risk factors they would not otherwise contemplate. It is unlikely, for instance, that jurors will be able to discern how a particular person reacts to stress and what types of stress are most likely to trigger violence in that person without some explanation by a clinician who is qualified to provide one.

As this last caveat suggests, however, only clinical prediction testimony that is based on factors derived from the risk literature should be considered helpful. The typical mental health professional is concerned with diagnosing and treating mental disorder, skills that are of limited utility in evaluating dangerousness. As George Dix has argued, a clinician unfamiliar with the research literature on dangerousness prediction should not be considered qualified to offer a clinical prediction of dangerousness, regardless of educational or experiential attainments.[14] Clinicians like Dr. Kozol are much more likely to meet these threshold requirements than someone like Dr. Grigson, whose testimony is not only deficient for the procedural reasons suggested earlier, but also often seemed to consist of little more than a bow to the type of past behavior that laypeople can evaluate for themselves. Grigson himself appeared to agree with this negative assessment of his expertise. As he told a journalist, "I think you could do away with the psychiatrist in these cases. Just take any man off the street, show him what the guy's done, and most of these things are so clear-cut he would say the same things I do."[15]

Compared to clinical prediction, actuarial and structured professional judgment assessments are more clearly useful to lay fact finders. Both are explicitly based on the risk literature. The specific probability estimates they provide are also beyond the ken of laypeople. Assuming such assessments are material and probative, as those terms were defined in earlier discussion, they are undoubtedly helpful as well.

Whether based on clinical or actuarial information, however, prediction testimony that goes beyond identifying risk factors and probability estimates to assert that a person is "dangerous," a "continuing threat to society," or "committable"—in other words, prediction testimony that addresses the ultimate legal issue—is not helpful, for the same sorts of reasons culpability testimony that declares an offender is insane is not helpful. The determination as to whether a person presents a risk to society sufficient to justify indeterminate commitment, an enhancement in sentence, or the death penalty is solely legal in nature, dependent on many factors other than those having to do with risk. For instance, a 20 percent probability that a person will harm others might justify short-term civil commitment, but not the death penalty. Other potential legal variables include the magnitude of the harm predicted (rape versus simple assault), its frequency, and its imminence.[16] Mental health professionals might be able to provide helpful information on each of these points, but they have no specialized insight into whether that information authorizes deprivation of life or liberty; thus, they cannot assist the fact finder on that ultimate issue.

Mental health professionals can sometimes helpfully address the *penultimate* issue—that is, whether an individual is "likely" or "substantially likely" to harm another—because that question is an empirical one. However, it is incumbent on the mental health professional to define what he or she means when using these terms. Furthermore, if such testimony is not associated with a specific probability estimate, based on actuarial data or structured professional judgment, then it should generally be barred as unduly prejudicial, for reasons developed in the next part of this chapter.

C. The Prejudicial Nature of Clinical Prediction Testimony

In his dissent in *Barefoot*, Justice Blackmun explained why he was unwilling to permit capital sentencing juries to hear expert prediction testimony (as opposed to lay testimony about past conduct): "The specious testimony of a psychiatrist, colored in the eyes of an impressionable jury by the inevitable untouchability of a medical specialist's words, equates with death itself."[17] Judge Garza, the lone Fifth Circuit judge willing to endorse Blackmun's prohibition of prediction testimony, expressed similar concerns about its prejudicial impact: "When a medical doctor testifies that 'future dangerousness' is a scientific inquiry on which [he or she has] particular expertise, and testifies that a particular defendant would be a 'continuing threat to society,' juries are almost always persuaded."[18]

Of course, the potent influence that Blackmun and Garza attribute to prediction experts would not be a significant concern if the experts were correct most or all of the time. But chapter 6 made clear that they are not. If Judge Garza's assertion that lay decision makers are "almost always persuaded" by expert prediction testimony is true, solid ground for exclusion would exist.

The *Barefoot* majority dismissed this concern, confident that the adversary system is "competent to uncover, recognize, and take due account of [prediction testimony's] shortcomings." Aided by this process, Justice White contended for the majority, the fact finder will be able to "separate the wheat from the chaff."[19] There is good reason to believe, however, that Blackmun and Garza are correct and White is wrong about the effect of prediction testimony in an adversarial proceeding, at least when it is clinical in nature.

As the *Barefoot* majority noted, cross-examination and rebuttal experts are usually viewed as adequate means of exposing the shortcomings of an expert witness, and indeed the first part of this book assumes that these traditional components of the adversary process can effectively expose weaknesses in expert testimony about culpability. But culpability testimony and prediction testimony differ from one another in a crucial way, one that significantly undermines the efficacy of adversarial techniques in the latter situation. Culpability testimony is proffered by a criminal defendant who has admitted, explicitly or implicitly, the commission of a crime and who must fight de jure or de facto presumptions of sanity and intentionality. As chapter 5 explained, the state's burden on rebuttal is substantially eased by the natural skepticism such a setting elicits. Prediction testimony, in contrast, is introduced by the government, either at sentencing, which directly follows conviction for a criminal offense, or at a commitment hearing, which is also preceded by a violent act of some sort. In this type of situation, the defense's case in rebuttal is a much tougher sell. Advocates against the state's position must convince the fact finder that the individual will not do again what he or she has just done.

Of course, sentencing and commitment are not the only proceedings in which a litigant must overcome a mind-set favoring the government; a criminal trial, initiated by a formal charge against the defendant, is another obvious example. But the potential pro-state bias at criminal trials is counteracted by the presumption of innocence and the high standard of proof, and can be further combated with concrete evidence that the defendant did not commit the claimed act or that someone else did. Prediction settings are vastly different: no "presumption of safeness" exists, either as a legal matter or in the minds of the decision makers; the quantum of proof demanded of the state in sentencing and commitment hearings, in practice, seldom approaches that required at trial, for reasons developed earlier, and demonstrating that a person will not act a certain way in the future is a much more problematic enterprise than proving he or she did not act a certain way in the past.

To these general points of concern can be added disquieting conjectures about the likely efficacy of specific rebuttal techniques. One might expect that providing the fact finder with information about false-positive rates (which I argued above should always occur) would diminish any tendency to hold the state expert's opinion in undue regard. But research on the well-documented "representativeness heuristic" demonstrates that people tend to lend significantly more credence to case-specific information than to generalized statistics.[20] Judges and jurors can tell themselves, with some basis, that regardless of their overall inaccuracy rate, the state's experts are right this time. Introduction of case-specific information through a rebuttal expert could, in theory, redress that problem. But if, as is often the case when offenders or respondents are indigent, there is no opposing expert,[21] or the expert can, in candor, do little more than identify a few "protective factors" meant to rebut the state's "risk factors," this stratagem will be unavailing as well. The one study directly on point found that even strong cross-examination and an opposing expert do not shake the influence of a state expert willing to pronounce the defendant dangerous.[22]

Also suggestive of clinical prediction's power are data on the outcome of proceedings in which it is offered. A survey of hearings under a Maryland criminal commitment program found that, despite the fact that the staff's prediction of dangerousness was virtually always contested (albeit not always by opposing experts), judges agreed with its recommendations in 86 percent of the cases.[23] Similarly, only 31 (or 12 percent) of the 257 patients that Kozol and his staff originally diagnosed as dangerous were released by the courts, many for reasons having nothing to do with perceived risk.[24] And Texas capital sentencing juries virtually never disagreed with Dr. Grigson's clinical predictions, despite cross-examination and rebuttal experts.[25] At least in these cases, Judge Garza appears to be right that lay fact finders *are* "almost always persuaded" by clinical prediction testimony proffered by the state, a conclusion that is particularly troubling given the very low likelihood that the judges and juries involved in them were correct in concluding that more than 85 percent of the individuals they committed or sentenced to death would have reoffended if released.[26]

One might be tempted to explain these results simply as a demonstration that, when given the opportunity, laypeople will almost always conclude that offenders and individuals subject to commitment are dangerous, whether or not experts confirm that view. In interesting contrast to these data, however, is research suggesting that other types of prediction testimony are much less likely to sway judges and juries. For instance, concordance between the government's expert witnesses and the ultimate decision in sexual predator proceedings, where actuarial testimony predominates, is much lower than 85 percent.[27] Numerous studies have confirmed that clinical prediction testimony is more persuasive to lay decision makers than actuarial testimony, despite the latter's superior accuracy.[28] Of particular import given the debate in *Barefoot* about the usefulness of the adversary process is a study finding not only that "jurors weigh clinical opinion expert testimony more heavily than actuarial expert testimony," but that "adversarial procedures may be insufficient to remove this bias."[29] A second study confirmed that, whereas cross-examination of clinical testimony has little impact on dangerousness ratings, cross-examination of actuarial testimony does reduce those ratings.[30]

These findings makes sense. Cross-examination and rebuttal experts aimed at attacking the risk factors underlying clinical prediction testimony will, at best, be able to suggest in some vague way that the subject is a lower risk than the state's expert believes. In contrast, when risk factors are associated with a precise probability of recidivism, as occurs under the actuarial approach, cross-examination and rebuttal can suggest in more concrete terms how that probability will be lowered if particular factors are not present or particular protective factors are present. Laypeople may also be less likely to give in to their preexisting inclination to find offenders and commitment respondents dangerous when the expert says "This person belongs to a group that reoffends at a [particular] rate," rather than simply pronounces that the person is a high risk or is likely to reoffend.

The implications of these observations and research findings are twofold. First, the government should not be permitted to introduce clinical prediction testimony in its case in chief. Contrary to the assertion of the *Barefoot* majority, the adversarial process cannot effectively expose the shortcomings of this type of opinion evidence, with the result that lay decision makers give it too much weight. Balancing the relatively low probative value and helpfulness of such testimony against its prejudicial impact requires its exclusion.

The same balancing analysis suggests the opposite result, however, when the government seeks to introduce prediction testimony tied to empirically based probability estimates of the type produced by actuarial assessment or associated with some structured professional judgment instruments. As earlier parts of this chapter demonstrated, the latter type of testimony is both more probative and more helpful than clinical prediction testimony. And, as just discussed, testimony based on empirically derived risk estimates is not as likely to be misused by the fact finder. Perhaps, given its quantified nature, laypeople are better able to judge the true import of such testimony, or perhaps they are simply more distrustful of information in the form of data than information that tells an idiographic story about the subject of the prediction.[31] Whatever the reason for the difference, it leads to the conclusion that the government should be able to use such testimony in its case in chief.

D. The Subject-First Regime

The foregoing analysis does not require a complete ban on clinical prediction testimony. The offender/respondent (who from now on will simply be called the subject) should still be able to use clinical prediction to undermine the state's claim that he or she is a menace to society. Although clinical prediction testimony is less probative and less helpful than testimony that reports empirically based risk estimates, it is also less likely to have a prejudicial impact when it is proffered by the subject as opposed to the state. That is because, when proffered by the subject, prediction testimony is aimed at dispelling preconceptions, not feeding them. Under such circumstances, it is much less likely to overinfluence the fact finder.

Furthermore, just as criminal defendants are entitled to tell their culpability stories using suspect testimony (as explained in chapter 3), the subjects of prediction hearings should be able to tell the best story they can about their future. Under what I will call a "subject-first regime," they would have the option of using clinical testimony to do so, knowing that this step will open the door to rebuttal using the same kind of evidence. When the state's actuarial evidence is weak, subjects are unlikely to opt for this strategy. When it is strong, they are more likely to do so, arguing, in effect, that the statistical estimates should be adjusted downward in light of personal characteristics that the actuarial analysis did not take into account.

The subject-first approach has a time-honored analogue in the character evidence rule.[32] Recognized in some form in every state and the federal courts,[33] this rule prohibits the prosecution from introducing evidence concerning the defendant's character in a criminal trial unless the defendant first raises the character issue. The rule's prohibition is motivated by the same type of evidentiary concerns that were just raised in connection with clinical prediction testimony. Evidence of bad character is relevant to the question of whether the defendant committed the crime because it shows that the defendant has a tendency to commit crimes or other bad acts and thus might have committed the one currently being prosecuted. But against the probative value of such evidence must be weighed the possibility that proof of bad character will lead the fact finder to convict the defendant merely because he or she has been a bad person, rather than because the state has proved its case. Because the risk is so great that negative character evidence will produce an erroneous decision, its introduction is barred unless and until the defendant decides that its potential for misleading the fact finder can be overcome (or at least neutralized) by countervailing evidence of good character.[34] Analogously, because the risk is great that clinical prediction testimony will prompt an erroneous prediction, its introduction should be prohibited unless the subject opens the door to its use.

The character evidence rule serves as a well-established precedent for the type of rule proposed here. However, there are some unique conceptual and practical issues that arise in applying a subject-first rule to clinical dangerousness testimony. The following three sections explore the most important of these issues.

The Type of Evidence the State May Use to Prove Dangerousness

If the state is barred from introducing clinical predictions, it will be deprived of a primary means of proving dangerousness. But it may still resort to two other sources of proof. First, for the reasons outlined above, it may rely on empirically based risk estimates, if they are material to the case. As indicated in chapter 6, for some populations and some types of harmful behavior, material statistical information is scarce. Courts will thus sometimes have to make difficult decisions as to whether a risk estimate derived from an actuarial instrument normed on a dissimilar population or using a definition of harm that varies from the applicable legal standard can reasonably be extrapolated to cover the case at hand.

A second permissible method of proving dangerousness, either in combination with or instead of empirical estimates, is the introduction of lay evidence describing prior antisocial acts. The strong consensus of the risk literature is that the number and type of prior violent acts committed by an individual are the most relevant factors to a prediction of future behavior.[35] The type of proceeding involved will dictate the type of prior acts that might be considered. If, as the Supreme Court suggested in *Jones v. United States*,[36] larceny is dangerous behavior for purposes of commitment of insanity acquittees, then evidence of past thefts would be admissible in such proceedings, even if those acts neither harmed nor threatened anyone. On the other hand, such evidence may not be admissible in a capital sentencing proceeding concerned with determining the defendant's potential for committing serious bodily harm in the future. Courts will also have to decide, as they do now in sentencing and other contexts, whether evidence short of conviction for an offense is sufficient proof of a particular prior bad act.[37]

Finally, of course, if the subject opts to use clinical prediction testimony, the state may do so as well. This follows from the analogy to the character evidence rule, as well as general fairness principles.

When the Subject Opens the Door

Determining when the subject should be said to have opened the door to state use of clinical prediction will not always be easy. Certainly, if the defense puts a clinician such as Dr. Kozol on the stand to discuss risk factors, the state may respond in kind. At the same time, the defense should be able to respond in kind to both actuarial-type prediction testimony and lay testimony about past acts *without* fear of triggering state use of clinical evidence. But other scenarios present harder questions.

In criminal commitment proceedings, a commonly contested threshold issue is whether the subject is mentally disordered.[38] Because this issue focuses on present mental state, use of a mental health professional to address it should not authorize state use of clinical prediction testimony. In sexual predator commitment proceedings, however, the issue of whether the subject has a "mental abnormality" is often explicitly defined in terms of whether the condition "predisposes" the individual to commit further violent acts.[39] If the defense decides to use a clinician to address this subject, it is in effect introducing clinical prediction testimony. In such situations, the state should be entitled to respond in similar fashion.

A second, closely related issue that arises in sexual predator proceedings (and perhaps in other commitment proceedings as well) is whether the subject is volitionally impaired. This inquiry appears to be mandated by the Supreme Court's decision in *Kansas v. Hendricks*, which upheld sexual predator commitment on condition that the state show that the individual is dangerous "beyond [his or her] control."[40] This language implies that the state must show some evidence of impulsivity or undeterrability in order to commit under these laws.[41] Although one's propensity to act impulsively might be distinguishable, in a technical sense, from one's dangerousness, the two concepts are so closely related that, once again, a defense decision to use a clinician on the former issue should permit the state to use a clinician to address either or both.

A third potential door-opening scenario involves sentencing. In sentencing proceedings, particularly capital sentencing, offenders frequently present clinical evidence about culpability in an attempt to mitigate the disposition. Thus, a defense witness might testify that the subject was suffering extreme mental or emotional distress at the time of the offense, or was unable to appreciate the wrongfulness of his or her criminal acts.[42] This testimony often is based on precisely the same type of information an an-amnestic approach to clinical prediction might collect. Here, however, the defense's expert is clearly focused on past mental state and culpability issues, not future acts and dangerousness. Such testimony should not authorize state use of clinical prediction testimony.

Finally, both criminal commitment and sentencing proceedings frequently focus on the treatability of the subject.[43] This scenario is the most difficult to resolve in a subject-first regime. Both dangerousness and treatability assessments involve predictions. More important, when the defense introduces clinical evidence based on the latter type of assessment, it is often suggesting that the individual either is not dangerous or will not be so for long, given proper treatment. Frequently, however, such testimony may focus on therapeutic modalities, such as antidepressant medication or occupational therapy, that are not directly aimed at preventing the reoccurrence of violent behavior. In such circumstances, the court may need to make a sensitive appraisal of the testimony's scope to determine whether the state should be able to use clinical prediction evidence.

As an efficiency mechanism, the defense should be required, analogous to common practice with respect to past mental state testimony,[44] to give notice to the state and the court whenever it is contemplating using a clinician at criminal commitment or sentencing. In that way, door-opening issues can be sorted out prior to adjudication and the state can prepare accordingly. Even with this adjustment, a subject-first regime should not involve a major shake-up of current defense practice. Defense use of clinicians on mental abnormality and volitional impairment issues in commitment hearings is and probably will remain rare, and when the defense does decide to have a clinician testify on those issues it will probably also want the prediction issue addressed, so the door will be opened in any event. A similar coincidence of aims usually is present when treatability is at issue. If not, the defense may often be able to structure the clinician's testimony about treatability so that it does not directly address dangerousness.

When the State May Use a Clinician

The state's prerogatives should mirror the subject's. If the defense uses a clinical prediction expert, as defined above, then the state should be able to do so. However, if the defense does not rely on expert clinical evidence to address dangerousness or issues that are really dangerousness in disguise ("predisposing" mental abnormality, volitional impairment, or treatability), the state should not be able to so either. Instead, it must rely on empirically derived probability estimates or lay testimony to address these issues.[45]

The one exception to this rule, consistent with what was said earlier in connection with the defense's prerogatives, is that the government should be able to present clinical testimony about treatability when it does not directly implicate dangerousness. For instance, in an insanity acquittee commitment hearing, the state should be able to introduce clinical evidence showing that, if the subject is found to be dangerous, treatment would be most efficacious in an inpatient unit rather than on an outpatient basis.[46] It also bears iteration, with respect to the treatability issue, that the state would always be permitted to present both hard actuarial data on the prognosis for given populations of patients and reports of prior treatment successes or failures with respect to a particular individual, analogous to the actuarial and lay proof of dangerousness that the state is always permitted to adduce.

E. Civil Commitment

The prohibition on state use of clinical prediction testimony in its case in chief and the associated subject-first rule, which I have argued should govern sentencing and criminal commitment, probably should not apply to civil commitment, at least at the front end. This is so for two reasons, one practical, one evidentiary.

The practical reason is simply that the proposed regime could probably not be implemented in the emergency commitment setting. A mentally ill person who has just threatened to kill his wife or has taken a sledgehammer to a neighbor's car should not be allowed to go free while the information necessary to use an actuarial or structured professional judgment instrument is collected. Such individuals are often brought to a mental health professional, who, using his or her best clinical judgment, must decide immediately whether to hospitalize them, against their will if necessary. Given the exigencies, state use of clinical predictions of dangerousness and treatability may not be avoidable, nor would there be time for the defense to assess its options and give pretrial notice of the type proposed earlier.

The second reason evidentiary restrictions on prediction testimony might be relaxed in the emergency commitment setting is that the prediction called for in such situations is likely to be more accurate than the long-term predictions that have been the focus of discussion to this point. John Monahan has summarized the theoretical grounds for this assertion as follows: "In emergency commitment...there is a small situational and temporal 'gap' between the behavior used as a predictor and the outcome that is being predicted. One is directly sampling actions, e.g., threatening words and gestures, that are 'as similar as possible to the behavior used on criterion measures,' e.g., fulfilled threats. In violence as in other areas, it is potentially true that 'predictions about individual behavior can be generated accurately from knowledge of the environments in which the behavior occurs.'"[47] If, in fact, as research to date suggests,[48] clinical predictions of imminent dangerousness based on recent behavior in the community can provide "clear and convincing proof" of dangerousness, the rationale for the subject-first rule disappears.

Both the practical and the evidentiary arguments against the defendant-first approach begin to lose their persuasiveness, however, as one moves out of the emergency detention context. If, for instance, a commitment proceeding takes place two or more weeks after the initial intervention (as provided for in several state statutes),[49] there will probably be time for the respondent to gather the appropriate nonclinical information and make a decision regarding the presentation of clinical testimony. More important, the accuracy of any clinical prediction of dangerousness will decrease as the "situational and temporal gap" between the precipitating behavior and the outcome that is being predicted (i.e., violence in the community) increases; prejudice concerns again become paramount. An added concern is that adversarial protections are notoriously lacking at civil commitment proceedings;[50] although previous discussion suggested that cross-examination and rebuttal witnesses are seldom successful at exposing flaws in clinical prediction testimony, their absence here nonetheless enhances the need for a subject-first rule outside the emergency setting.

——

F. Conclusion

Expert prediction testimony, whether based on actuarial assessment, structured professional judgment, or clinical assessment, will usually be material, probative, and helpful if certain tenets are followed. When prediction testimony is based on group data, the materiality factor requires courts to pay close attention to norming and criterion variable issues. To ensure that prediction testimony is both adequately probative and optimally helpful, courts should qualify as experts only those mental health professionals who are familiar with the risk literature and modern risk methodologies and who utilize appropriate assessment procedures; courts should also ensure that those experts they permit to testify describe, or at least respond to, the pertinent error rates and avoid the ultimate legal issue of whether a subject's risk factors require legal action. Finally, in sentencing and criminal commitment proceedings, courts should exclude even qualified testimony when it is clinical in nature (rather than grounded on empirically derived probability estimates) unless it is presented by the defense to support a claim of nondangerousness or by the state to rebut the same.

8

Conclusions: The Structure of Expertise in Criminal Cases

Difficult problems of proof pervade the legal system. But perhaps the two most daunting tasks legal fact finders must face are assessing why the perpetrator of a harmful act committed it and whether it will happen again. Not only are culpability and dangerousness determinations impossible to make with a high degree of certainty, but the consequences of getting them wrong are drastic: either an unjust deprivation of liberty or life, or a failure to confine a person who deserves to be punished or who poses a threat to society.

In the past half-century, mental health professionals have come to play a crucial role in these important decisions. Indeed, they always testify for the government in civil and criminal commitment cases, virtually always provide expert evidence for the defense in cases involving insanity and related legal defenses, and are routinely involved in prediction issues that arise in sentencing. This book has been an attempt to assess whether these roles should continue and, if so, in what form.

As this book has documented, the courts have generally taken a relaxed approach to opinion evidence from mental health professionals in criminal and commitment cases. On those rare occasions when the courts have refused to accept particular testimony it has been for a mix of reasons: its threat to doctrinal boundaries, its nomothetic nature, its novelty, its propensity for usurping the jury's role, and last, and sometimes least, its shaky reliability. Ironically, evidence that is demonstrably based on empirical evidence is more likely to be meet judicial resistance than testimony based on clinical intuition.

In the past decade or so, however, the Supreme Court's decision in *Daubert v. Merrell Dow Pharmaceutical Co.* and its reaffirmation of that decision in *Kumho Tire Co. v. Carmichael* have focused greater attention on the accuracy of expert testimony as a threshold admissibility factor. In particular, these decisions have provided impetus for the critics of forensic psychiatry and psychology, who argue that *Daubert*'s emphasis on reliability spells doom for much, if not all, opinion testimony from mental health professionals on culpability and dangerousness issues. And some courts have begun to listen.

As a way of summarizing the basic themes of this book, this final chapter explains why a rigid interpretation of *Daubert* would be an unfortunate development for "criminal justice" (here meant to include the civil and criminal commitment settings as well as criminal adjudication and sentencing). The argument proceeds in three stages, laid out in the first three sections of this chapter. First, it is clear that *Daubert* and *Kumho Tire* push the criminal justice system away from the notion that knowledge is socially constructed and toward a positivist epistemology that assumes we can know things objectively. Second, in the long run, that development will be good for prosecutors and bad for criminal defendants and those subjected to criminal and civil commitment. Third, the consequence of that differential impact will be a criminal justice system that is not only less fair, but also less reliable. To put the issues in perspective, the discussion in these first three sections of the chapter will range beyond analysis of testimony from mental health professionals to look at other types of forensic evidence presented by experts, including testimony about ballistics, handwriting, and the interrogation process.

The final section recanvasses the prescriptions in this book in explaining how we should go about proving culpability and dangerousness. It also makes a few predictions about the future of expert testimony by mental health professionals.

A. The Positivist Push

There is no doubt that, in theory, *Daubert* moves the admissibility analysis in a positivist direction. *Daubert* and *Kumho Tire* establish reliability as the linchpin of admissibility analysis. The best-known pre-*Daubert* approaches were much less aggressive in this regard. The balancing test admits expert testimony unless its probative value is substantially outweighed by its potential for confusing or overawing the jury, and *Frye*'s general acceptance test looks at the extent to which the basis of the testimony has found favor in the relevant professional community. *Daubert* mandates that testimony be subject to verification through the scientific method or some other transparent methodology, whereas the other two tests come close to relying solely on the ipse dixit of a single individual or of a group, so long as he, she, or it is well credentialed.[1]

Thus, on their face, the balancing and general acceptance tests are much more likely than the *Daubert* trilogy to give legal fact finders wide-ranging, "socially constructed" information.[2] Under the balancing test, virtually all expertise is admissible, and under the general acceptance test all expertise that is not novel should get in. Under the reliability standard, on the other hand, only verifiable information is admissible. The first two tests are likely to permit any expert testimony the reliability test would let in, with the possible exception of testimony based on new, verifiable findings (which might not be admissible under *Frye* but would be under *Daubert*). In contrast, the reliability test is likely to exclude a substantial amount of expert testimony that is admissible under the balancing and general acceptance tests. That means that, under *Daubert*, legal fact finders will be exposed to much less soft science and much less speculation based on experience. In short, the reliability standard should make the epistemology of the courtroom decidedly more scientific, in the classic sense.

Of course, in criminal and commitment cases that prediction has not been entirely borne out. Courts in *Daubert* jurisdictions still admit scientifically weak expert testimony, proffered by both the prosecution and the defense. Suspect testimony from handwriting and fingerprint experts continues unabated in many jurisdictions, and, as this book has made clear, the prosecution often benefits from soft testimony about subjects such as dangerousness and the behavior of child sex abuse victims.[3] Defense experts may be somewhat more likely to be rejected post-*Daubert*, but, as chapter 2 indicated, many trial courts still routinely allow them to testify about syndromes and other unusual mental states that are only weakly supported by data.

At the same time, the clear trend is toward more exclusion. Paul Gianelli has noted that *Daubert* has triggered attacks, some of them successful, on handwriting evidence, hair comparisons, fingerprint examinations, firearms identification, bite marks, and intoxication testing.[4] An empirical study of criminal cases concluded in 1998 found that, although there was only a marginally significant decline in the proportion of expert evidence admitted, judges were clearly scrutinizing such evidence more closely after *Daubert*.[5] It is likely that momentum in this direction will increase, now that *Kumho Tire* and the Federal Rules of Evidence have closed the "technical and specialized knowledge" loophole by applying the reliability standard to that type of expertise as well as to scientific testimony.[6]

B. Daubert's Disadvantages for the Defense

Proponents of *Daubert* think that the trend toward rigorous screening of expert evidence is all to the good and would like to see it accelerated. I am much more ambivalent on this score, at least in the criminal and commitment contexts. Most of the reasons for this ambivalence were expressed in the foregoing chapters. A final overarching reason, not yet fully explored in these pages, begins with the assertion that the scientific way of seeing the world is much better for prosecutors than for the defense.

The preliminary reaction to this assertion is likely to be that it gets things backward. Prosecutors stand to lose a significant amount of expert support if *Daubert* is applied rigorously to testimony about handwriting, fingerprints, and the like. Defense attorneys would also find many of their experts excluded or limited under a strict *Daubert* regime, but many might be willing to put up with that development if the prosecution were prevented from presenting suspect forensic evidence.

In the long run, however, the likelihood is high that criminal defendants will suffer much more than the state if *Daubert* is taken seriously. That is because prosecutors and defense attorneys need different types of experts to make their cases in chief. The types of facts on which the prosecution relies are more easily subjected to testing, more likely to be perceived as material to the case, more likely to produce useful error rate information, and institutionally and financially more feasible to develop.

Testability

The prosecution uses experts primarily to support assertions about physical facts. It most often needs opinion evidence to prove identity, as in testimony that ties a fingerprint, a strand of hair, or a signature to the defendant, or a bullet to a particular gun. Of more relevance to this book, it also frequently uses experts to prove that a physical act occurred, such as abuse, or will occur, as in dangerousness determinations.

In contrast, the defense is most likely to use experts in its affirmative case to support claims about the defendant's mental state at the time of the offense, such as insanity, lack of premeditation, extreme mental or emotional stress, or learned helplessness. Although the prosecution sometimes bears the burden of proving mental states, the defense always bears the burden of production on these issues.[7] The prosecution needs experts on mental state issues only if and when the defense decides to use a mental health professional. Thus, it is up to the defense to put mental health experts into play.

This difference in the type of experts the prosecution and defense need for their prima facie cases becomes extremely significant in a strict *Daubert* regime. Assertions about physical facts are eminently more verifiable than assertions about past mental state. Testing the hypothesis that a single fingerprint is enough to provide a match or that a certain handwriting expert is proficient at identifying authors of script is relatively easy as science goes.[8] A similar procedure can be undertaken in studying prediction expertise. Although, as chapter 6 pointed out, perfect data about recidivism will probably never be available, researchers can, through both retrospective and cross-validation studies, come reasonably close to pinpointing the risk factors that correlate with individuals who end up reoffending.

The same cannot be said for research on past mental state, for reasons described in detail in chapter 3. Put briefly, the point is that mental states such as insanity, lack of premeditation, extreme mental and emotional stress, and reasonable fear of harm are closer to social constructions than to objective facts; a scientist or technician can tell us the extent to which fingerprints match or whether a person predicted to be violent was in fact violent, but only juries can tell us whether a defendant premeditated, appreciated the wrongfulness of his or her actions, or experienced irresistible urges or overwhelming fears. Further, even if such constructions are somehow reducible to objective referents, gaining access to them is extremely difficult. For obvious ethical and legal reasons they cannot be replicated in the lab. And even if they could be, or can be discovered through ex post interviewing, scientific measurement of their existence at the time of a criminal offense is very difficult; the stability of intent, the depth of appreciation, and the strength of urges and fears are not easily susceptible to calibration even in the present, much less the past. In a strict *Daubert* regime, the typical defense expert may be able to do little more than describe a criminal defendant's alleged thoughts and actions and leave further inferences to the fact finder.

Fit

A second, more subtle difference between prosecution and defense expertise is that, on those occasions when verifiability is possible, the latter type of expertise is more prone to lack fit. *Daubert* and *Kumho Tire* have made the fit inquiry a fundamental aspect of admissibility analysis.[9] The key issue here, as Denbeaux and Risinger indicate, is "the reliability of the proffered expertise specifically as it applies to the task for which it is being utilized in the litigation in which it is offered, not in some more global sense."[10] This reliability-for-a-specific-purpose test is likely to exclude more defense expertise than prosecution expertise because, given the greater ease with which they can be found in the real world or simulated in the laboratory, physical facts of the type prosecutors need to prove can be investigated with much more specificity than the usual types of claims defendants make.

For instance, if investigators want to determine the accuracy of fingerprint identification when there are only two partial prints or only three match points, they can simply replicate those situations using known individuals, in as many variations as they desire, and ascertain the experts' ability to match the prints with the full prints of the sample. In scientific terms, the research can be carried out with objective criterion variables, having high external validity.

Scenarios useful to criminal defense experts, by contrast, are much more difficult to arrange. This is most obvious with respect to mental states during criminal events. Even if they could somehow be discovered and measured, these states are so varied in content and process that obtaining scientific data about them that is generalizable to legal proceedings is close to futile.

This problem with defense evidence does not afflict just past mental state evidence. Consider two other types of defense expertise: false confession and eyewitness testimony. Ideal research material to determining whether a confession is false would either locate people who have confessed to a crime they did not commit and then try to trace the factors that led to the confession or simulate the types of police techniques hypothesized to cause such confessions. The first type of research—finding people who have confessed falsely and then classifying possible causal variables—is virtually impossible because of the low base rate of false confessions and the difficulty of determining when confessions are in fact false.[11] The second type of study—analogue research—would have the most potent external validity if police subjected individuals to various interrogation techniques, such as prolonged questioning, promises of leniency, and deception about the strength of the evidence, in situations where it was known that the suspect did not commit the act police want him or her to admit to. But, for obvious reasons, practical and ethical problems with this type of research abound. An alternative analogue study might involve accusing innocent subjects of something noncriminal and subjecting them to lesser pressures; if false confessions occurred under such circumstances, one might be able to draw conclusions about the effects of police techniques. But the prosecutor confronted with such research would rightly point to the fact that the consequences of a false admission in the noncriminal context do not approximate imprisonment and thus make such admissions easier.[12]

Most important for present purposes, even if it can be carried out, neither kind of research about the interrogation process is likely to produce results that easily fit a proposition in criminal adjudication. Rather, the findings are likely to read something like "The longer the interrogation, the more likely a false confession occurs" or "People who are diagnosed as submissive based on personality testing are more likely to give in to suggestions." These general pronouncements say very little about the case at hand.

Simulation of eyewitness situations is somewhat easier because here the criterion variable is a physical fact: whether a particular person is the perpetrator of a particular act. Researchers can subject experimental eyewitnesses to crime-relevant scenarios varying the race of the perpetrator, the presence of a weapon, the length of the encounter, lighting and distance, and a host of factors having to do with the nature of the identification procedure (lineups, photo arrays, etc.), and then gauge the ability of the subjects to describe and identify the actual perpetrators.[13] For this reason, as chapter 2 noted, study of eyewitness accuracy tends to be among the most reliable research, as far as it goes. But in the end, it does not go very far. Similar to false confession research, all eyewitness research is likely to tell us is something comparative, to wit: "All else being equal, an eyewitness who is confronted with a gun is less likely to be accurate in identifying the perpetrator than someone who was not confronted by a weapon."[14]

It should not be surprising that courts have tended to exclude this type of testimony.[15] Sometimes the exclusion is explicitly on unreliability grounds, but more commonly, consistent with the foregoing comments, it results from a judicial determination that the evidence is not helpful to the trier of fact because, given its general nature, it is within the ken of the jury and will not help resolve the particular issues in the case.[16] A study of appellate court decisions verifies that the type of behavioral science expert most likely to be excluded by the courts is the experimental psychologist—precisely the type of expert who testifies about eyewitness and confession issues—and that the usual reason given for the exclusion is the testimony's failure to assist the fact finder.[17] These types of holdings, though questionable as a matter of policy,[18] are easily traceable to *Daubert*'s concern with fit; trial judges can tell themselves that, although the research is interesting, it does very little to resolve whether *this* confession or *this* eyewitness identification is false.

The reader who remembers the materiality discussion in chapter 6 may be thinking that there is at least one type of *prosecution* evidence—actuarial prediction testimony—that also suffers from a serious fit problem. The nomothetic nature of this testimony does make it seem less individualized. But in this case the difficulties with fit are countered by another aspect of *Daubert*—its declaration that the availability of error rates goes far toward making expert testimony admissible.

Error Rates

Emphasis on errors rates, like the emphasis on testability and fit, will hinder the defense much more than the prosecution. Forensic labs working for the prosecution can produce error rates for all sorts of scenarios, for the reasons indicated earlier. Prediction research can also easily generate false positive and false negative data. In contrast, particularized error rates are much harder to generate in connection with the type of social science research used by the defense because of the multiplicity of potential variables that might explain criminal behavior or its perception. Even with respect to eyewitness testimony, which is based on the most sophisticated of all the social science research canvassed here, meaningful error rates are hard to come by. As Gary Wells, a prominent researcher in this area, has noted, "Unfortunately . . . effect size measures from [eyewitness] experiments are not necessarily applicable to actual cases (even when measured as standard deviation units), because experiments tend to hold constant and ensure the independence of other variables that could influence eyewitness accuracy. The result of this is that most eyewitness experts are reluctant to make firm statements regarding effect sizes."[19] And when experts demonstrate this reluctance, courts have been quite willing to find it grounds for exclusion.[20]

The dichotomy between prosecution and defense expertise would be even greater under one interpretation of *Daubert*. Suppose research shows that forensic investigators with a two-point match can make a correct fingerprint identification only 20 percent of the time; in other words, there is an 80 percent error rate in such situations. Or suppose that the false-positive rate for a given prediction methodology is 80 percent. As chapter 7 noted, one can make a good argument that, under *Daubert*, even this relatively high error rate should not be a bar to admission because the error rate can be communicated to the jury, and the jury can act accordingly. Only the failure to have the error rate handy would lead to exclusion. The defense is much more likely to fail in this regard because of the aforementioned methodological difficulties.

Ease of Production

This latter comment suggests the final way *Daubert* hurts the defense more than the prosecution. Research takes money. The state has more of it. Of course, the defense is always resource-disadvantaged when it comes to expert testimony. But *Daubert* exacerbates that disadvantage by putting a premium on verifiability, rather than allowing anyone with credentials to testify.

The state not only has more money but is better equipped, in an institutional sense, to use it. Prosecutors are much better than defense attorneys at sharing information. That is partly because the government is by its nature a more coherent entity than the defense bar, but it is also because the state is better able to anticipate the scientific issues that will arise and act accordingly. Indeed, *Daubert* has already stimulated massive federal efforts to validate the type of forensic expertise typically relied on by the prosecution; in 2001 alone, for instance, Congress appropriated over $12 million to the FBI for scientific research on projects such as identification of latent fingerprints and gunshot residue.[21] There is no analogous criminal defense effort to generate scientific research on past mental states, false confessions, and eyewitnesses and, given the atomistic nature of defense work, unlikely to be any. Further, any one attorney's attempt to obtain research for a particular case is likely to meet a hostile reception from the courts because it is so obviously motivated by litigation needs.[22]

Independent academic researchers have often come to the aid of defense attorneys. But their resources pale when compared to the government's. The $12 million of federal support appropriated for government researchers in 2001 represents three times the amount the National Science Foundation dispensed in *thirteen* years (from 1989 to 2002) to researchers investigating issues connected with eyewitness testimony, confessions, and insanity issues.[23] More important for the thesis of this book, any alliance between academics and the defense that does exist might not survive more rigorous application of *Daubert*. In contrast to the effect of exclusion on prosecution experts, who often work for the government, exclusion of academics' testimony will not necessarily work any change in research agenda because neither the reputation nor the livelihood of these professional scholars necessarily depends on the courtroom. This fact, together with the fact that defense attorneys are typically not repeat players for these types of expertise, may mean that the hope that strict admissibility standards will trigger better research will not be borne out in this context.[24]

C. Daubert's Potential Damage to Criminal Justice

These observations lead to the following question, which gets at the third and final proposition I want to address: Assuming *Daubert* has the differential impact on prosecution and defense expertise just described, is it something we should worry about, or is it merely a sensible consequence of focusing criminal cases on reliability? My answer is that we should worry, because *Daubert's* reliability test, if it does lead to significant exclusion of defense evidence, will make the system both less fair and less reliable.

As many commentators have pointed out, *Daubertian* reliability is not the only objective of the criminal justice system. Chapter 4 of this book speaks of the defendant's entitlement to voice, derived in the first instance from the Supreme Court's due process case law establishing the right to testify, but also from the idea that the criminal justice system's legitimacy is undermined when courts squelch the defendant's efforts, however tenuous, to tell his or her story. Other commentators have made a similar point based on the procedural justice literature, which suggests that an important component of adjudication, from society's as well as the individual's perspective, is the perception that people have an opportunity to make their point of view known.[25] Katherine Goldwasser has additionally argued that reliability-based exclusionary rules, when used against the defendant, impair the Sixth Amendment right to jury trial. That right, she notes, is "founded on the notion that juries are likely to be more protective of an accused than are judges" because, as a diverse group of laypeople, they will more likely "be receptive to—or at least give meaningful consideration to—the unusual, unexpected, or even implausible stories criminal defendants sometimes bring to court."[26] And Janet Hoeffel has forcefully contended that the Sixth Amendment Compulsory Process Clause has been and should be read to accord the criminal defendant the right to present all material evidence. To interpret *Daubert* to require something more than materiality, she argues, undermines the fair process goals of rationality, predictability, and consistency, as judges futilely try to implement an amorphous reliability threshold in a wide array of contexts.[27]

I will not rehearse these arguments any further here. They all suggest that, whatever might be the case in the civil context out of which *Daubert* and *Kumho Tire* arose, in the criminal setting concerns about process should trump concerns about reliability: the defense should be able to use clinical experts both to bolster lack-of-culpability arguments and to attack contentions about risk. But we should also recognize that reliability is not necessarily sacrificed when the defense is permitted to use evidence that fails the positivist threshold dictated by a stringent interpretation of *Daubert*. There are at least five reasons for thinking so.

The Inscrutability of Culpability and Dangerousness Determinations

The first reason has already been suggested, in this chapter and throughout the book. When the expert addresses inferences about past mental state or future violence of a particular individual, we cannot *know* whether the opinion is unreliable, and thus exclusion may work a real harm to accuracy goals. Aside from the malingerer (who can often be detected), defendants who say they suffered mental aberrations during the offense may well be right; at least, we have no scientific way of proving them wrong. And although we do have a scientific methodology for evaluating dangerousness, at bottom even the individual who is the subject of prediction cannot say for sure what he or she will do in the future. Thus, legal decision makers are ultimately guessing on both of these issues.

This reasoning also explains why defense-proffered expert opinion about mental state or dangerousness should not be excluded simply because it is based on diagnoses or other concepts that are unreliable in the social science sense. Disagreement between two evaluators assessing the same individual does mean that one is wrong, but it does not mean that *both* are wrong. If the only grounds for declaring a defense evaluator's opinion unreliable is interrater comparison data, we should err on the side of letting the testimony in. (At the same time, in an effort to improve consistency, we can insist on assessment techniques that consider, in a structured way, the legally relevant variables, as chapters 4, 5, and 7 suggested.)

Fact Finder Heuristics

The second reason the admission of scientifically untested defense evidence may not undermine, and may even enhance, ultimate reliability (now returning to use of that term to mean valid or accurate) relates to the typical heuristics of legal decision makers described in chapters 5 and 7. In cases where the defense makes claims based on past mental state, false confessions, or mistaken identification, the defendant is left with very little ammunition for creating reasonable doubt if he or she is deprived of an expert. In these cases the defendant is trying to overcome assumptions, legal or otherwise, that are quite strong: that people who commit criminal acts intend their actions, control them, and do not grossly misperceive the surrounding circumstances; that people who are innocent do not confess to crimes; and that eyewitnesses who are sure about their identification do not get it wrong. The same dynamic occurs in connection with prediction testimony. The natural assumption in commitment and sentencing hearings is that the individual will do again what he or she just did. As I have argued throughout this book, expert testimony provides the decision maker with plausible reasons for challenging all of these assumptions. Without the testimony, however, judicial and jury decisions are very likely to be uninformed. Alternative explanations will never be heard, or they will never be seriously considered because they are supported only by the presumably self-serving statements of the defendant-subject and the attorney.

The result could be truly unreliable decisions. With respect to past mental state, that conclusion is obvious, given the indeterminacy of culpability determinations described in chapter 3. The manner in which exclusion of soft defense evidence on dangerousness can undermine accuracy should also be apparent from the discussion in chapters 6 and 7. Although prediction testimony based on actuarial evidence can be very helpful to the fact finder, it still leaves out many variables that only unscientific, clinical testimony can address. A rigid interpretation of *Daubert* that limited the defense to empirically verifiable predictions would present the fact finder with a skeletal view of the subject's violence potential that may well represent an inaccurate view of his or her risk. It should not be forgotten that the false-positive rate for even the best actuarial prediction scheme is well over 20 percent (certainly a reasonable doubt under any definition of that term).

The same type of observation can be made about defense testimony supporting false confession and mistaken identification claims. Mistaken identifications are the single most significant cause of wrongful convictions, and coerced confessions are not too far behind in that category.[28] Using *Daubert* to exclude defense expert testimony supporting such claims could easily increase the chances of such mistakes.

Effect on Members of the Legal System

Defense experts can also enhance accuracy in more subtle ways. Articulate credentialed witnesses can help make up for the woefully inadequate representation often accorded criminal defendants and respondents in commitment proceedings, another cause of wrongful convictions and detentions.[29] Additionally, their presence can keep the government on its toes. If defense experts are kept out of the courtroom, police, prosecutors, and state experts, knowing their interrogation, identification, and prediction processes will not be meaningfully challenged, may be less careful, producing further risk of erroneous verdicts.[30]

Fact Finder Skepticism

A fourth reason we should not be overly concerned about expert defense evidence that fails a stringent *Daubert* reliability test is that judges and juries know what to do with it. As detailed in chapter 5, most research shows that juries do not attribute undue significance to syndrome testimony, eyewitness testimony, and the like; if anything, such testimony is undervalued because of a pervasive skepticism about social science claims. The one study that found to the contrary, discussed in chapter 7, involved prediction testimony by a *prosecution* witness, which even strong cross-examination and an opposing expert could not shake.[31] That study does not suggest that *defense* witnesses need to be kept from the jury, but rather supports the point made earlier that the state naturally benefits from assumptions against defendants, so much so that defense evidence rarely dents its case. That is all the more reason to put as few obstacles in the way of defense efforts to do so, if reliability of outcome is really our ultimate goal.

Some data do suggest that judges and jurors are distracted by an expert's style or educational attainments, thus sometimes missing substantive information.[32] Even if that is so, it is not clear why adjusting expert admissibility standards is the appropriate response. Arguably, the proper prescription for any lay tendency to pay too much attention to demeanor, amount of fee, credentials, and other peripheral factors is not a reliability threshold— because even reliable evidence will be ignored under the appropriate peripheral conditions—but rather presentation of expert evidence in as bland a manner as possible, perhaps through documents without identifying the source. That, for better or worse, runs afoul of our adversarial tradition in criminal cases.[33]

The Consequences of an Erroneous Outcome

In sum, defense use of material expert testimony on past mental state, dangerousness, eyewitnesses, and interrogation may well enhance reliability even when it is not demonstrably valid or of questionable fit. Occasionally, of course, a person will erroneously be acquitted or escape preventive detention because a judge or jury, misled by speculative expert testimony, mistakenly ignores a confession or an eyewitness or mistakenly sympathizes with a psychopath asserting that he or she is insane or not dangerous. But the consequences of these mistakes should not be exaggerated. The final reason defense reliance on unverified expertise should be permitted is because the cost of an error will usually not be high.

Note first that, in insanity and other cases in which the expert testimony involves past mental state, a win for the defense will still often result in incarceration, either in a hospital or a prison. People who are acquitted by reason of insanity are usually confined at least as long as those convicted of the same crime, and a successful diminished capacity or diminished responsibility defense usually still results in conviction of a lesser included offense.[34] Even an undeserving defense victory in prediction cases will not necessarily cause more harm to society than a defense loss. In the latter instance, dangerous individuals who are confined may still be violent in confinement, or once released from that confinement.

Second, and most important, the small number of cases in which a guilty or dangerous person actually walks free because of unreliable defense expertise will probably fall far below the number of cases in which that expertise vindicates an innocent, excusable, or nonviolent person. In scientific terms, the number of false positives such testimony prevents is likely to be greater than the number of false negatives it causes. If so, the reasonable doubt standard strongly suggests that the experts should be allowed to testify.

D. Conclusion: Achieving Balance through Asymmetry

Daubert, a decision meant to make adjudication more reliable, will not do so if reliability is the only factor courts consider in making admissibility decisions. Construed so as to require strong verifiability and vigorous fit to the task at hand, *Daubert* and its sister case, *Kumho Tire*, will create an imbalance between the government and the defense in criminal and commitment cases. Once it has adjusted to the more stringent standards, the state, with its superior resources, its institutional incentives, and its focus on expertise that relies on observance of physical facts, will have little difficulty producing admissible evidence, especially if the main admissibility criterion is the existence of error rates rather than the existence of low ones. The defense, on the other hand, will struggle to produce positivist-oriented expertise with sufficient external validity because of the socially constructed nature of its claims, the difficulty of simulating relevant scenarios, and the general disorganization of the defense bar. The result will be a criminal process that is unfair in appearance and in fact, and one that will produce more unreliable results than one that is more generous toward defense-produced expertise.

These considerations suggest that very few limitations should be placed on defense expertise in criminal and commitment cases. Some have gone so far as to suggest that defense expert evidence should always be admitted unless it is completely untrustworthy and immune to the traditional means of evaluating credibility, such as cross-examination, rebuttal witnesses, and jury instructions (in other words, these commentators endorse the balancing test of yore).[35] In this book, I have suggested a somewhat more demanding standard. Culpability testimony proffered by the defense must not only be material, but must also demonstrate generally accepted content validity and add to the factors that lay decision makers would normally consider in making judgments about past mental state. Clinical prediction testimony should be based on the risk literature and generally accepted professional evaluation procedures. Both types of testimony should avoid ultimate issue language. With the exception, perhaps, of the last principle, expert testimony from mental health professionals is already moving in this direction. The prescriptions in this book hopefully will accelerate and help guide that trend.

Whatever the evidentiary standard, it should ensure that defense expertise is not subject to a rigorous *Daubert* test. At the same time, forensic expertise offered by the prosecution in its case in chief generally should be. Some have objected to this differential treatment. Roger Park, for instance, argues that an "asymmetrical" approach to *Daubert* would create dissonance outside the courtroom (because the public won't be able to understand why prosecution experts have to jump through more hoops than defense experts do) as well as inside the courtroom (because, if the defendant decides to use particular questionable types of evidence, it can be difficult figuring out how much the prosecution may respond in kind). He also suggests that loosened evidentiary standards will come back to haunt the defense because the system will make up for this advantage by shifting burdens, enhancing penalties, and so on.[36]

The regime that I advocate would not be directly asymmetrical, in that the government, as well as the defense, would be the beneficiary of laxer reliability and fit rules when the expert testimony concerns past mental state, eyewitness, and confession testimony; only forensic identification and prediction evidence would be subject to stricter standards and, in the latter case, the government would still be able to introduce soft testimony if the defense opens the door. In this regime, Park's concerns may dissipate.

To the extent they do not, they are no different from the concerns that are routinely associated with constitutionally mandated adversarial advantages, ranging from the exclusion of illegally seized evidence to the reasonable doubt standard itself. Presumably Park would not eliminate these latter advantages simply because the public may not understand them, courts have trouble implementing them, or the system adjusts in various ways to their impact. These types of speculative harms do not outweigh the clear harm that would occur if, because of a rigid application of *Daubert*, criminal defendants are no longer able to tell their exculpatory or mitigating stories through experts.

Given the structure of expertise, asymmetry between defense and government use of expertise in criminal cases should be sought, not avoided. Because the government's expert evidence tends to be easier to verify, better funded, less favored under constitutional doctrine, more prone to feed jury preconceptions, and more likely to cause dramatic harm if erroneous, *Daubert* and the rules of evidence must be read flexibly, with a bow to the defense. If they are not, the imbalance between the government and the individual that already exists in cases involving deprivations of life and liberty will only worsen.

Notes

Chapter 1

1. A search on Westlaw for criminal cases involving psychiatrists or psychologists over twenty-year intervals beginning in 1945 indicates significant increases in state and federal appellate court use of clinical experts, which presumably reflects increases in trial court usage of experts as well: 1945 (23); 1965 (239); 1985 (1,018); 2005 (2,098).

2. Senate Floor Amendment 1 to Senate Bill 459, 42d Leg., 1st Sess (N.M. 1995), cited in Scott E. Sundby, "The Jury as Critic: An Empirical Look at How Capital Juries Perceive Expert and Lay Testimony," 83 *Virginia Law Review* 1109 (1997).

3. The Citizens Commission on Human Rights, *Psychiatry Eradicating Justice* 8 (1995) (quoting Jeffrey Harris, executive director of the Attorney General's Task Force on Violent Crime).

4. Stephen J. Morse, "Crazy Behavior, Morals, and Science: An Analysis of Mental Health Law," 51 *Southern California Law Review* 527, 604–05, 620 (1978); Stephen J. Morse, "Failed Explanations and Criminal Responsibility: Experts and the Unconscious," 68 *Virginia Law Review* 971, 1037 (1982).

5. Morse, "Crazy Behavior," 601, 615–16.

6. David Faigman, "To Have and Have Not: Assessing the Value of Social Science to the Law as Science and Policy," 38 *Emory Law Journal* 1005, 1073–77 (1989).

7. David Faust & Jay Ziskin, "The Expert Witness in Psychology and Psychiatry," 241 *Science* 31 (1988).

8. Lee Coleman, *The Reign of Error* 45, 61–64, 86–87 (1984).

9. Alan A. Stone, *Law Psychiatry and Morality* 96 (1984).

10. Bruce Ennis & Thomas Litwack, "Psychiatry and the Presumption of Expertise: Flipping Coins in the Courtroom," 62 *California Law Review* 693, 700–702 (1974).

11. Morse, "Crazy Behavior," 621–22 (stating that only actuarial prediction should be permitted); Faust & Ziskin, "Expert Witness," 33–35 (same); Daniel W. Shuman & Bruce D. Sales, "The Admissibility of Expert Testimony Based upon Clinical Judgment and Scientific Research," 4 *Psychology, Public Policy & Law* 1226, 1250 (1998) (same).

12. The M'Naghten case was decided by the House of Lords in 1843 but soon made its way to the United States; see M'Naghten's Case, 8 Eng. Rep. 718 (H.L. 1843).

13. For a review of this history, see Christopher Slobogin, "An End to Insanity: Recasting the Role of Mental Disability in Criminal Cases," 86 *Virginia Law Review* 1199, 1208–15 (2000). See also Christopher Slobogin, *Minding Justice: Laws That Deprive People with Mental Disability of Life and Liberty* 28–32 (2006).

14. See Gary Melton et al., *Psychological Evaluations for the Courts: A Handbook for Mental Health Professionals and Lawyers* 186–90 (2d ed. 1997).

15. Slobogin, "An End to Insanity," 1214.

16. See Melton et al., *Psychological Evaluations*, 187 & n. 6.

17. Ibid., 204–08.

18. American Law Institute, *Model Penal Code* § 212.3(1)(b).

19. Ibid., §3.04(2)(b), §2.09(1).

20. Wayne LaFave, *Criminal Law* 497, 785, 543 (4th ed. 2003).

21. See Lockett v. Ohio, 438 U.S. 586, 604 (1978) ("The Eighth and Fourteenth Amendments require that the sentencer, in all but the rarest kind of capital case, not be precluded from considering, as a mitigating factor, any aspect of a defendant's character or record and any of the circumstances of the offense that the defendant proffers as a basis for a sentence less than death.").

22. Ellen Fels Berkman, "Mental Illness as an Aggravating Circumstance in Capital Sentencing," 89 *Columbia Law Review* 291, 297 (1989).

23. See, e.g., Minnesota Sentencing Guidelines, Guideline II.D.103.2(a).

24. Fed. R. Evid. 405(a) & Advisory Committee Note.

25. 28 U.S.C. §994(c) (stating that sentences should be based only on offense characteristics and deterrence); 28 U.S.C. §994(k) (rejecting rehabilitation as a goal of sentencing); 18 U.S.C. §3624(a)(b) (abolishing parole).

26. Susan R. Klein, "The Return of Federal Judicial Discretion in Criminal Sentencing," 39 *Valparaiso Law Review* 693, 726–27, 732–33 (2005) (describing the impact of the *Apprendi, Blakely,* and *Booker* cases—all post-1999 U.S. Supreme Court cases that significantly restructured sentencing—and predicting much more variation in sentencing, based in part on predictive criteria).

27. At least six states have such provisions. Mitzi Dorland & Daniel Krauss, "The Danger of Dangerousness in Capital Sentencing: Exacerbating the Problem of Arbitrary and Capricious Decision-Making," 29 *Law & Psychology Review* 63, 64 n. 5 (2005).

28. See Ralph Reisner et al., *Law and the Mental Health System: Civil and Criminal Aspects* 666 (4th ed. 2004).

29. Ibid., 668–70.

30. Ibid., 842.

31. For a description of the laws and the disorders that form the basis for commitment, see W. Lawrence Fitch, "Sex Offender Commitment in the United States: Legislative and Policy Concerns," 989 *Annals of the New York Academy of Science* 489 (2003).

32. Samuel Brakel & Richard Rock, *The Mentally Disabled and the Law* 341 (1971).

33. See W. Lawrence Fitch & Debra A. Hammen, "The New Generation of Sex Offender Commitment Laws: Which States Have Them and How Do They Work?," in *Protecting Society from Sexually Dangerous Offenders* 27, 33 (Bruce J. Winick & John Q. LaFond eds., 2003); Kansas v. Hendricks, 521 U.S. 346 (1997)(upholding laws against double jeopardy, ex post facto and due process claims); Seling v. Young, 531 U.S. 250 (2001) (upholding laws against due process claim).

34. See Christopher Slobogin, "The Civilization of the Criminal Law," 58 *Vanderbilt Law Review* 121 (2005). See also Slobogin, *Minding Justice*, ch. 5.

35. See Andrew Von Hirsch, *Doing Justice: The Choice of Punishments* 19–26 (1976) (sentencing); Alan Stone, *Mental Health and the Law: A System in Transition* 66–91 (1975) (commitment).

36. 3 John Weinstein & Margaret Berger, *Weinstein's Evidence* § 702(02), at 702–10 (1996) (noting that prior to the enactment of the Federal Rules, the test for expert testimony typically was whether the testimony was "within the common knowledge of the average layman").

37. 1 *McCormick on Evidence* § 15, 62 (John William Strong ed., 4th ed. 1992). See § 12, 47–48 ("Until about 35 years ago, a very substantial number of courts...had announced the general doctrine that witnesses would not be permitted to give their opinions or conclusions upon an ultimate fact in issue.").

38. 293 F. 1013, 1014 (D.C. Cir. 1923).

39. Andre A. Moenssens et al., *Scientific Evidence in Civil and Criminal Cases* 8 (4th ed. 1995).

40. See Coppolino v. State, 223 So. 2d 68, 70 (Fla. Dist. Ct. App.), appeal dismissed, 234 So. 2d 120 (Fla. 1969); Commonwealth v. Fatalo, 191 N.E.2d 479, 480–81 (Mass. 1963); see also John William Strong, "Questions Affecting the Admissibility of Scientific Evidence," 1970 *University of Illinois Law Forum* 1, 14 ("The *Frye* standard...tends to obscure...proper considerations by asserting an undefinable general acceptance as the principle if not sole determinative factor.").

41. See 1 *McCormick on Evidence*, § 13, 54 ("Rule 702 should permit expert opinion even if the matter is within the competence of the jurors if specialized knowledge will be helpful.").

42. See Reisner et al., *Law and the Mental Health System*, 519.

43. See Moenssens et al., *Scientific Evidence*, 12 (discussing the post-1975 division of jurisdictions into at least three groups: one that rejected *Frye* in favor of the Federal Rules, one that held that *Frye* survived the Rules and is complementary to Rule 702, and one that adopted neither approach).

44. United States v. Gillis, 773 F.2d 549, 558 (4th Cir. 1985); State v. Kim, 645 P.2d 1330, 1336 (Haw. 1982).

45. See 1 *McCormick on Evidence*, § 203, 872. In 1992, one year before *Daubert*, the authors of *McCormick on Evidence* found the "relevancy" or balancing approach "the most appealing." 1 *McCormick on Evidence*, § 203, at 874. They cite a long list of commentators who agree, including David W. Louisell & Christopher B. Mueller, 1 *Federal Evidence* § 105 (1977); Margaret A. Berger, "A Relevancy Approach to Novel Scientific Evidence," 115 *Federal Rules of Decision* 89, 89–91 (1987); and Edward J. Imwinkelried, "The Standard for Admitting

Scientific Evidence: A Critique from the Perspective of Juror Psychology," 28 *Villanova Law Review* 554 (1983).

46. 509 U.S. 579, 588–89, 592–93, 593–94 (1993).

47. See "Post-*Daubert* Standards for Admissibility of Scientific and Other Expert Evidence in State Courts," 90 *American Law Reports*, § 2, 453 (2001).

48. See, e.g., United States v. Rouse, 100 F.2d 560, 567–68 (1996) (suggesting that "social science" should be treated differently from testimony from the "scientific context").

49. 526 U.S. 137 (1999).

50. Ibid., 150 (stating "We can neither rule out, nor rule in, for all cases and for all time the applicability of [*Daubert's* factors], nor can we now do so for subsets of cases categorized by category of expert or by kind of evidence").

51. Ibid., 152 (stating that the *Daubert* gatekeeping requirement "make[s] certain that an expert, whether basing testimony upon professional studies or personal experience, employs in the courtroom the same level of intellectual rigor that characterizes the practice of an expert in the relevant field").

52. Ibid., 149.

53. Michael J. Gottesman, "Admissibility of Expert Testimony after *Daubert*: The 'Prestige' Factor," 43 *Emory Law Journal* 867, 975–76 (1996); Michael H. Graham, "Daubert v. Merrell Dow Pharmaceuticals, Inc.: No *Frye*, Now What?," 30 *Criminal Law Bulletin* 153, 162 (1994).

54. 1 *McCormick on Evidence* § 185, 541 ("There are two components to relevant evidence: materiality and probative value.").

Chapter 2

1. For a much longer list, see Alan Dershowitz, *The Abuse Excuse and Other Cop Outs, Sob Stories, and Evasions of Responsibility* (1994) (describing adopted child syndrome, American dream syndrome, black rage syndrome, computer addiction, fetal alcohol syndrome, self-victimization syndrome, and UFO survivor syndrome). See also Werner v. State, 711 S.W.2d 639, 649 (Tex. Crim. App. 1986) (Teague, J., dissenting) (describing other syndromes). It should be noted, however, that not all of these syndromes have been used in criminal trials.

2. Ian Freckleton, "When Plight Makes Right: The Forensic Abuse Syndrome," 18 *Criminal Law Journal* 29 (1994).

3. The initial, although not the most coherent, description of the syndrome is found in Lenore E. Walker, *The Battered Woman* (1979). See also Mary Ann Dutton, "Understanding Women's Responses to Domestic Violence: A Redefinition of Battered Woman Syndrome," 21 *Hofstra Law Review* 1191, 1197 (1993) (noting the traditional view that included learned helplessness as an element of BWS and arguing for a reconceptualization that focuses on the experiences of battered women rather than learned helplessness alone).

4. See, e.g., People v. Humphrey, 921 P.2d 1 (Cal. 1996) (examining BWS in self-defense context); State v. McClain, 591 A.2d 652 (N.J. Super. Ct. App. Div. 1991) (examining BWS in terms of adequate provocation). See generally Susan Murphy, "Assisting the Jury in Understanding Victimization: Expert Psychological Testimony on Battered Woman Syndrome and Rape Trauma Syndrome," 25 *Columbia Journal of Law & Social Problems* 277 (1992) (examining use of BWS testimony to support claims of insanity or self-defense). The syndrome appears to

be less prominent as an explanation for domestic violence than it was several years ago. See Diane Follingstad, "Battered Woman Syndrome in the Courts," in *Comprehensive Handbook of Psychology: Forensic Psychology* 485 (Alan Goldstein ed., 2003).

5. See generally Roland C. Summit, "The Child Sexual Abuse Accommodation Syndrome," 7 *Child Abuse & Neglect* 177 (1983) (providing the first explicit treatment of CSAAS); Ann Wolbert Burgess & Lynda Lytle Holmstrom, "Rape Trauma Syndrome," 131 *American Journal of Psychiatry* 981 (1974) (providing the first scholarly article on RTS); Lisa R. Askowitz & Michael H. Graham, "The Reliability of Expert Psychological Testimony in Child Sexual Abuse Prosecutions," 15 *Cardozo Law Review* 2027, 2040–44 (1994) (discussing cases in which testimony based on CSAAS has been admitted); Karla Fischer, "Defining the Boundaries of Admissible Expert Psychological Testimony on Rape Trauma Syndrome," 1989 *University of Illinois Law Review* 691, 710–26 (outlining admissibility of RTS evidence in various contexts).

6. See generally Chaim Shatan, "Soldiers in and after Vietnam," 31 *Journal of Social Science* 25 (1975) (describing the existence of a delayed reaction to the stress of combat during the Vietnam War); Chaim Shatan, "The Grief of Soldiers: The Vietnam Combat Veterans' Self-Help Movement," 43 *American Journal of Orthopsychiatry* 640 (1973) (same).

7. See, e.g., United States v. Crosby, 713 F.2d 1066 (5th Cir. 1983); State v. Felde, 422 So. 2d 370 (La. 1982); State v. Coogan, 453 N.W.2d 186 (Wis. Ct. App. 1990).

8. See Wally Owens, Case Note, "State v. Osby, the Urban Survival Defense," 22 *American Journal of Criminal Law* 809 (1995).

9. See, e.g., State v. Hungerford, No. 94-S-045 et al., 1995 WL 378571 (N.H. Super. Ct. May 23, 1995), aff'd, 697 A.2d 916 (N.H. 1997); Commonwealth v. Crawford, 682 A.2d 323 (Pa. Super. Ct. 1996), appeal granted, 693 A.2d 965 (Pa. 1997). False memory syndrome "refers to a condition in which the victim's personality or identity and interpersonal relationships revolve around a traumatic memory which is objectively false, but in which the person strongly believes." Douglas R. Richmond, "Bad Science: Repressed and Recovered Memories of Childhood Sexual Abuse," 44 *University of Kansas Law Review* 517, 521 (1996).

10. Peter Arenella, "Demystifying the Abuse Excuse: Is There One?," 19 *Harvard Journal of Law & Public Policy* 703, 706–09 (1996).

11. For example, virtually everyone who is hospitalized after being found not guilty by reason of insanity is categorized according to a standard diagnosis listed in the American Psychiatric Association's *Diagnostic and Statistical Manual of Mental Disorders*. See Gary Melton et al., *Psychological Evaluations for the Courts: A Handbook for Mental Health Professionals and Lawyers* 216–17 (2d ed. 1997).

12. For instance, only a handful of the veteran forensic mental health experts that I have trained in Florida, Virginia, and elsewhere over the past twenty-five years have given such testimony.

13. See Zamora v. State, 361 So. 2d 776, 779 (Fla. Dist. Ct. App. 1978) (discussing admissibility of psychological testimony on "involuntary subliminal television intoxication" in the context of an insanity defense); People v. Poddar, 103 Cal. Rptr. 84, 88–89 (Cal. Ct. App. 1972) (discussing admissibility of

anthropological testimony on relationships in India in the context of a diminished capacity defense), rev'd, 518 P.2d 342 (Cal. 1974); United States v. Hearst, 412 F. Supp. 889, 891 (N.D. Cal. 1976) (discussing expert testimony about whether treatment of the defendant by her captors "deprived her of the requisite general intent to commit the offense charged"), aff'd, 563 F.2d 1331 (9th Cir. 1977); United States v. Alexander 471 F.2d 923, 957–65 (D.C. Cir. 1972) (discussing "rotten social background" as a defense); People v. Tanner, 91 Cal. Rptr. 656 (Cal. Ct. App. 1970). See generally Lawrence B. Kessler, Note, "The XYY Chromosomal Abnormality: Use and Misuse in the Legal Process," 9 *Harvard Journal on Legislation* 469 (1972) (describing research into "the XYY anomaly" and its correlation to socially deviant behavior).

14. See Carolyn Anspacher, *The Trial of Dr. Dekaplany* 115 (1965) (describing the defendant as having two personalities, one courageous and gentle, the other cowardly, brutal, and sadistic); People v. Gorshen, 336 P.2d 492, 496 (Cal. 1959) (involving psychological testimony that stated, "For this man to go insane, means to be permanently . . . under the influence of the devil. . . . An individual in this state of crisis will do anything to avoid the threatened insanity."); United States v. Pollard, 282 F.2d 450, 460–64 (6th Cir.) (discussing psychological testimony to the effect that the defendant committed the crime as a result of an unconscious need for punishment), mandate clarified, 285 F.2d 81 (6th Cir. 1960); United States v. Batchelor, 19 C.M.R. 452, 489–94 (A.C.M.R. 1954) (addressing claim based on "induced political psychosis"), aff'd, 22 C.M.R. 144 (C.M.A. 1956).

15. In 1987, for instance, Professors Walker and Monahan noted, "Within the past several years . . . courts have increasingly begun to use [general research of the type described in the text]. . . . Notable examples can be found in cases concerning eyewitness identification, assessments of dangerousness, battered women, and sexual victimization." Laurens Walker & John Monahan, "Social Frameworks: A New Use of Social Science in Law," 73 *Virginia Law Review* 559, 563 (1987).

16. Ibid., 560 (defining "social framework" as the use of "general conclusions from social science research in determining factual issues in a specific case").

17. See Ibn-Tamas v. United States, 407 A.2d 626, 631–39 (D.C. 1979) (describing testimony by Dr. Lenore Walker about her research concerning battered women); People v. Taylor, 552 N.E.2d 131, 133–35 (N.Y. 1990) (discussing studies concerning RTS); see also Shahzade v. Gregory, 923 F. Supp. 286, 287–90 (D. Mass. 1996) (discussing Dr. Bessel van der Kolk's testimony describing "several studies which focused on the concept of repressed memories").

18. See United States v. Lewellyn, 723 F.2d 615, 619 (8th Cir. 1983) (noting "recent" recognition of pathological gambling as a disease); United States v. Shorter, 618 F. Supp. 255 (D.D.C. 1985), aff'd, 809 F.2d 59 (D.C. Cir. 1987) (discussing "the impact of pathological gambling disorder on the volitional faculties"); Robert Mark Carney & Brian D. Williams, "Recent Decision: Premenstrual Syndrome, a Criminal Defense," 59 *Notre Dame Law Review* 253 (1983) (examining the validity of PMS as a criminal defense); United States v. Hadley, 918 F.2d 848, 853 (9th Cir. 1990) (allowing expert to testify based on professional experience, without using special techniques or models, because testimony was not based on a "novel scientific technique"); *Lewellyn*, 723 F.2d at 619 (discussing expert's basis as "experience with pathological gamblers"); *Santos*, No.

K046229 (N.Y. Crim. Ct. Nov. 3, 1982) (discussing expert who had worked with women who were violent prior to menstruation).

19. See *Lewellyn*, 723 F.2d at 617–20 (discussing inability of pathological gambler to resist impulses to gamble); *Santos*, No. 1K046229 (involving argument by defendant that she "blacked out" as a result of PMS); People v. Yukl, 372 N.Y.S.2d 313, 319–20 (N.Y. Sup. Ct. 1975) (examining evidence of XYY syndrome as biological cause of deviant behavior).

20. See, e.g., Dang Vang v. Vang Xiong X. Toyed, 944 F.2d 476, 480–82 (9th Cir. 1991) (discussing expert testimony regarding defendant's cultural background); State v. Coogan, 453 N.W.2d 186, 187 (Wis. Ct. App. 1990) (involving claim by defendant that, at the time of the killings, he "believed he was in a combat situation in Vietnam"); Owens, "State v. Osby," 810 (noting claim by defendant that, because of his upbringing in a violent, urban environment, he believed his only option was to kill his two victims).

21. See generally Dershowitz, *Abuse Excuse*, 3 (defining the abuse excuse as "the legal tactic by which criminal defendants claim history of abuse as an excuse for violent retaliation"); 19 (noting that each of the various abuse excuse claims shares in common "a goal of deflecting responsibility from the person who committed the criminal act onto someone else who may have abused him or her or otherwise caused him or her to do it").

22. See Zamora v. State, 361 So. 2d 776, 779–81 (Fla. Dist. Ct. App. 1978) (involving research-based testimony on the effects of television violence on children); United States v. Alexander, 471 F.2d 923 (D.C. Cir. 1973) (involving rotten social background); United States v. Hearst, 412 F. Supp. 863 (N.D. Cal. 1975) (involving brainwashing defense).

23. Professor Lewin's 1975 article, focusing on psychological evidence presented in criminal trials for purposes other than insanity, discussed only diminished capacity cases. See Travis H. D. Lewin, "Psychological Evidence in Criminal Cases for Purposes Other Than the Defense of Insanity," 26 *Syracuse Law Review* 1051 (1975).

24. See, e.g., Shepard v. State, 847 P.2d 75 (Alaska Ct. App. 1993) (holding that posttraumatic stress disorder testimony should have been admitted to prove self-defense); People v. Sandoval, 841 P.2d 862 (Cal. 1992) (allowing forensic psychiatrist to testify regarding a self-defense claim that ingestion of PCP made the victim angry, aggressive, and violent), aff'd, 511 U.S. 1 (1994); State v. Purcell, 669 N.E.2d 60 (Ohio Ct. App. 1995) (holding psychological testimony admissible to prove self-defense); Commonwealth v. Kacsmar, 617 A.2d 725 (Pa. Super. Ct. 1992) (holding battered person syndrome admissible to establish self-defense); State v. Maelega, 907 P.2d 758 (Haw. 1995) (using battered spouse expert evidence to support extreme mental or emotional disturbance defense in an effort to reduce murder charge to manslaughter); United States v. Brown, 891 F. Supp. 1501 (D. Kan. 1995) (using battered spouse syndrome to prove duress and compulsion); State v. Duncan, 830 P.2d 554 (N.M. Ct. App. 1990) (holding the exclusion of psychological testimony on duress to be reversible error), aff'd, 805 P.2d 621 (N.M. 1991); State v. Riker, 869 P.2d 43, 47 (Wash. 1994) (examining use of BWS testimony to support a duress defense); United States v. Bastanipour, 41 F.3d 1178 (7th Cir. 1994) (excluding expert testimony on coercion in drug possession case); United States v. Newman, 849 F.2d 156 (5th Cir. 1988) (holding

admissible testimony regarding mental disease or subnormal intelligence to show defendant was peculiarly susceptible to inducement by government).

25. See People v. Shelton, 385 N.Y.S.2d 708 (N.Y. Sup. Ct. 1976), aff'd, 434 N.Y.S.2d 649 (N.Y. App. Div. 1980); State v. Ott, 686 P.2d 1001 (Or. 1984).

26. See People v. Jones, 266 P.2d 38 (Cal. 1954); United States v. MacDonald, 688 F.2d 224, 227–28 (4th Cir. 1981) (supporting trial court's exclusion of expert testimony that defendant's personality was inconsistent with outrageous and senseless murders of his family); State v. Treadaway, 568 P.2d 1061, 1066 (Ariz. 1977) (allowing testimony that defendant was incapable of "inflicting grievous harm to anyone"); Kanaras v. State, 460 A.2d 61, 72–73 (Md. Ct. Spec. App. 1983) (allowing testimony that defendant is passive and thus unable to commit violent crime).

27. See United States v. Hiss, 88 F. Supp. 559 (S.D.N.Y. 1950); see also Judson Fauknor, *Annual Survey of American Law Evidence* 804–08 (1950), reprinted in Jon R. Waltz & Roger C. Park, *Cases and Materials on Evidence* 484–86 (8th ed. 1995) (describing the use of psychological testimony in *Hiss*).

28. See, e.g., State v. Foret, 628 So. 2d 1116 (La. 1993) (involving child witness's credibility); State v. Kim, 645 P.2d 1330 (Haw. 1982) (involving rape victim's credibility); State v. Wilson, 456 N.E.2d 1287 (Ohio 1982) (involving rape victim's credibility); see also Munoz v. State, 763 S.W.2d 30, 32 (Tex. Ct. App. 1988) (involving credibility testimony in a murder trial).

29. See generally Elizabeth F. Loftus & James M. Doyle, *Eyewitness Testimony* 36–39, 51–52, 90–94 (1979) (examining the effects of weapons focus, memory of events over time, and police suggestion).

30. See Cole v. Shults-Lewis Child and Family Services, Inc., 681 N.E.2d 1157, 1159–60 (Ind. Ct. App. 1997) (holding that a party asserting repressed memory must also provide expert testimony to support "the scientific validity of the phenomenon"); Barrett v. Hyldburg, 487 S.E.2d 803, 806 (N.C. Ct. App. 1997) (holding "testimony regarding recovered memories . . . may not be received at trial absent accompanying expert testimony on the phenomenon of memory repression").

31. See Shahzade v. Gregory, 923 F. Supp. 286, 290 (D. Mass. 1996) (noting that, despite the inability to test repressed memories empirically, the theory of repressed memory has been generally accepted and applies in this case); Isely v. Capuchin Province, 877 F. Supp. 1055, 1067 (E.D. Mich. 1995) (allowing expert to testify in a civil case "as to whether Mr. Isely's behavior is consistent with someone who is suffering repressed memory").

32. See Paul Giannelli, "The Supreme Court's Criminal *Daubert* Cases," 33 *Seton Hall Law Review* 1071, 1097–109 (2003) (describing successful and unsuccessful *Daubert* challenges against forensic scientists); Lloyd Dixon & Brandon Gill, "Changes in the Standards for Admitting Expert Evidence in Civil Cases," 8 *Psychology, Public Policy & Law* 251 (2001) (discussing *Daubert*'s impact in toxic tort cases); Robert G. Badal & Edward J. Suzewski, "Economic Testimony Under Fire," *ABA Journal* 56 (Nov. 2001) (describing *Daubert*'s impact on economists' testimony).

33. I base this statement on conversations with participants in training programs that I have taught, as well as the results of an informal survey sent out in December 1996 and September 2005 on Psy-Law, a listserve with more than nine hundred members, most of whom are practicing forensic mental health professionals. All respondents in the two surveys ($N = 32$) agreed with the statement in

the text. Representative are statements like the following: "In 99 percent of what we do we don't have to worry about *Frye, Daubert* or 702," and "I have been involved with hundreds of criminal cases over the past ten years and testified in federal and state court dozens and dozens of times, and yes, you are correct, I have rarely had my testimony challenged on the grounds you mention." Most respondents had never been challenged on lack-of-expertise grounds, and none had been challenged more than once in criminal responsibility cases.

34. See Daniel W. Shuman, "Expertise in Law, Medicine and Health Care," 26 *Journal of Health Policy & Law* 267, 282 (2001).

35. A survey on Westlaw of all federal and state cases involving insanity cases in which *Daubert* challenges were raised found one case in which testimony was excluded: State v. George, 768 So.2d 748, 753–54 (La. 2000) (excluding testimony about limbic psychotic trigger reaction because there were no published papers on the topic). See also Henry F. Fradella et al., "The Impact of *Daubert* on the Admissibility of Behavioral Science Testimony," 30 *Pepperdine Law Review* 403 (2003) (finding that exclusion rarely occurs outside of cases where the expert testimony is about eyewitness accuracy, the falseness of a particular confession, or the credibility of a witness).

36. See United States v. Salamanca, 990 F.2d 629, 636 (D.C. Cir. 1993) (permitting expert testimony that "someone who had drunk as much as [the defendant] would have a diminished capacity to think and plan"); United States v. Kristiansen, 901 F.2d 1463, 1466 (8th Cir. 1990) (permitting defense counsel to ask whether the mental disease of the type the defendant allegedly had "would affect a person's ability to appreciate their actions"); United States v. Davis, 835 F.2d 274, 276 (11th Cir. 1988) (approving the trial court's inquiry of appellant's expert regarding the capability of an individual diagnosed with multiple personalities to understand what he or she was doing).

37. See United States v. Lewellyn, 723 F.2d 615, 619 (8th Cir. 1983) (pathological gambling); United States v. Fosher, 590 F.2d 381, 382–83 (1st Cir. 1979) (eyewitness identification testimony); Ibn-Tamas v. United States, 455 A.2d 893, 894 (D.C. 1983) (BWS); State v. Kim, 645 P.2d 1330, 1335 (Haw. 1982) (child sexual abuse situation); State v. Black, 745 P.2d 12, 14 (Wash. 1987) (RTS); State v. Roberts, 544 P.2d 754, 758 (Wash. Ct. App. 1976) (XYY syndrome).

38. Note, "Developments in the Law: Confronting the New Challenges of Scientific Evidence," 108 *Harvard Law Review* 1490, 1493 (1995).

39. Veronica Dahir et al., "Judicial Application of *Daubert* to Psychological Syndrome and Profile Evidence: A Research Note," 11 *Psychology, Public Policy & Law* 62, 78 (2005).

40. Donald N. Bersoff et al., "The Admissibility of Psychological Evidence Six Years after *Daubert*: Floodgates or Gatekeeping?," presentation at American Psychology-Law Society meeting, New Orleans, March 4, 2000 (study of all appellate cases decided from five and one-half years prior to *Daubert* to five and one-half years after *Daubert*). This study also found that these courts rarely referred to *Daubert*'s precepts in such cases, noting that out of 428 appellate cases involving psychological testimony, only 17 referred to falsifiability and only 13 referred to error rate.

41. Jennifer L. Groscup et al., "The Effects of *Daubert* on the Admissibility of Expert Testimony in State and Federal Criminal Cases," 8 *Psychology, Public Policy & Law* 339 (2002).

42. People v. Stoll, 783 P.2d 698, 710 (Cal. 1989). See also State v. Varela, 873 P.2d 657, 663–64 (Ariz. Ct. App. 1993) (holding that psychological testimony that "is not 'new, novel or experimental scientific evidence'... does not require the additional screening provided by *Frye*").

43. Samaniego v. City of Kodiak, 80 P.3d 216, 220 (Ala. 2003).

44. Barefoot v. Estelle, 463 U.S. 880, 896 (1983).

45. State v. Borelli, 629 A.2d 1105, 1111 (Conn. 1993).

46. See Steven D. Penrod et al., "Expert Psychological Testimony on Eyewitness Reliability before and after *Daubert*: The State of the Law and the Science," 13 *Behavioral Science & Law* 229, 256 (1995) (arguing that such testimony meets the reliability requirements of *Daubert*); Scott Woller, "Rethinking the Role of Expert Testimony Regarding the Reliability of Eyewitness Identifications in New York," 48 *New York Law School Law Review* 323, 324–37 (2003).

47. Commonwealth v. Francis, 390 Mass. 89, 101, 453 N.E.2d 1204 (1983), quoted in State v. McClendon, 730 A.2d 1107, 1116 (Conn. 1999). See also Lewis v. State, 572 So. 2d 908, 911 (Fla. 1990) (upholding trial court discretion to exclude expert testimony on eyewitness identification); State v. Gardiner, 636 A.2d 710, 713–14 (R.I. 1994) (excluding expert testimony based on general research findings).

48. State v. Saldana, 324 N.W.2d 227, 230 (Minn. 1982).

49. 471 F.2d 923, 965 (dictum), 968 (D.C. Cir. 1973).

50. See United States v. Brawner, 471 F.2d 969, 1032 (D.C. Cir. 1972) (Bazelon, J., concurring) (advocating adoption of a test that would require a person to be found insane "if at the time of his unlawful conduct his mental or emotional processes or behavior controls were impaired to such an extent that he cannot justly be held responsible for his act").

51. See *Alexander*, 471 F.2d at 957–61 (Bazelon, J., dissenting).

52. Zamora v. State, 361 So. 2d 776, 784 (Fla. Dist. Ct. App. 1978).

53. 723 F.2d 615, 619–20 (8th Cir. 1983).

54. See ibid., 618–20 (describing the testimony of Drs. Taber and Custer); 619 (noting that the diagnosis was in the third edition of the *DSM*, published in 1980, and that both experts testified that this meant it was a "generally accepted" diagnosis). The court justified its contrary holding on the general acceptance issue by noting that pathological gambling was not recognized in the second edition of the *DSM*, published in 1968, and that only twenty to twenty-five doctors were experienced with the diagnosis. Ibid., 619–20.

55. See Richard Bonnie, "Compulsive Gambling and the Insanity Defense," 9 *Newsletter of the American Academy of Psychiatry & Law* 6, 7 (1984).

56. Jahnke v. State, 682. P.2d 991, 997 (Wyo.1984).

57. State v. Hulbert, 481 N.W.2d 329, 332 (Iowa 1992) ("Our cases also hold... that expert psychological evidence may not be used to merely bolster a witness's credibility... because veracity is not a 'fact in issue' subject to expert opinion [and]... is uniquely within a lay jury's common understanding."); Commonwealth v. Seese, 517 A.2d 920, 922 (Pa. 1986) (rejecting credibility testimony about a child witness because it "would be an invitation for the trier of fact to abdicate its responsibility to ascertain the facts relying upon the questionable premise that the expert is in a better position to make such a judgment").

58. 99 F.3d 870, 884 (8th Cir. 1996).

59. State v. Taylor, 663 S.W.2d 235, 241 (Mo. 1984) (en banc).

60. See People v. Stoll, 783 P.2d 698, 710 (Cal. 1989).

61. Ibid., 109.

62. See David McCord, "Syndromes, Profiles and Other Mental Exotica: A New Approach to the Admissibility of Nontraditional Psychological Evidence in Criminal Cases," 66 *Oregon Law Review* 19, 66 (1987).

63. According to one source, "the courts have not been as generous" toward admissibility of evidence of CSAAS as they have been toward admissibility of RTS evidence. Andre Moenssens et al., *Scientific Evidence in Civil and Criminal Cases* 1154 (4th ed. 1995). See United States v. Whitted, 994 F.2d 444, 447 (8th Cir. 1993) (holding that expert testimony on CSAAS impermissibly invaded the province of the jury); State v. Saldana, 324 N.W.2d 227, 230 (Minn. 1982) (holding that to allow RTS to prove "whether [a rape] has occurred...would...invade the jury's province of factfinding"); Commonwealth v. Gallagher, 547 A.2d 355, 357 (Pa. 1988) (noting that expert testimony regarding RTS "was introduced for the sole purpose of shoring up the credibility of the victim on the crucial issue of identification").

64. See, e.g., State v. Hickson, 630 So. 2d 172 (Fla. 1993); State v. Anaya, 438 A.2d 892 (Me. 1981); State v. Kelly, 478 A.2d 364 (N.J. 1984); State v. Hill, 339 S.E.2d 121 (S.C. 1986); State v. Allery, 682 P.2d 312 (Wash. 1984). According to Professor Mosteller, at least eleven states have a specific statutory authorization mandating admissibility of BWS evidence. See Robert P. Mosteller, "Syndromes and Politics in Criminal Trials and Evidence Law," 46 *Duke Law Journal* 461, 484 n. 77 (1996).

65. See Moenssens, *Scientific Evidence*, 1135 (noting that in early battered spouse cases, "women were foreclosed altogether from using a self defense claim because the killing was not committed during an abusive attack").

66. See Mosteller, "Syndromes and Politics," 486–91, 488–89 ("Despite the fact that change is coming through an evidentiary rule rather than a modification of self-defense law, my point remains: courts and legislatures are altering the substantive law by admitting a new class of evidence that will produce predictably different outcomes.").

67. For an interesting debate about the substantive and evidentiary issues connected with BWS, see Charles P. Ewing, "Psychological Self-Defense: A Proposed Justification for Battered Women Who Kill," 14 *Law and Human Behavior*, 579 (1990); Stephen J. Morse, "The Misbegotten Marriage of Soft Psychology and Bad Law: Psychological Self-Defense as a Justification for Homicide," 14 *Law and Human Behavior*, 595 (1990).

68. See James Q. Wilson, *Moral Judgment: Does the Abuse Excuse Threaten Our Legal System?* 89, 90 (1997).

69. See, e.g., United States v. Dupre, 339 F.Supp.2d 534 (S.D.N.Y., 2004); United States v. Mezvinsky, 206 F.Supp.2d 661 (E.D. Pa., 2002); United States. v. Boykoff, 186 F.Supp.2d 347 (S.D.N.Y., 2002).

70. For an account of this case, see Anthony V. Alfieri, "Defending Racial Violence," 95 *Columbia Law Review* 1301, 1310–12 (1995).

71. The first "Rodney King trial," in Simi Valley, resulted in an acquittal on all serious charges of four white police officers, three of whom were captured on videotape beating King after they had stopped him in a high-speed chase. See George P. Fletcher, *With Justice for Some: Victims' Rights in Criminal Trials* 38 (1995).

72. Williams was acquitted on attempted murder and aggravated mayhem charges but convicted of simple mayhem. Ibid., 234.

73. Cal. Penal Code § 28 (2002).

74. People v. Sekona, 32 Cal. Rptr. 2d 606, 609 (Cal. Ct. App. 1994). The California Court of Appeals stated, "No specific intent to maim or disfigure is required [to convict for mayhem], the necessary intent being inferable from the types of injuries resulting from certain intentional acts; one who unlawfully strikes another without the specific intent to commit the crime of mayhem is still guilty of that crime if the blow results in the loss or disfigurement of a member of the body or putting out of the eye of the victim."

75. People v. Montes, 112 Cal. App. 4th 1543, 1549, 5 Cal. Rptr. 3d 800 (2003).

76. People v. Weinstein, 156 Misc.2d 34, 591 N.Y.S.2d 715 (1992).

77. Cf. People v. Tanner, 91 Cal. Rptr. 656, 659 (Ct. App. 1970) (holding XYY testimony inadmissible because, inter alia, the experts could not state that an extra Y chromosome prevented defendant from knowing the nature and quality of his act or that it was wrong). See also Millard v. State, 261 A.2d 227, 231 (Md. Ct. Spec. App. 1970) (noting that the presence of the XYY "genetic abnormality" would not, of itself, indicate a lack of "substantial capacity" to appreciate the criminality of particular conduct); People v. Yukl, 372 N.Y.S.2d 313, 318 (N.Y. Sup. Ct. 1975) (noting inadequacy of existing research in determining a causal connection between "XYY genetic phenomenon" and "a predisposition toward violent criminal conduct").

78. See Michael S. Moore, "Causation and the Excuses," 73 *California Law Review* 1091, 1130 (1985).

79. See ibid., 1129–30.

80. See, e.g., Richard Delgado, "'Rotten Social Background': Should the Criminal Law Recognize a Defense of Severe Environmental Deprivation?," 3 *Law & Inequality* 9, 12–23 (1985) (examining the debate over the validity of rotten social background as a defense); Patricia J. Falk, "Novel Theories of Criminal Defense Based upon the Toxicity of the Social Environment: Urban Psychosis, Television Intoxication, and Black Rage," 74 *North Carolina Law Review* 731, 809 (1996) ("If the criminal law restricts itself to the consideration of only short-term causal explanations for criminal behavior, it will miss the rich contribution these theories of defense can make by elucidating more diffuse and long-term pathogenic factors in criminal behavior."); David Skeen, "The Genetically Defective Offender," 9 *William Mitchell Law Review* 217 (1983) (arguing inter alia that testimony about chromosomal abnormality ought to be admissible); cf. Michael L. Perlin, *The Jurisprudence of the Insanity Defense* 120–28 (1994) (suggesting that the law's adherence to intentionality and free will paradigms may be outmoded given science's "remarkable contrary evidence").

81. See Reisner et al., *Law and the Mental Health System*, 533.

82. See generally Robert Mosteller, "Legal Doctrines Governing the Admissibility of Expert Testimony Concerning Social Framework Evidence," 52 *Law & Contemporary Problems* 85 (Autumn 1989).

83. See, e.g., State v. Ritt, 599 N.W.2d 802, 811 (Minn. 1999) (limiting BWS testimony to "a description of the syndrome's general nature").

84. See generally Reisner et al., *Law and the Mental Health System*, 575–82 (detailing the "mental disease or defect," "capacity," and "crime" limitations on diminished capacity testimony).

85. 517 F.2d 584 (2d Cir. 1975).
86. Ibid., 586.

Chapter 3

1. See, e.g., United States v. Cantu, 12 F.3d 1506, 1509 & n.1 (9th Cir. 1993) (taking judicial notice that a condition listed in the *DSM* is a recognized psychiatric condition). For an interesting description of the *DSM* development process, see David Goleman, "Who's Mentally Ill?," *Psychology Today* 34 (Jan. 1978).

2. Research using the diagnostic criteria found in the third edition of the *DSM* reported reliability rates between 69 percent and 85 percent for the major diagnostic categories. American Psychiatric Association, *Diagnostic and Statistical Manual of Mental Disorders* 470–71 (3d ed. 1980). Compare Samuel Fennig et al., "Comparison of Facility and Research Diagnoses in First-Admission Psychotic Patients," 151 *American Journal of Psychiatry* 1423, 1426 (1994) (showing 57.1 percent agreement on schizophrenia); Paul B. Lieberman & Frances M. Baker, "The Reliability of Psychiatric Diagnosis in the Emergency Room," 36 *Hospital & Community Psychiatry* 291, 292 (1985) (showing 41 percent agreement on schizophrenia, 50 percent agreement on mood disorders, and 37 percent agreement on organic brain syndromes).

3. See Lieberman & Baker, "Reliability of Psychiatric Diagnosis," 292 (describing reliability of diagnostic opinions); Graham Mellsop, "The Reliability of Axis II of DSM-III," 139 *American Journal of Psychiatry* 1360, 1361 (1982) (finding that reliability of personality disorder diagnoses in everyday clinical settings ranged from 49 percent for antisocial personality to 1 percent for schizoid personality). See generally David Faust & Jay Ziskin, "The Expert Witness in Psychology and Psychiatry," 241 *Science* 31 (1988) ("A number of subsequent studies showed that rate of disagreement of specific diagnostic categories often equals or exceeds rate of agreement.").

4. See Michael Flaum et al., "The Reliability of 'Bizarre' Delusions," 32 *Comprehensive Psychiatry* 59, 62 (1991) ("In this study, the interrater reliability of distinguishing bizarre versus non-bizarre delusions was poor, using an unstructured definition, as well as DSM-III and DSM-III-R definitions."); Thomas F. Oltmanns, "Approaches to the Definition and Study of Delusions," in *Delusional Beliefs* 3–11 (Thomas F. Oltmanns & Brendan A. Maher eds., 1988) (discussing low reliability of judgments regarding bizarreness of beliefs).

5. Richard Rogers & Daniel W. Shuman, *Fundamentals of Forensic Practice: Mental Health and Criminal Law* 11–13 (2005). See, e.g., Pamela Taylor et al., "Delusion and Violence," in *Violence and Mental Disorder: Developments in Risk Assessment* 161 (John Monahan & Henry Steadman eds., 1994) (finding roughly 82 percent agreement using Maudsley Assessment of Delusions Schedule).

6. See Richard Rogers, *Handbook of Diagnostic and Structured Interviewing* (2001); Charles E. Holzer II et al., "Reliability of Diagnoses in Mental Disorders," 19 *Psychiatric Clinics of North America* 73 (1996); Fennig et al., "Comparison of Facility and Research Diagnoses," 1426.

7. For instance, interrater reliability on the issue of whether a person is insane can be relatively high. Kenneth K. Fukunaga et al., "Insanity Plea: Inter-Examiner Agreement and Concordance of Psychiatric Opinion and Court Verdict,"

5 *Law & Human Behavior* 325 (1981) (finding 92 percent reliability); Michael R. Phillips et al., "Psychiatry and the Criminal Justice System: Testing the Myths," 145 *American Journal of Psychiatry* 605 (1988) (finding 76 percent agreement).

8. Thomas Grisso, *Evaluating Competencies: Forensic Assessments and Instruments* 12 (2d ed. 2003).

9. Ronald J. Rychlak & Joseph Rychlak, "Mental Health Experts on Trial: Free Will and Determinism in the Courtroom," 100 *West Virginia Law Review* 193, 195, 209 (1997).

10. Stephen J. Morse, "Excusing and the New Excuse Defenses: A Legal and Conceptual Review," 23 *Crime & Justice* 329, 367 (1998).

11. Max Hamilton, "Mood Disorders: Clinical Features," in 1 *Comprehensive Textbook of Psychiatry V* 894 (Harold I. Kaplan & Benjamin Sadock eds., 1989).

12. Paul E. Meehl, "Theoretical Risks and Tabular Asterisks: Sir Karl, Sir Ronald, and the Slow Progress of Soft Psychology," 46 *Journal of Consulting & Clinical Psychology* 806, 806 (1978).

13. Ibid., 829. Meehl describes twenty "difficulties in scientizing the human mind" that have only been alluded to here. Ibid., 808–17.

14. Thomas Grisso, "Pretrial Clinical Evaluations in Criminal Cases: Past Trends and Future Directions," 23 *Criminal Justice & Behavior* 90, 97–98 (1996).

15. Michael H. Graham, "*Daubert v. Merrell Dow Pharmaceuticals, Inc.*: No *Frye*, Now What?," 30 *Criminal Law Bulletin* 153, 162 (1994).

16. Christopher B. Mueller & Laird C. Kirkpatrick, *Evidence* 1008 (1999).

17. See *Daubert*, 509 U.S., 591.

18. See, e.g., Susan J. Brison, "Outliving Oneself: Trauma, Memory, and Personal Identity," in *Feminists Rethink the Self*, 12 (Diana Tietjens Meyers ed., 1977); Jaegwon Kim, *Philosophy of Mind* (1996); Robin West, *Caring for Justice* (1997).

19. Andrew E. Taslitz, "A Feminist Approach to Social Scientific Evidence: Foundations," 5 *Michigan Journal of Gender and the Law* 1, 12–27, 78 (1998) (discussing mental state as an interpretive activity).

20. Ibid., 19–20.

21. Ibid., 24.

22. Ibid., 26.

23. See ibid., 34 ("It is narrative thinking that dominates our conceptions of the self: 'Our plannings, our rememberings, even our loving and hating, are guided by narrative plots,'" quoting Theodore R. Sarbin, "The Narrative as a Root Metaphor for Psychology," in *Narrative Psychology: The Storied Nature of Human Conduct* 3, 11 (Theodore R. Sarbin ed., 1986)).

24. Alexander Rosenberg, "The Explanation of Human Action," in *Philosophy of Social Science* 47–49 (1988).

25. Stephen J. Morse, "Crazy Behavior, Morals and Science: An Analysis of Mental Health Law," 51 *Southern California Law Review* 527, 584 (1978).

26. See Thomas D. Lyon & Jonathan J. Koehler, "The Relevance Ratio: Evaluating the Probative Value of Expert Testimony in Child Sexual Abuse Cases," 82 *Cornell Law Review* 43, 46–50 (1996).

27. Ibid., 47.

28. See ibid., 67 (describing "selection bias," which "occurs when the abused and nonabused children who are selected for study differ in ways that may affect the variables measured in the studies").

29. 509 U.S., 591 ("Scientific validity for one purpose is not necessarily scientific validity for other, unrelated purposes.").

30. Ellen Hochstedler Steury & Michelle Choinski, " 'Normal' Crimes and Mental Disorder: A Two-Group Comparison of Deadly and Dangerous Felonies," 18 *International Journal of Law & Psychiatry* 183, 197 (1995).

31. Pamela J. Taylor, "Motives for Offending among Violent and Psychotic Men," 147 *British Journal of Psychiatry* 491, 493 (1985).

32. See, e.g., Robert F. Schopp, *Automatism, Insanity, and the Psychology of Criminal Responsibility* 185–87 (1991) (reporting research indicating that people with schizophrenia have trouble with cognitive focus [e.g., distraction by irrelevant stimuli, thought blocking]; reasoning [e.g., attribution of elaborate meanings to ordinary events]; and concept formation [e.g., tendency to include information in categories to which they bear no relationship]).

33. Morse, "Crazy Behavior," 587–88.

34. David L. Faigman, "The Evidentiary Status of Social Science under *Daubert*: Is It 'Scientific,' 'Technical,' or 'Other' Knowledge?," 1 *Psychology, Public Policy & Law* 960, 971–77 (1995).

35. See Peter Arenella, "Demystifying the Abuse Excuse: Is There One?," 19 *Harvard Journal of Law & Public Policy* 703, 703–05 (1996) (noting that successful abuse excuses are very rare and that typically only those defendants claiming insanity are eligible to be excused under abuse excuse theories); Richard J. Bonnie, "Excusing and Punishing in Criminal Adjudication: A Reality Check," 5 *Cornell Journal of Law & Public Policy* 1, 3–4, 15 (1995) (describing lack of success of novel psychiatric defenses in several cases); Stephanie B. Goldberg, "Fault Lines: Has a Talk-Show Mentality Softened Jurors to Accept Any Excuse?," *American Bar Association Journal* 40, 42 (June 1994) (indicating such defenses are usually unsuccessful).

36. See, e.g. Rule 404(a) (permitting the prosecution to introduce evidence of character if the defendant does so first). This defendant-first idea is developed further in chapter 7.

37. The defendant has a Fifth Amendment right to refuse to take the stand. Malloy v. Hogan, 378 U.S. 1 (1964). Although most courts hold that the defendant may be compelled to undergo evaluation on past mental state issues once a defense has been raised, some hold otherwise. Christopher Slobogin, "Estelle v. Smith: Constitutional Contours of the Forensic Evaluation Process," 31 *Emory Law Journal* 71, 97–98 (1982).

38. See Note, "Incompetency to Stand Trial," 81 *Harvard Law Review* 454, 459 (1967) (noting that, despite fairness concerns, enlarging the class of people found incompetent to include all defendants who "lack the intelligence or the legal sophistication to participate actively in the conduct of their defense . . . would fundamentally alter the administration of the criminal law").

39. For instance, people with schizophrenia are often said to "lack insight" into their condition, *DSM-IV-TR*, 279, and large percentages of defendants state they have diminished memory of the offense. See generally John Bradford & Selwyn Smith, "Amnesia and Homicide: The Padola Case and a Study of Thirty Cases," 7 *Bulletin of the American Academy of Psychiatry & Law* 219 (1979) (finding 60 percent of defendants studied claimed amnesia); Pamela J. Taylor & Michael L. Kopelman, "Amnesia for Criminal Offenses," 14 *Psychological Medicine* 581 (1984) (finding 23 percent claimed amnesia).

40. Morse, "Crazy Behavior," 601–24.

41. Ryder v. State, 83 P.3d 856, 859 n.3 (Okla. Crim. App., 2004).

42. Morse, "Crazy Behavior," 618.

43. Michael L. Perlin, "Unpacking the Myths: The Symbolism Mythology of Insanity Defense Jurisprudence," 40 *Case Western Reserve Law Review* 599, 709–30 (1989–1990).

44. Gary Melton et al., *Psychological Evaluations for the Courts: A Handbook for Mental Health Professionals and Lawyers* 245–46 (2d ed. 1997).

45. People v. Gorshen, 336 P.2d, 492, 497 (Cal. 1959). See also Richard J. Bonnie & Christopher Slobogin, "The Role of Mental Health Professionals in the Criminal Process: The Case for Informed Speculation," 66 *Virginia Law Review* 427, 486–88 (1980).

46. Melton et. al., *Psychological Evaluations*, 592.

47. Meehl, "Theoretical Risks," 817.

48. Ralph Underwager & Hollida Wakefield, "A Paradigm Shift for Expert Witnesses," 5 *Issues in Child Sex Abuse Accusations* 156, 158–59 (1993).

49. See Pointer v. Texas, 380 U.S. 400 (1965) (applying the right of confrontation to the states); Washington v. Texas, 388 U.S. 14 (1967) (applying the compulsory process clause to the states).

50. 483 U.S. 44, 61 (1987).

51. The majority's sweeping language in *Scheffer* suggesting that per se exclusion was warranted did not attract even five members of the Court. Justice Kennedy, joined by three other justices, wrote a concurring opinion which agreed that the lower courts could reach the result affirmed in *Scheffer* but also stated, "I doubt . . . that the rule of per se exclusion is wise." 523 U.S. 303, 318 (1998). Justice Stevens, the lone dissenter, argued that defendants should be permitted to at least tell the jury of the polygraph results. Ibid., 320.

52. Ibid., 309.

53. Ibid., 314, 313–14.

54. As Stevens noted, several studies have found that jurors are not "unduly swayed" by polygraph evidence. Ibid., 322 n. 2 (Stevens, J., dissenting).

55. Ibid., 313.

56. Ibid., 316 (quoting *Rock*, 483 U.S. at 52).

57. Ibid., 317.

58. Tom R. Tyler, *Why People Obey the Law* 63 (1990) ("Respondents are almost equally likely to comply with the law because they view it as legitimate whether they think the likelihood of their being caught is high or low, whether or not they think their peers would disapprove of law breaking, and whether or not they think law breaking is morally wrong.").

59. Paul Robinson & John Darley, *Justice, Liability and Blame: Community Views and the Criminal Law* 7 (1995) ("The legal system that the community perceives as unjustly criminalizing certain conduct is one that is likely to cause the society governed by those laws to lose faith in the system—not only in the specific laws that lead to the unjust result, but in the entire code and criminal justice system enforcing that code.").

60. E. Allan Lind & Tom R. Tyler, *The Social Psychology of Procedural Justice* 70 (1988) ("There is a growing body of research showing that the experience of procedural justice not only enhances evaluations of persons, institutions, and specific outcomes, but also leads to greater overall satisfaction with the legal

experience and more positive affect with respect to an encounter with the justice system.").

61. Based on a scanning of news media reports, Perlin concluded, "Society is simply overwhelmingly skeptical about the use of the insanity defense in virtually any case." Michael Perlin, "'The Borderline Which Separated You from Me': The Insanity Defense, the Authoritarian Spirit, the Fear of Faking, and the Culture of Punishment," 82 *Iowa Law Review* 1375, 1403–04 (1997).

62. See Joan H. Krause, "Of Merciful Justice and Justified Mercy: Commuting the Sentences of Battered Women Who Kill," 46 *Florida Law Review* 699, 719–42 (1994) (describing commutations and review panels in several states.

Chapter 4

1. Holloway v. United States, 148 F.2d 665, 666 (D.C. Cir. 1945).

2. Robert I. Simon, "Retrospective Assessment of Mental States in Criminal and Civil Litigation: A Clinical Review," in *Retrospective Assessment of Mental States in Litigation: Predicting the Past* 2 (Robert I. Simon & Daniel W. Shuman eds., 2002).

3. See Gary Melton et al., *Psychological Evaluations for the Courts: A Handbook for Mental Health Professionals and Lawyers* 230–32 (2d ed. 1997) (describing studies).

4. Julian L. Simon & Paul Burstein, *Basic Research Methods in Social Science* 22 (3d ed. 1985). See generally Samuel Messick, "The Once and Future Issues of Validity: Assessing the Meaning and Consequences of Measurement," in *Test Validity* 33, 40 (Howard Waine & Henry Braun eds., 1988).

5. Melton et al., *Psychological Evaluations*, 216–18.

6. Kenneth W. Eckhardt & M. David Ermann, *Social Research Methods: Perspective, Theory, and Analysis* 99 (1977).

7. Daniel B. Fishman, *The Case for Pragmatic Psychology* (1999).

8. Ibid., 130, 131, 131–32.

9. Ibid., 132, 169, 170–72, 186–87, 168, 170.

10. Daniel B. Fishman, "Call for Papers for Special Issue of Psychology," *Psychology, Public Policy & Law*, www.apa.org/journals/law/papercall3.html (retrieved November 30, 2001).

11. Research indicates that a high percentage of war veterans suffer from PTSD and that many also experience flashbacks, but is silent on whether these latter individuals know right from wrong or feel compelled to act. See, e.g., Arthur Egendor, "The Postwar Healing of Vietnam Veterans: Recent Research," 33 *Hospital & Community Psychiatry* 901 (1981).

12. Richard Rogers et al., *Structured Interview of Reported Symptoms (SIRS) and Professional Manual* (1992).

13. See, e.g., Richard Rogers & James Cavanaugh, "The Rogers Criminal Responsibility Assessment Scales," 160 *Illinois Medical Journal* 164 (1981) (providing a structured interview format for insanity evaluations, although also unfortunately suggesting that cognitive and volitional impairment can be "quantified"); Steven L. Golding et al., "The Assessment of Criminal Responsibility: Current Controversies," in *The Handbook of Forensic Psychology* 379, 390–95 (Alan K. Hess & Irving B. Weiner eds., 1999) (suggesting how the Present State Examination can be used to evaluate legally relevant delusional thinking).

14. See Fed. R. Crim. P. 3.211(b).

15. Evans v. State, 800 So.2d 182, 188 (2001).

16. Cf. American Academy of Psychiatry and Law, "Ethical Guidelines for the Practice of Forensic Psychiatry," in *American Academy of Psychiatry and Law Membership Directory* xi–xiv (2000) ("The psychiatrist maintains confidentiality to the extent possible given the legal context.").

17. Although a court-ordered evaluation can be conducted over the individual's objection, use of the materials beyond the scope of the court order may well be actionable. See, e.g., Doe v. Roe, 93 Misc.2d 201, 400 N.Y.S.2d 668 (1977) (finding a psychiatrist liable for publication of a book that reported verbatim and extensively the patients' thoughts, feelings, and emotions, despite some attempt to disguise the patients' identity).

18. Government works are generally not copyrightable. But federal law provides copyright protection for all "literary works" created by independent contractors (as opposed to regular government employees). See 17 U.S.C.A. § § 102(a)(1), 201(a) & (b). That rule would probably include most forensic evaluators. Of course, the evaluator submitting his or her report might waive copyright protection, but other evaluators whose reports were submitted along with it would have to do so as well to ensure no violation of federal law.

19. See Daniel Fishman, "From Single Case to Database: A New Method for Enhancing Psychotherapy, Forensic, and Other Psychological Practice," 10 *Applied and Preventive Psychology* 275 (2001).

20. Max Hamilton, "Mood Disorders: Clinical Features," in 1 *Comprehensive Textbook of Psychiatry V* 894 (Harold I. Kaplan & Benjamin Sadock eds., 1989).

21. See, e.g., Thomas Grisso et al., "The MacArthur Treatment Competence Study II: Measures of Abilities Related to Competence to Consent to Treatment," 19 *Law & Human Behavior* 127, 130–36 (1995).

22. Philip H. Witt, "Transfer of Juveniles to Adult Court: The Case of H.H.," 9 *Psychology, Public Policy & Law* 361, 375 (2003).

23. Ibid., 368 (concluding that H.H. had both a dissociative disorder and a paranoid personality disorder and that she was not significantly depressed).

24. Fishman, *The Case for Pragmatic Psychology*, 172, 218.

25. American Bar Association, *Standards Relating to Pleas of Guilty* xi–xii (1988) (93 percent of cases in federal system and 91 percent of cases in state systems resolved through guilty plea); Melton et al., *Psychological Evaluations for the Courts* 188 (reporting studies indicating that 60 percent to 90 percent of all insanity acquittals result from a bench trial where the issue is stipulated or dealt with summarily).

26. See generally Melton et al., *Psychological Evaluations*, 190–93 (describing various insanity tests).

27. Wayne R. LaFave et al., 1 *Criminal Procedure* 147 (2d ed. 1999) ("The total number of appeals to the intermediate appeals court is likely to amount to less than 10% of all convictions entered by the state's general trial court."). If a criminal defendant is acquitted, the prosecution may not appeal, even if the court or jury improperly applied the law or was wrong as to the relevant facts. Charles H. Whitebread & Christopher Slobogin, *Criminal Procedure: An Analysis of Cases and Concepts* 858–61 (4th ed. 2000). Of those cases appealed, most never reach the state supreme court but end at the intermediate appellate court, and thus no uniform ruling on a statewide basis exists.

28. Fishman, "Call for Papers."

29. Fishman, *The Case for Pragmatic Psychology*, 192 ("A good model for pragmatic psychology . . . is judicial law.").

30. See Christopher C. Langdell, "Address to Harvard Law School Association," in *A Record of the Commemoration, November 5th through 8th, 1886, on the 250th Anniversary of the Founding of Harvard College* 84, 86–87 (Justin Winsor ed., 1887).

31. Charles W. Collier, "The Use and Abuse of Humanistic Theory in Law: Reexamining the Assumptions of Interdisciplinary Legal Scholarship," 41 *Duke Law Journal* 191, 200 (1991).

32. Thomas F. Cotter, "Legal Pragmatism and the Law and the Law & Economics Movement," 84 *Georgetown Law Journal* 2072, 2082 (1996).

33. Fishman, *The Case for Pragmatic Psychology*, 173–74.

34. Mock jurors routinely arrive at different conclusions about insanity and other issues on the same facts. See, e.g., Norman J. Finkel, "The Insanity Defense: A Comparison of Verdict Schemas," 15 *Law & Human Behavior* 533, 544 (1991) (Table 2) (finding significant disagreement among mock jurors on whether particular individuals should be found insane or guilty, regardless of verdict scheme used).

35. In some ways, this notion parallels the premise underlying the legal process movement, which emphasized the need to recognize certain immutable principles of process, such as the requirement that judges state reasons for their decisions, in an effort to minimize the relativizing aspects of substantive law. See generally, Calvin Woodard, "The Limits of Legal Realism: An Historical Perspective," 54 *Virginia Law Review* 689 (1968).

36. United States v. Sims, 514 F.2d 147 (9th Cir. 1973); United States v. Wright, 783 F.2d 1091 (D.C. Cir.1986); United States v. Bramlet, 820 F.2d 851 (7th Cir. 1987).

37. *Wright*, 783 F.2d, 1100.

38. Advisory Committee Notes, Rule 703.

39. Cf. Richard Bonnie & Christopher Slobogin, "The Role of Mental Health Professionals in Criminal Cases: The Case for Informed Speculation," 66 *Virginia Law Review* 427, 503–08 (1981).

40. 541 U.S. 36 (2004).

41. Ibid., 51.

42. People v. Goldstein, 6 N.Y.3d 119, 843 N.E.2d 727 (2005).

Chapter 5

1. Gary Melton et al., *Community Mental Health Centers and the Courts: An Evaluation of Community-Based Forensic Services* 43–55 (1985) (reporting a study showing that forensic mental health professionals were far more knowledgeable about clinical syndromes commonly observed in criminal and juvenile forensic practice, and the research relevant to those syndromes, than trial judges).

2. See David Faust & Barry Nurcombe, "Improving the Accuracy of Clinical Judgment," 52 *Psychiatry* 197, 202 (1989) (defining incremental validity as "the advantage gained by adding a sign").

3. See, e.g., Brian L. Cutler & Steven D. Penrod, *Mistaken Identification: The Eyewitness, Psychology, and Law* 240 (1995) (concluding, based on several studies,

that without expert testimony, "jurors appear insensitive to the factors that influence eyewitness identification accuracy").

4. See generally Michael H. Shapiro, "Is Bioethics Broke? On the Idea of Ethics and Law 'Catching Up' with Technology," 33 *Indiana Law Review* 17 (1999).

5. Ibid., 34.

6. Ibid.

7. See Wayne LaFave, *Criminal Law* 426 (4th ed. 2003) ("On the issue of lack of responsibility because of insanity, the initial burden of going forward is everywhere placed upon the defendant."); see also Davis v. United States, 160 U.S. 469, 470 (1895) (recognizing a presumption of sanity). At one time a person was "presumed" to intend the natural and probable consequences of his or her acts, but since Sandstrom v. Montana, 442 U.S. 510, 522–23 (1979), courts are permitted to instruct juries only that they may draw an inference about intent from behavior.

8. For instance, the presumption of sanity has been described as a device for saving "the state the fruitless trouble of proving sanity in the great number of cases where the question will not be raised" and as "a description of the initial assignment of the burden of producing evidence to the defendant." 2 *McCormick on Evidence*, § 343, 455 n.7 (John William Strong ed., 4th ed. 1992).

9. See, e.g., People v. Day, 2 Cal. Rptr. 2d 916, 923 (Cal. Ct. App. 1992) (noting prosecution argument that defendant "could have easily left" the abusive relationship), overruled by People v. Humphrey, 921 P.2d 1 (Cal. 1996).

10. See, e.g., People v. Karst, 560 N.Y.S.2d 577 (N.Y. App. Div. 1990) (involving victim's failure to promptly report the alleged rape).

11. See Lisa R. Askowitz & Michael H. Graham, "The Reliability of Expert Psychological Testimony in Child Sexual Abuse Prosecutions," 15 *Cardozo Law Review* 2027, 2040 (1994) ("The overwhelming majority of jurisdictions will allow testimony based on CSAAS when it is used to explain the significance of the child complainant's seemingly self-impeaching behavior, such as delayed reporting or recantation."); Karla Fischer, "Defining the Boundaries of Admissible Expert Psychological Testimony on Rape Trauma Syndrome," 1989 *University of Illinois Law Review* 691, 713–17 (detailing cases that allow RTS evidence "when it is used to rebut misconceptions about victim behavior"); Robert P. Mosteller, "Syndromes and Politics in Criminal Trials and Evidence Law," 46 *Duke Law Journal* 461, 479 (1996) ("When BWS is used for the purpose of restoring the credibility of the defendant by countering prosecutorial impeachment . . . the evidence, almost regardless of form, is readily accepted.").

12. See, e.g., Kenneth A. Deffenbacher & Elizabeth F. Loftus, "Do Jurors Share a Common Understanding Concerning Eyewitness Behavior?," 6 *Law & Human Behavior* 15 (1982) (examining lay beliefs about potential eyewitness inaccuracy); Patricia Frazier & Eugene Borgida, "Juror Common Understanding and the Admissibility of Rape Trauma Syndrome Evidence in Court," 12 *Law & Human Behavior* 101, 111–15 (1988) (reporting study comparing expert and nonexpert beliefs about rape); Gail S. Goodman et al., "Jurors' Reactions to Child Witnesses," 40 *Journal of Social Issues* 139, 142 (1984) (examining beliefs about the accuracy of child witnesses).

13. As Professor LaFave points out, the presumption of innocence is not really a presumption, in that it does not require proof of an underlying fact that

then allows the assumption of innocence. Rather, it is designed to overcome, inter alia, the assumption that the "fact of accusation is . . . evidence of . . . guilt." LaFave, *Criminal Law*, 69.

14. See Fed. R. Evid. 404(a)(2) (providing that "evidence of a person's character or a trait of character is not admissible for the purpose of proving action in conformity therewith on a particular occasion, except . . . (1) evidence of a pertinent trait of character offered by an accused, or by the prosecution to rebut same").

15. Cf. Fed. R. Evid. 608(a). The rule states, "The credibility of a witness may be attacked or supported by evidence in the form of opinion or reputation, but subject to these limitations: (1) the evidence may refer only to character for truthfulness or untruthfulness, and (2) evidence of truthful character is admissible only after the character of the witness for truthfulness has been attacked by opinion or reputation evidence or otherwise."

16. See, e.g., Shahzade v. Gregory, 923 F. Supp. 286, 289 (D. Mass. 1996) (characterizing repressed memory evidence as helpful); Isely v. Capuchin Province, 877 F. Supp. 1055, 1063–64 (E.D. Mich. 1995) (allowing expert testimony on repressed memory). Research in this area may be difficult to assemble. See Gary M. Ernsdorff & Elizabeth F. Loftus, "Let Sleeping Memories Lie? Words of Caution about Tolling the Statute of Limitations in Cases of Memory Repression," 84 *Journal of Criminal Law & Criminology* 129, 133 (1993) ("The traumatic nature of events that lead to repression . . . virtually precludes experimental probing of the theory; researchers have yet to design experiments that will enable them to study the repression and subsequent retrieval of a memory.").

17. See, e.g., Stephen Morse, "Crazy Behavior, Morals, and Science: An Analysis of Mental Health Law," 51 *Southern California Law Review* 527, 554–60 (1978); Barbara Weiner, "Mental Disability and the Criminal Law," in *The Mentally Disabled and the Law* 693, 721 (Jan Brakel et al. eds., 3d ed. 1985).

18. See, e.g., United States v. Hearst, 563 F.2d 133 (9th Cir. 1977); Atkinson v. State, 391 N.E.2d 1170 (Ind. Ct. App. 1979); Melton et al., *Community Mental Health Centers and the Courts* 94–95 (description of Virginia lawyers' and judges' negative reaction to ban on ultimate issue testimony); Richard Rogers & Daniel W. Shuman, *Fundamentals of Forensic Practice: Mental Health and Criminal Law* 75–76 (2005).

19. American Law Institute, Model Penal Code 4.01 (1962 Draft).

20. American Bar Association, *Criminal Justice Mental Health Standards*, standard 7-6.6 (1989); American Psychiatric Association, *Statement on the Insanity Defense* 14 (1982); see, e.g., Cal. Penal Code 28(a) (1982).

21. See "Report of the Task Force on the Role of Psychology in the Criminal Justice System," Recommendation 5, in *Who Is the Client?* (John Monahan ed. 1981) ("Since it is not within the professional competence of psychologists to offer conclusions on matters of law, psychologists should resist pressure to offer such conclusions.").

22. American Bar Association, *Criminal Justice Standards*, 336–38.

23. Solomon M. Fulero & Norman J. Finkel, "Barring Ultimate Issue Testimony: An 'Insane' Rule?" 15 *Law & Human Behavior* 495 (1991).

24. See Melton et al., *Psychological Evaluations for the Courts*, 94–95, 367; Norman Poythress, "Concerning Reform in Expert Testimony: An Open Letter from a Practicing Psychologist," 6 *Law & Human Behavior* 39, 40–42 (1982).

25. I was the reporter for the American Bar Association standard concerning the insanity defense and the ultimate issue issue and wrote the above-mentioned commentary. However, the commentary reflected the views of the ABA's task force on the insanity defense; my personal view is found in the text.

26. See, e.g., John Petrila, "The Insanity Defense and Other Mental Health Dispositions in Missouri," 5 *International Journal of Law & Psychiatry* 81 (1982); Kenneth K. Fukunaga et al., "Insanity Plea: Inter-examiner Agreement and Concordance of Psychiatric Opinion and Court Verdict," 5 *Law & Human Behavior* 325, 327–28 (1981); Wright Williams & Kent S. Miller, "The Processing and Disposition of Incompetent Mentally Ill Offenders," 5 *Law & Human Behavior* 245 (1981); Virginia Hiday, "Reformed Commitment Procedures: An Empirical Study in the Courtroom," 11 *Law & Society Review* 651 (1977); Serena Stier & Kurt Stoebe, "Involuntary Hospitalization of the Mentally Ill in Iowa: The Failure of the 1975 Legislation," 64 *Iowa Law Review* 1284 (1979). Cf. R. C. Howard & Charles R. Clark, "When Courts and Experts Disagree: Discordance between Insanity Recommendation and Adjudications," 9 *Law & Human Behavior* 385, 394 (1984) (speculating that opposing expert testimony and attorney skill explained discordances found between state examiner and court opinions on insanity).

27. Gare Smith & James Hall, "Evaluating Michigan's Guilty but Mentally Ill Verdict," 16 *University of Michigan Journal of Law Reform* 77, 94 (1982); Jeffrey Rogers et al., "Insanity Defenses: Contested or Conceded?," 141 *American Journal of Psychiatry* 885 (1984).

28. Compare United States v. Manley, 893 F.2d 1221 (11th Cir. 1999) (defense counsel not permitted to ask expert whether persons with manic-depressive psychosis would "be able to appreciate the nature and quality or the wrongfulness of their actions") to United States v. Salamanca, 990 F.2d 629 (D.C. Cir. 1993) (permitting an expert to testify that "someone who had drunk as much [as the defendant] would have a diminished capacity to seek and plan") and United States v. Kristiansen, 901 F.2d 1463 (8th Cir. 1990) (permitting defense counsel to ask whether the mental disease of the type defendant allegedly had "would affect a person's ability to appreciate their actions").

29. Morse, "Crazy Behavior."

30. See Charles Bleil, "Evidence of Syndromes: No Need for a 'Better Mousetrap,'" 32 *South Texas Law Review* 37, 66 (1990) (arguing that psychological testimony is probably "the least over-awing" of the various types of expert testimony "because jurors have some innate knowledge of human behavior" but are unlikely to have similar knowledge of physics, genetics, or aeronautics).

31. Dennis J. Devine et al., "Jury Decision Making: 45 Years of Empirical Research on Deliberating Groups," 7 *Psychology, Public Policy & Law* 622, 689 (2001).

32. Lisa Callahan et al., "The Volume and Characteristics of Insanity Defense Pleas: An Eight State Study," 19 *Bulletin of the American Academy of Psychiatry & Law* 331 (1991) (estimating 26 percent success rate for insanity defense across eight states); Stuart M. Kirschner & Gary M. Galperin, "The Defense of Extreme Emotional Disturbance in New York County: Pleas and Outcomes," 10 *Behavioral Science & Law* 47 (2002) (contested diminished responsibility claims failed in ten of eleven jury trials and in all five cases in which a bench trial was held). For research rejecting the jury gullibility hypothesis, see Neil J. Vidmar & Regina A. Schuller, "Juries and Expert Evidence: Social Framework Testimony," 52

Law & Contemporary Problems 133, 173 (1989). See also Regina Schuller, "The Impact of Battered Woman Syndrome Evidence on Jury Decision Processes," 16 *Law & Human Behavior* 597, 616 (1992).

33. People v. Enis, 564 N.E.2d 1155, 1165 (Ill. 1990) (upholding trial court's exclusion of testimony on eyewitness identification because "it would be inappropriate for a jury to conclude, based on expert testimony, that all eyewitness testimony is unreliable").

34. In Bayesian terms, the court would admit the evidence only if there was some concrete probability, independent of the expert testimony, that the event occurred.

35. Indeed, a barely positive relevance ratio might lead to presumptive exclusion. After detailing methodological problems that could promote bias in studies comparing abused and nonabused children, Lyon and Koehler state, "Because these biases are difficult to eliminate . . . courts should treat as presumptively irrelevant symptoms that are only slightly more common among abused children than among nonabused children." Thomas D. Lyon & Jonathan J. Koehler, "The Relevance Ratio: Evaluating the Probative Value of Expert Testimony in Child Sexual Abuse Cases," 82 *Cornell Law Review* 43, 70 (1996).

36. See Flanagan v. State, 625 So. 2d 827, 828–29 (Fla. 1993) (holding testimony based on "sex offender profile" inadmissible).

37. See Fed. R. Evid. 404(b) ("Evidence of other crimes, wrongs, or acts . . . may . . . be admissible [to prove] motive, opportunity, intent, preparation, plan, knowledge, identity, or absence of mistake or accident.").

38. 628 A.3d 696, 701 (1993).

39. Nancy J. Brekke et al., "Of Juries and Court-Appointed Experts: The Impact of Nonadversarial versus Adversarial Expert Testimony," 15 *Law & Human Behavior* 451, 471 (1991).

40. See Redevelopment Agency v. Tobriner, 264 Cal. Rptr. 481, 488 n.5 (Cal. Ct. App. 1989) (noting that "courts routinely conduct hearings in limine to determine the scope of admissible evidence"); E. Donald Elliot, "Toward Incentive-Based Procedure: Three Approaches for Regulating Scientific Evidence," 69 *Boston University Law Review* 487, 501 (1989) (noting "inherent power of a trial judge to appoint an expert").

41. The rule provides that "the court may appoint any expert witnesses agreed upon by the parties and may appoint expert witnesses of its own selection." See also Elliot, "Three Approaches," 507–08 (recommending that the court appoint its own expert if it finds expert testimony proffered by one of the parties would be subject to "substantial doubt in peer review by the scientific community").

42. See Hope Viner Samborn, "Changing the Jury Tool Box: ABA Task Force Invites Criticism of Trial Proposals—And Gets It," *American Bar Association Journal* 22 (Dec. 1997) (reporting on the Civil Trial Practice standards drafted by the American Bar Association's Litigation Section Task Force on Civil Trial Practice, which include a provision for permitting jurors to submit written questions for witnesses). Under this provision, "after receiving a question, the judge should disclose it to the attorneys and give them an opportunity to object outside the presence of the jury. A cautionary instruction should explain, among other things, that some queries may be rejected or rewritten." Ibid. The ABA also proposes that judges distribute "jury notebooks" containing selected admitted exhibits and other materials not subject to dispute). Ibid.

43. See, e.g., American Psychological Association, Ethical Principles of Psychologists and Code of Conduct §2.01 (Boundaries of Competence); §2.03 (Maintaining Competence); §9.01 (b) (Bases for Assessments) ("Psychologists clarify the possible impact of their limited information on the reliability and validity of their opinions, and appropriately limit the nature and extent of their conclusions or recommendations."); American Bar Association, *Model Rules of Professional Conduct*, Rule 1.1 (1983) ("A lawyer shall provide competent representation to a client. Competent representation requires the legal knowledge, skill, thoroughness and preparation reasonably necessary for the representation."). One commentator has proposed that experts be liable in tort if the testimony deviates from what the expert knows or should know would be acceptable by peers in his or her area of expertise. Jeffrey Harrison, "Reconceptualizing the Expert Witness: Social Costs, Current Controls and Proposed Responses," 8 *Yale Journal on Regulation* 253 (2001).

44. Shelby A. D. Moore, "Battered Women Syndrome: Selling the Shadow to Support the Substance," 38 *Howard Law Journal* 297, 301 (1995) (arguing that the syndrome "reinforces an image of women as weak, crazy, powerless 'victims' in need of protection").

45. Anthony V. Alfieri, "Defending Racial Violence," 95 *Columbia Law Review* 1301, 1324 (1995).

46. Ibid., 341.

47. See George P. Fletcher, *With Justice for Some: Victims' Rights in Criminal Trials* 38 (1995).

48. Williams was acquitted on attempted murder and aggravated mayhem charges but convicted of simple mayhem. Ibid., 234.

49. Alfieri, "Defending Racial Violence," 1312, 1314–15.

50. Ibid.,1304, 1324 (asserting that "by privileging a narrative of racial deviance, the defense teams help constitute black men and their communities in terms of pathological violence").

51. Ibid., 1341, 1342, 1316–20 (describing "defiance narratives," generally in positive terms), 1306.

52. As noted in chapter 2, the "reasonable battered woman" standard owes its current prominence in statutory and case law as much to feminist persuasiveness as to anything else. Mosteller has proffered the admission of BWS as an illustration that "political forces are now openly shaping a field of law—the law of evidence—where such forces have been previously less overt." Mosteller, "Syndromes and Politics in Criminal Trials," 515.

53. Alfieri, "Defending Racial Violence," 1311.

54. Ibid., 1312 (quoting from trial transcript).

55. See Fletcher, *With Justice for Some*, 234 (calling the testimony in the Williams case a "parody of scientific thinking"). It is worth noting, however, that scientific research bearing on this question does exist and that, had it been proffered, it might have been admissible under *Daubert*, although a lack-of-fit objection might apply. See, e.g., Edward Diener, "Deindividuation: The Absence of Self-Awareness, and Self-Regulation in Group Members," in *The Psychology of Group Influence* 231 (Paul B. Paulus ed., 1980) (discussing research showing how involvement in groups may cause "deindividuation," which can "release the person from both societal norms and personal standards that normally influence behavior," although the precise actions taken "will depend on his or her

motivations and desires at the time and on situational influences such as the behavior of models").

56. See Fed. R. Evid. 403, Advisory Committee's Note (" 'Unfair prejudice' within its context means an undue tendency to suggest [a] decision on an improper basis, commonly, though not necessarily, an emotional one.").

57. See, e.g., Washington v. Texas, 388 U.S. 14, 23 n.21 (1967) (stating that the defendant's right to present a defense should not be construed "as disapproving testimonial privileges, such as the privilege against self-incrimination or the lawyer-client or husband-wife privileges"); United States v. Abbas, 74 F.3d 506, 511 (4th Cir. 1996) (stating that in a conflict between the defendant's Sixth Amendment right and a potential witness's Fifth Amendment privilege, the privilege prevails); United States v. Doyle, 1 F. Supp. 2d 1187, 1190 (D. Or. 1998) (stating that a defendant's Sixth Amendment right to compulsory process does not trump a victim's right to confidentiality of psychotherapy records).

58. See, e.g., Christopher B. Mueller & Laird C. Kirkpatrick, *Evidence* 230 (1995) (noting that the federal rape shield law was passed in part "to encourage greater reporting of sex offenses" and thus help ensure that rapists are caught and convicted).

59. See, e.g., Shaw v. United States, 892 F. Supp. 1265, 1277 (D.S.D. 1995) ("The limited interest in encouraging reporting [underlying rape shield laws] would not in and of itself outweigh Shaw's interest in presenting relevant evidence. Nevertheless, this interest is one that must be considered along with other legitimate interests in determining whether a victim's alleged sexual conduct should be admitted."). See generally Michigan v. Lucas, 500 U.S. 145, 149 (1991) ("The right to present relevant testimony is not without limitation. The right 'may, in appropriate cases, bow to accommodate other legitimate interests in the criminal trial process [including assuring the efficient administration of justice],' " quoting Rock v. Arkansas, 483 U.S. 44, 55 (1987)).

60. Alfieri, "Defending Racial Violence," 1309–10 (referring to the "intersection of defiance and deviance narratives" and "double images of black defiance and deviance"); see also Anthony V. Alfieri, "Race Prosecutors, Race Defenders," 89 *Georgetown Law Journal* 2227, 2258 (2001) (discussing the "interlacing and sometimes dissonant deviance and defiance narratives").

61. For an account of the Colin Ferguson case, see David van Biema, "A Fool for a Client," *Time*, 66 (Feb. 6, 1995).

62. See United States v. Alexander, 471 F.2d 923, 958–60 (D.C. Cir. 1973).

63. A better example of a defiance-deviance dichotomy occurs in the battered women situation, where scholars discussing defenses to homicide (of the batterer) have differentiated between a defense based on survivorship and a defense based on "learned helplessness" arguments. See Martha R. Mahoney, "Legal Images of Battered Women: Redefining the Issue of Separation," 90 *Michigan Law Review* 1, 34–43 (1991) (critiquing the learned helplessness theory). But Alfieri does not provide any equivalently persuasive examples in the racialized defense context. For an approach that moves in that direction, see Paul Harris, *Black Rage Confronts the Law* 274 (1997).

64. See generally Bruce J. Winick, "Reforming Incompetency to Stand Trial and Plead Guilty: A Restated Proposal and a Response to Professor Bonnie," 85 *Journal of Criminal Law & Criminology* 571, 581–82 (1995) (arguing for a "presumption of competence" in the client decision-making context in large part

because the incompetency label can become a self-fulfilling prophecy, acting to diminish self-esteem, inhibit initiative and motivation, and cause depression).

65. Peter Margulies, "Identity on Trial: Subordination, Social Science Evidence, and Criminal Defense," 51 *Rutgers Law Review* 45, 131 (1998).

66. Ibid., 124.

67. Social scientists would say that this defense tries to overcome "fundamental attribution error." That concept posits that when people judge the unusual behavior of others they are prone to try to explain the behavior in terms of the person's psychological disposition (e.g., anger) rather than in terms of the person's situation (e.g., the degree of stress recently experienced by the individual). See generally Richard E. Nisbett & Lee Ross, *Human Inference: Strategies and Shortcomings of Social Judgment* 133–34 (1980).

68. For a description of the facts, see People v. Goetz, 497 N.E.2d 41, 43–44 (N.Y. 1986).

69. This is, in fact, very close to the standard the appellate court found appropriate in the case. See ibid., 52.

70. Lori Montgomery, "Teen Guilty of Murder: Urban Theory Not Allowed," *Detroit Free Press*, 6A (Nov. 12, 1994) (describing the trial of Daimian Osby).

71. Margulies, "Identity on Trial," 74–100.

Chapter 6

1. American Psychiatric Ass'n Task Force, *Clinical Aspects of the Violent Individual* 33 (1974).

2. "Report of the Task Force on the Role of Psychology in the Criminal Justice System," 33 *American Psychologist* 1099, 1110 (1978).

3. John Monahan, *The Clinical Prediction of Violent Behavior* 47–49 (1981).

4. 463 U.S. 880 (1983).

5. Shah identified eleven other stages of the legal process at which dangerousness assessments occur, including pretrial release hearings, juvenile transfer decisions, and transfer of prisoners to special prisons for disruptive offenders. Saleem Shah, "Dangerousness: A Paradigm for Exploring Some Issues in Law and Psychology," 33 *American Psychologist* 224, 225 (1978).

6. See, e.g., Idaho Code §19–2515(9)(h) (requiring "propensity to commit murder which will probably constitute a continuing threat to society"); Tex. Code Crim. Pro. art. 37.071 § 2(b)(1) (requiring "probability that the defendant would commit criminal acts of violence that would constitute a continuing threat to society"); Va. Code § 19.2–264.4C (same).

7. With respect to danger to property, see, e.g., Ark. Stat. §5-2-315(a)(1) (release of insanity acquittees required if they "no longer create a substantial risk of bodily injury to another person or serious damage to the property of another"); Hawai'i Rev. Stat. §334-1 (permitting civil commitment if threat of substantial damage to property); Del. Code tit. 16, § 5001(6) (same); Kan. Stat. §59-2946(3)(a) (same); North Dakota Cent. Code § 25-03.1-02(12)(b) (same); Jones v. United States, 463 U.S. 354, 364 (1983) (stating, in the context of criminal commitment proceedings, "We do not agree with petitioner's suggestion that the requisite dangerousness is not established by proof that a person committed a non-violent crime against property"). With respect to emotional harm, see Hawaii Rev. Stat. §334-1 (dangerous to others defined as "likely to do substantial physical or

emotional injury on another"); Iowa Code Ann. §229.1(16)(b) ("serious emotional injury on members of the person's family or others who lack reasonable opportunity to avoid contact with the person").

8. Compare Idaho Code § 19–2515(9)(h) (requiring proof beyond a reasonable doubt for all aggravating factors in capital cases) to Addington v. Texas, 441 U.S. 418 (1979) (permitting civil commitment by clear and convincing evidence).

9. For descriptions of these techniques, see R. Karl Hanson, "What Do We Know about Sex Offender Risk Assessment?," 4 *Psychology, Public Policy & Law* 50, 52–53 (1998); Kevin S. Douglas & Jennifer L. Skeem, "Violence Risk Assessment: Getting Specific about Being Dynamic," 11 *Psychology, Public Policy & Law* 347, 352–53 (2005).

10. Harry L. Kozol et al., "The Diagnosis and Treatment of Dangerousness," 18 *Crime & Delinquency* 371, 383 (1972).

11. 452 U.S. 454, 457–60 (1981).

12. Harry L. Kozol, "The Diagnosis of Dangerousness," in *Violence and Victims* 3, 8 (S. Pasternack ed., 1975).

13. Kozol et al., "The Diagnosis and Treatment of Dangerousness," 379.

14. Gary Melton et al., *Psychological Evaluations for the Courts: A Handbook for Mental Health Professionals and Lawyers* 284–85 (2d ed. 1997).

15. 463 U.S. at 918–19 (Blackmun, J., dissenting). Barefoot shot at point-blank range a police officer who wanted to ask him questions about a fire that Barefoot apparently had started to divert attention from a planned robbery. Barefoot v. State, 596 S.W.2d 875, 879–80 (5th Cir. 1980).

16. The best description of the VRAG and pertinent research is found in Vernon Quinsey, *Violent Offenders: Appraising and Managing Risk* (2d. ed. 2005). See also Grant T. Harris et al., "Violent Recidivism of Mentally Disordered Offenders: The Development of a Statistical Prediction Instrument," 20 *Criminal Justice & Behavior* 315 (1993).

17. A more recent prospective study found that, over a five-year period, these two categories were associated with a 42 percent and 71 percent chance of reoffending, respectively. Grant T. Harris et al., "Prospective Replication of the Violence Risk Appraisal Guide in Predicting Violent Recidivism among Forensic Patients," 26 *Law & Human Behavior* 377, 385 (2002).

18. A good description of the conceptual work for this instrument is found in John Monahan et al., *Rethinking Risk Assessment: The MacArthur Study of Mental Disorder and Violence* 134 (2001). See also Henry Steadman et al., "A Classification Tree Approach to the Development of Actuarial Violence Risk Assessment Tools," 24 *Law & Human Behavior* 83 (2000).

19. D. Epperson et al., "Minnesota Sex Offender Screening Tool–Revised (MnSOST-R): Development, Validation, and Recommended Risk Level Cut Scores" (2003), available at www.psychology.iastate.edu/faculty/epperson/ TechUpdatePaper12-03.pdf. See also Richard Hamill, "Recidivism of Sex Offenders: What You Need to Know," 15 *Criminal Justice* 24, 30 (2001).

20. See R. Karl Hanson, "The Development of a Brief Actuarial Scale for Sexual Offense Recidivism" 13 (1997), available at www.sgc.gc.ca/publications/ corrections/199704_e.pdf.

21. See generally R. Karl Hanson, "What Do We Know about Sex Offender Risk Assessment?," 4 *Psychology, Public Policy & Law* 50, 65–67 (1998) (discussing

the types of factors that might adjust an actuarial prediction). Note, however, that the VRAG's developers would oppose using the VRAG this way. Vernon Quinsey et al., *Violent Offenders: Appraising and Managing Risk* 171 (1st ed. 1998).

22. See Kevin Douglas & Christopher Webster, "The HCR-20 Violence Risk Assessment Scheme: Concurrent Validity in a Sample of Incarcerated Offenders," 26 *Criminal Justice & Behavior* 3 (1999).

23. Kevin Douglas et al., "Assessing Risk for Violence among Psychiatric Patients: The HCR-20 Violence Risk Assessment Scheme and the Psychopathy Checklist: Screening Version," 67 *Journal of Consulting & Clinical Psychology* 917, 921 (1999).

24. Robert D. Hare, "The Hare PCL-R: Some Issues Concerning Its Use and Misuse," 3 *Legal & Criminal Psychology* 99 (1998).

25. Steven Wong, "Recidivism and Criminal Career Profiles of Psychopaths: A Longitudinal Study," 24 *Issues in Criminological & Legal Psychology* 147 (1995). See also Marnie E. Rice et al., "An Evaluation of a Maximum Security Therapeutic Community for Psychopaths and Other Mentally Disordered Offenders," 16 *Law & Human Behavior* 399 (1992) (reporting that 77 percent of those who scored higher than 25 on the PCL-R committed a violent offense despite treatment).

26. Unlike the actuarial predictor, "a clinical decisionmaker is not committed in advance of decision to the factors that will be considered and the rule for combining them." Barbara Underwood, "Law and the Crystal Ball: Predicting Behavior with Statistical Inference and Individualized Judgment," 88 *Yale Law Journal* 1408, 1423 (1979).

27. Seymour Halleck, *Psychiatry and the Dilemmas of Crime* 314 (1967).

28. See Melton et al., *Psychological Evaluations*, 278–79 (discussing judgment errors and biases that can affect clinical prediction).

29. See generally Paul Meehl, "What Can the Clinician Do Well?," in *Psychodiagnosis: Selected Papers* 165, 169–70 (1973) (discussing factors favoring clinical prediction); Underwood, "Predicting Behavior," 1427. Note that structured professional judgment approaches, like the HCR-20, can take individual characteristics into account.

30. Note that the developers of the VRAG considered fifty variables and found that only twelve were significantly related to violence. Grant Harris et al., "Psychopathy and Violent Recidivism," 15 *Law and Human Behavior* 625, 631 (Table 1) (1991). Thus, there is some basis for considering the thirty-eight excluded variables irrelevant to prediction.

31. Monahan et al., *Rethinking Risk Assessment*, 134.

32. Hare, "The Hare PCL-R," 100.

33. Grant T. Harris, "The Construct of Psychopathy," 28 *Crime & Justice* 197, 217 (2001) ("The PCL-R has yielded high interrater reliability and test-retest reliability on prisoners and forensic psychiatric patients.").

34. See Melton et al., *Psychological Evaluations* 283 (reporting a study finding that self-reports increased base rates from 3 percent to 40 percent).

35. See Christopher Slobogin, "Dangerousness and Expertise," 133 *University of Pennsylvania Law Review* 97, 110–11, 117–18 (1984) (describing eight clinical prediction studies and three actuarial prediction studies finding false-positive rates ranging from 54 percent to 94 percent).

36. John Monahan, *Clinical Prediction of Violent Behavior*, 47.

37. John Monahan et al., "An Actuarial Model of Violence Risk Assessment for Persons with Mental Disorders," 56 *Psychiatric Services* 810, 814 (2005).

38. For studies of clinical prediction, see Diana S. Sepejak et al., "Clinical Predictions of Dangerousness: Two Year Follow-up of 408 Pre-Trial Forensic Cases," 11 *Bulletin of the American Academy of Psychiatry & Law* 171 (1983) (44 percent false positives); Charles Lidz et al., "The Accuracy of Predictions of Violence to Others," 269 *Journal of the American Medical Association* 1007 (1993) (47 percent); Jay Apperson et al., "Short-Term Clinical Prediction of Violent Behavior: Artifacts of Research Methods," 150 *American Journal of Psychiatry* 1374 (1993) (25 percent). For studies of actuarial prediction, see Deidre Klassen & William O'Connor, "A Prospective Study of Predictors of Violence in Adult Male Mental Patients," 12 *Law and Human Behavior* 143 (1988) (40 percent) and the research reported in the text following.

39. John Monahan, "The Prediction of Violent Behavior: Toward a Second Generation of Theory and Policy," 141 *American Journal of Psychiatry* 10, 11 (1984). See also Randy Otto, "On the Ability of Mental Health Professionals to 'Predict Dangerousness': A Commentary on Interpretations of the 'Dangerousness' Literature," 18 *Law & Psychology Review* 43, 63 & n.63 (1994) ("Whereas first generation research suggested that perhaps one out of three people predicted to engage in some kind of violent behavior will actually go on to do so, more recent studies suggest that one out of every two people predicted to be violent would go on to engage in some kind of legally relevant, violent behavior.").

40. I first pointed this out in 1984. Slobogin, "Dangerousness and Expertise," 112–14.

41. Kevin Douglas & John Weir, "HCR-20 Violence Risk Assessment Scheme: Overview and Annotated Bibliography" 4 (2005), available at www.sfu.ca/psyc/faculty/hart.

42. Douglas Mossman, "Assessing Predictions of Violence: Being Accurate about Accuracy," 62 *Journal of Consulting & Clinical Psychology* 783, 789 (1994). I focus on the medians from studies using cross-validation samples because AUC values so derived tend to reflect more accurately the real-world validity of a device than AUC values obtained on the sample used to derive the instrument.

43. For the VRAG, Quinsey et al., *Violent Offenders: Appraising and Managing Risk* 148 (2d ed. 2006); Harris et al., "Prospective Replication of the VRAG," 386. For the COVR, John Monahan et al., "An Actuarial Model of Violence Risk Assessment for Persons with Mental Disorders," 56 *Psychiatric Services* 810, 814 (2005). For the RRASOR, R. Karl Hanson et al., "Research Summary, Corrections Research and Development" 13 (Jan. 1997).

44. For the HCR-20, Douglas & Weir, "HCR-20 Violence Risk Assessment Scheme," 5–9. For the PCL-R, M. Dolan & M. Doyle, "Violence Risk Prediction: Clinical and Actuarial Measures and the Role of the Psychopathy Checklist," 177 *British Journal of Psychiatry* 303, 305 (2000).

45. Quinsey et al., *Violent Offenders* (1st ed.), 171.

46. Thomas R. Litwack, "Actuarial versus Clinical Assessments of Dangerousness," 7 *Psychology, Public Policy and Law* 409, 437 (2001).

47. 463 U.S. at 896–97.

48. Ibid., 901.

49. See generally Cass R. Sunstein, *One Case at a Time: Judicial Minimalism on the Supreme Court* (1999).

50. 970 S.W.2d 549, 562 (Tex. Crim. App. 1998).

51. Johnson v. Cockrell, 306 F.3d 249, 254 (5th Cir. 2002).

52. See, e.g., Martinez v. Dretke, 99 Fed.App. 538, 542 (5th Cir. 2004); United States v. Barnette, 211 F.3d 803 (2000) (holding that testimony in a capital case based on the PCL-R is admissible under *Daubert*).

53. Randy K. Otto & John Petrila, "Admissibility of Testimony Based on Actuarial Scales in Sex Offender Commitments: A Reply to Doren," 3 *Sex Offender Law Reporter* 1 (2002). Trial courts in Iowa, Arizona, Florida, and Missouri have excluded predictive opinion, but appellate courts in the first two states overruled those decisions, and appellate courts in the latter two states have yet to address the issue. See In re Detention of Holtz, 653 N.W.2d 613, 614–16 (Iowa Ct. App. 2002) ("Our research has revealed no state appellate court decision which has found actuarial instruments inadmissible at [sexually violent predator] proceedings."). For post-2002 decisions, see In re Detention of Traynoff, 831 N.E.2d 709 (Ill. App. Ct. 2005); Com. v. Bradway, 62 Mass.App.Ct. 280, 287, 816 N.E.2d 152, 157–58 (Mass. App. Ct., 2004). But see State v. Holtz, 653 N.W. 613, 619–20 (Iowa Ct. App. 2002) (permitting actuarial evaluation only when used "in conjunction with a full clinical evaluation").

54. Alexander Scherr, "Daubert & Danger: The 'Fit' of Expert Predictions in Civil Commitment," 55 *Hastings Law Journal* 1, 60 (2003). For a long list of cases in which prediction testimony has been held admissible, see John Monahan, "A Jurisprudence of Risk Assessment: Forecasting Harm among Prisoners, Predators and Patients," 92 *Virginia Law Review* 391, 410 n.74 (2005).

55. 463 U.S. at 938 (Blackmun, J., dissenting).

56. 210 F.3d 456 (5th Cir. 2000).

57. U.S. v. Sampson, 335 F.Supp.2d 166 (D. Mass. 2004).

58. People v. Taylor, 782 N.E.2d 920, 932 (Ill. App. Ct. 2002); In re Valdez, No. 99-000045CI (Fl. Cir. Ct. Aug. 21, 2000); Eric S. Janus & Robert A. Prentky, "Forensic Use of Actuarial Risk Assessment with Sex Offenders: Accuracy, Admissibility and Accountability," 40 *American Criminal Law Review* 1443, 1459 & n.90 (2003).

59. Compare In re Coffel, 117 S.W.3d 116, 129 (Mo. App. Ct. 2003) (excluding clinical prediction testimony) to In re Care and Treatment of Kapprelian, 168 S.W.3d 708, 715 (Mo. App. Ct. 2005) (distinguishing *Coffel*, and admitting clinical testimony, because here the expert's opinion was not based "solely on clinical judgment").

60. In re Linehan, 518 N.W.2d 609, 616 (Coyne, J., dissenting).

61. Gordon Allport, "The Use of Personal Documents in Psychological Science," 49 *S.S.R.C. Bulletin* 156 (1942), quoted in Paul Meehl, *Clinical versus Statistical Prediction* 19 (1954).

62. Monahan, *The Clinical Prediction of Violent Behavior*, 66.

63. Joseph T. McCann, "Standards for Expert Testimony in New York Death Penalty Cases," *New York State Bar Journal* 39, 31 (July–Aug. 1996) (stating that in every one of the 144 capital cases in which Grigson testified up to 1992 he stated he was sure the defendant would kill again).

64. Cf. Underwood, "Predicting Behavior," 1427 ("Although the clinician need not identify in advance the characteristics he will regard as salient, he must nevertheless evaluate the applicant on the basis of a finite number of salient

characteristics, and thus, like the statistical decisionmaker, he treats the applicant as a member of a class defined by those characteristics.").

65. Marnie Rice & Grant T. Harris, "Cross-validation and Extension of the Violence Risk Appraisal Guide for Child Molesters and Rapists," 21 *Law & Human Behavior* 231 (1997).

66. Donna Cropp Bechman, "Sex Offender Civil Commitments: Scientists or Psychics?," 16 *Criminal Justice* 24, 29 (2001).

67. See Litwack, "Actuarial versus Clinical Assessments," 428.

68. Idaho Code § 19-2515(9)(h); Tex. Code Crim. Pro. art. 37.071 sec. 2(b)(1).

69. Quinsey et al., *Violent Offenders* (1st ed. 1998), 177–78 ("There is good evidence that clinicians' appraisals of patients' current clinical conditions are unrelated to recidivism. . . . It is now clear that the 'getting to know' individuals that occurs in typical interviews does not improve the prediction of behavior in any domain.").

70. Note, for instance, that none of the variables excluded by the VRAG researchers involved the factors mentioned in the text, nor any of the other factors that were earlier hypothesized in discussing adjusted actuarial assessments (treatment, gang membership, specific threats) or clinical variables (e.g., anger). Harris et al., "Psychopathy and Violent Recidivism," 631.

71. Monahan, *The Clinical Prediction of Violent Behavior*, 74–75.

72. See generally Regents of U. of Cal. v. Bakke, 438 U.S. 265, 360 (1978) (stating "race, like gender . . . is an immutable characteristic which its possessors are powerless to escape or set aside" and thus subject to constitutional protection under the Equal Protection Clause). One is also powerless to escape one's age, although the Supreme Court has held that discrimination on the basis of relative youth (the type of discrimination most relevant to violence prediction) is not cognizable under the Age Discrimination Employment Act. General Dynamics Land Systems, Inc. v. Cline 540 U.S. 581 (2004).

73. Daniel Goodman, "Demographic Evidence in Capital Sentencing," 39 *Stanford Law Review* 499, 521 (1987).

74. Monahan, "A Jurisprudence of Risk Assessment," 428. See also Underwood, "Predicting Behavior," 1416.

75. See John E. Nowak & Ronald D. Rotunda, *Principles of Constitutional Law* 378–79 (2d ed. 2005).

76. Monahan et al., *Rethinking Risk Assessment*, 163 (showing a correlation of .12 between race and violence). As I argued in a different context: "[A government] action which depends upon factors such as race denigrates the state's interest in maintaining a democratic society and the allegiance of the populace. . . . Some citizens might see the state's behavior as a justification for using race as a surrogate in their own decisionmaking. Other, more sensitive, citizens who experience or hear about such [actions] will question the legitimacy not only of the [actions] themselves, but of the government that would permit them. In either case, the democratic state's interests are severely damaged." See Christopher Slobogin, "The World without a Fourth Amendment," 39 *UCLA Law Review* 1, 85–86 (1991).

77. Norval Morris, "Predicting Violence with Statistics," 34 *Stanford Law Review* 249, 253 (1981).

78. See, e.g., Paul Robinson, "Punishing Dangerousness: Cloaking Preventive Detention as Criminal Justice," 114 *Harvard Law Review* 1429 (2001) (arguing that desert and incapacitative principles are inherently incompatible, and that the latter principle should play no role in the criminal justice system, which should be based entirely on desert).

79. Even many of the states with sentencing guidelines, which are normally an attribute of a desert-based system, permit dangerousness assessments to influence the length of sentence, usually through a parole board determination. Richard S. Frase, "State Sentencing Guidelines: Diversity, Consensus, and Unresolved Policy Issues," 105 *Columbia Law Review* 1190, 1200 (2005).

80. Monahan, *A Jurisprudence of Risk Assessment*, 429.

81. See Kansas v. Hendricks, 521 U.S. 346, 361–62 (1997) (holding that sexual predator laws do not implicate "either of the two primary objectives of criminal punishment: retribution or deterrence").

Chapter 7

1. 509 U.S. 579, 592 (1993).

2. Michael J. Saks, "The Legal and Scientific Evaluation of Forensic Science (Especially Fingerprint Expert Testimony)," 33 *Seton Hall Law Review* 1167, 1168 (2003). See also Richard D. Friedman, "Squeezing *Daubert* Out of the Picture," 33 *Seton Hall Law Review* 1047, 1058–59 (2003).

3. In re Valdez, No. 99-000045CI (Fla. 2000) (reported in Randy K. Otto & John Petrila, "Admissibility of Testimony Based on Actuarial Scales in Sex Offender Commitments: A Reply to Doren," 3 *Sex Offender Law Reporter* 1, 5 (2002)).

4. Gary Melton et al., *Psychological Evaluations for the Courts: A Handbook for Mental Health Professionals and Lawyers* 284-93 (2d ed. 1997)(describing risk assessment procedures).

5. Addington v. Texas, 441 U.S. 418, 433 (1979).

6. Cf. Stephen Morse, "A Preference for Liberty: The Case against Involuntary Commitment of the Mentally Disordered," 70 *California Law Review* 54, 74–76 (1982).

7. Kenneth S. Brown et al., *McCormick on Evidence* § 185 at 640–41 (John W. Strong ed., 5th ed. 1999).

8. See, e.g., People v. Superior Court (Ghilotti), 44 P.3d 949, 954 (Cal. 2002) (holding that commitment under California's sexual predator law does not require proof that violence is "better than even" but only proof of "substantial danger— that is, a serious and well-founded risk of criminal sexual violence").

9. John Monahan & David Wexler, "A Definite Maybe: Proof and Probability in Civil Commitment," 2 *Law and Human Behavior* 37 (1978).

10. Cf. Mont. Code 53-21-126(2) (requiring proof of any "physical facts or evidence" beyond a reasonable doubt, while requiring only clear and convincing evidence for other facts); Michael J. Corrado, "Punishment and the Wild Beast of Prey: The Problem of Preventive Detention," 86 *Journal of Criminal Law & Criminology* 778, 792 (1996) (arguing that even when risk is low, if the detained person belongs to the designated risk group, "there is a one hundred percent chance that person presents a risk of harm").

11. Christopher Slobogin, *Minding Justice: Laws that Deprive People with Mental Disability of Life and Liberty*, 109-11 (2006); Christopher Slobogin, "A Jurisprudence of Dangerousness," 98 *Northwestern University Law Review* 1, 6–9, 53–58 (2003).

12. See Daniel W. Shuman & Bruce D. Sales, "The Admissibility of Expert Testimony Based upon Clinical Judgment and Scientific Research," 4 *Psychology, Public Policy & Law* 1226, 1228 (1998) ("Expert judgments that are clinically derived, as opposed to actuarially derived, are as susceptible to error as lay judgments."); Alan Stone, *Mental Health and the Law: A System in Transition* 33 (1975) ("There are many situations in which a layperson could predict dangerousness as well as the experts—for example, drug addicts in need of money."); Stephen Morse, "Crazy Behavior, Morals and Science: An Analysis of Mental Health Law," 51 *Southern California Law Review* 527, 620 (1978) (reasoning that "without hard, methodologically sound quantitative data, the guess of an expert is unlikely to be better than the guess of laypersons").

13. Douglas Mossman, "Assessing Predictions of Violence: Being Accurate about Accuracy," 62 *Journal of Consulting and Clinical Psychiatry* 783, 790 (1994).

14. George Dix, "The Death Penalty, 'Dangerousness,' Psychiatric Testimony, and Professional Ethics," 5 *American Journal of Criminal Law* 151, 175–77 (1977).

15. John Bloom, "Killers and Shrinks," *Texas Monthly* 64, 68 (July 1978). For the reasons suggested in the text, Dr. Grigson's career as a prosecution witness was sharply curtailed in 1995, when he was expelled from the American Psychiatric Association. See Hugh Aynesworth, "Texas 'Dr. Death' Retires after 167 Capital Case Trials," *Washington Times*, Dec. 21, 2003, at A2.

16. See Alexander Brooks, "Dangerousness Defined," in *Law, Psychiatry & Mental Health Systems* 680 (1974) (listing magnitude, probability, frequency, and imminence as factors that should be considered in determining dangerousness).

17. 463 U.S. at 916 (Blackmun, J., dissenting).

18. Flores v. Johnson, 210 F.3d 456, 466 (5th Cir. 2000) (Garza, J., concurring).

19. 463 U.S., 899 n.7 & § 901.

20. Saks and Kidd note that the "consistent overprediction of dangerousness is in part due to experts' insensitivity to the low frequency of such behavior and reliance on the representativeness heuristic wherein the person threatened with commitment is compared to the stereotype of a dangerous person." Michael Saks & Robert Kidd, "Human Information Processing and Adjudication: Trial by Heuristics," 15 *Law & Society Review* 123, 133 (1980–81), citing Daniel Kahneman & Amos Tversky, "Subjective Probability: A Judgment of Representativeness," 3 *Cognitive Psychology* 430 (1972). If experts do not respond to generalized data, it is unlikely laypersons will.

21. At the time of Barefoot's trial, for instance, indigent defendants in death penalty cases were entitled to $500 for "investigation and experts." 463 U.S. at 899 n.5. The Supreme Court has held that indigent defendants are entitled to state-paid assistance on the dangerousness issue, but only one such expert, who can be a state employee and who does not have to agree with the defense position. Ake v. Oklahoma, 470 U.S. 68, 83 (1985).

22. Shari Seidman Diamond et al., "Juror Reactions to Attorneys at Trial," 87 *Journal of Criminal Law & Criminology* 17, 52–53 & Table 4 (1996). Only

when the government expert admitted that he might be wrong two out of three times did study subjects tend to change their minds.

23. See Albert Hoff, "Patuxent and Discretion in the Criminal Justice System," 5 *Bulletin of American Academy of Psychiatry and Law* 144, 154 (1977).

24. George Dix, "Clinical Evaluation of the 'Dangerousness' of 'Normal' Criminal Defendants," 66 *Virginia Law Review* 523, 538 (1980).

25. According to one report, Grigson "has testified for the prosecution in at least 140 Texas capital trials; jurors imposed death sentences in more than 98 percent of these cases." Amnesty International Report, *The Death Penalty in Texas: Lethal Injustice* 12 (March 1998).

26. One study found that only 21 percent of those sentenced to death as dangerous by Texas jurors committed any type of violent act while in prison. James W. Marquart et al., "Gazing into the Crystal Ball: Can Jurors Accurately Predict Dangerousness in Capital Cases?," 23 *Law & Society Review* 449, 463 (1989).

27. See W. Lawrence Fitch & Debra A. Hamen, "The New Generation of Sex Offender Commitment Laws: Which States Have Them and How Do They Work?," in *Protecting Society from Sexually Dangerous Offenders* 27, 32 (Bruce J. Winick & John Q. LaFond eds., 2003) (indicating that, between 1999 and 2001, only 473 individuals had been committed under sexual predator laws, despite several thousand petitions for such commitments).

28. Daniel Krauss & D. Lee, "Deliberating on Dangerousness and Death: Jurors' Ability to Differentiate between Expert Actuarial and Clinical Predictions of Dangerousness," 26 *International Journal of Law and Psychiatry* 113 (2003); Randy Borum, "Improving the Clinical Practice of Violence Risk Assessment," 51 *American Psychologist* 945 (1996); William Gardner et al., "Clinical versus Actuarial Predictions of Violence in Patients with Mental Illness," 64 *Journal of Consulting and Clinical Psychology* 602 (1996).

29. Daniel A. Krauss & Bruce D. Sales, "The Effects of Clinical and Scientific Expert Testimony on Juror Decision Making in Capital Cases," 7 *Psychology, Public Policy & Law* 267, 305 (2003).

30. Daniel A. Krauss et al., "The Effects of Rational and Experiential Information Processing of Expert Testimony in Death Penalty Cases," 22 *Behavioral Science and Law* 801, 814 (2004).

31. See Krauss & Sales, "The Effects of Clinical and Scientific Testimony," 301.

32. Fed. R. Evid. 404(a)(1) ("Evidence of a person's character or a trait of his character is not admissible for the purpose of proving that he acted in conformity therewith on a particular occasion, except: (1) Character of accused. Evidence of a pertinent trait of his character offered by an accused, or by the prosecution to rebut the same.").

33. Indeed, the advisory committee note to the federal character evidence rule states that the rule "is so deeply imbedded in our jurisprudence as to assume almost constitutional proportions."

34. See Michelson v. United States, 335 U.S. 469, 476 (1948) ("The overriding policy of excluding such evidence, despite its admitted probative value, is the practical experience that its disallowance tends to prevent confusion of issues, unfair surprise and undue prejudice.").

35. Julian V. Roberts, "The Role of Criminal Record in the Sentencing Process," 22 *Crime & Justice* 303, 316–17 (1997) ("Research on the prediction of

criminal behavior repeatedly demonstrated criminal record to be the single best predictor of future offending."); John Monahan, *The Clinical Prediction of Violent Behavior* 71 (1981) ("If there is one finding that overshadows all others in the area of prediction, it is that the probability of future crime increases with each prior criminal act.").

36. 463 U.S. 354, 365 n.14 (1983) ("To describe the theft of watches and jewelry as 'non-dangerous' is to confuse danger with violence. Larceny is usually less violent than murder or assault, but in terms of public policy the purpose of the statute is the same as to both.") (quoting Overholser v. O'Beirne, 302 F.2d 852, 861 (D.C. Cir. 1961)).

37. After the Supreme Court's decision in Apprendi v. New Jersey, 530 U.S. 466 (2000), sentencing courts are no longer permitted to rely on evidence of prior bad acts to enhance a sentence beyond the statutory or guidelines maximum unless they resulted in conviction, are stipulated to by the defense, or were found by a jury to have occurred beyond a reasonable doubt. It remains to be seen whether this rule applies in commitment hearings, where the Sixth Amendment right to jury trial in criminal cases—the basis for the *Apprendi* ruling—probably does not apply.

38. See, e.g., Fla. Stat. §916.15(1) (requiring a showing of "mental illness" as a predicate for commitment of insanity acquittees).

39. See, e.g., Kan. Stat. §59-29a02(b) (defining "mental abnormality" as a "congenital or acquired condition affecting the emotional or volitional capacity which predisposes the person to commit sexually violent offenses in a degree constituting such person a menace to the health and safety of others").

40. 421 U.S. 646, 358 (1997).

41. I have argued that *Hendricks* should be construed to require true "undeterrability," that is, a showing that the individual will commit violent acts even when the likelihood of apprehension and significant punishment is very high. Slobogin, *Minding Justice*, 129-41.

42. For instance, roughly two-thirds of state capital sentencing statutes recognize these two conditions as mitigating factors. Ellen Fels Berkman, "Mental Illness as an Aggravating Circumstance in Capital Sentencing," 89 *Columbia Law Review* 291, 296–98 (1989).

43. See, e.g., American Bar Association, *Criminal Justice Mental Health Standards,* standard 7-7.4(d) ("If the court is persuaded that acquittee will continue to receive the needed treatment or habilitation, it may order . . . that acquittee be released."); American Law Institute, Model Penal Code § 7.01(2)(j) (Official Draft 1980) (mitigation possible if "the defendant is particularly likely to respond affirmatively to probationary treatment").

44. Every jurisdiction requires the defense to provide the prosecution with notice of an intent to raise an insanity defense. Wayne R. LaFave et al., *Criminal Procedure* 919 (2d ed. 1999).

45. This limitation is meant to be strict. Thus, for instance, a prediction based on structured professional judgment would not be admissible in the prosecution's case in chief unless tied to a probability estimate in the manner described in chapter 6. Even when such estimates exist, exclusion might occur. For example, the developers of the HCR-20 indicate that risk assessments may be based on information not elicited through the instrument, such as threats of harm. Christopher Webster et al., *HCR-20: Assessing Risk for Violence (Version 2)* 21–23

(1997). That information would not be associated with an empirically derived probability estimate, and thus would not be admissible in the prosecution's case in chief through expert testimony (it might be admissible through a lay witness report, however).

46. Cf. American Bar Association, *Mental Health Standards*, standard § 7-7.4(d) (providing that if the court finds that the only reason an insanity acquittee does not meet the commitment criteria is because of the effect of treatment or habilitation, "the acquittee may be committed unless the court is persuaded by a preponderance of the evidence that the acquittee will continue to receive such treatment or habilitation following release for as long as the treatment or habilitation is required").

47. Monahan, *The Clinical Prediction of Violent Behavior*, 59 (quoting W. Mischel, *Personality and Assessment* 168 (1968)).

48. Jay Apperson et al., "Short-Term Clinical Prediction of Assaultive Behavior: Artifacts of Research Methods," 150 *American Journal of Psychiatry* 1374 (1993) (finding a 25 percent false-positive rate for short-term predictions in emergency commitment context); Renee Binder, "Are the Mentally Ill Danger-ous?," 27 *Bulletin of the American Academy of Psychiatry and Law* 189, 197 (1999) (summarizing research indicating that short-term predictions are better than long-term predictions); Earl Rofman et al., "The Prediction of Dangerous Behavior in Emergency Civil Commitment," 137 *American Journal of Psychiatry* 1061, 1063 (1980) (producing a 59 percent false-positive rate but noting that those predicted to be dangerous were immediately medicated, and thus that "the probability of the patients in [the] experimental group (who would be un-medicated outside the hospital) committing assaults in the community would have far exceeded 41% without emergency commitment"). See generally Thomas Litwack & Louis Schlesinger, "Assessing and Predicting Violence: Research, Law and Applications," in *Handbook of Forensic Psychology* 205, 224 (Irving B. Weiner & Allen K. Hess eds., 1987) (specifying conditions in which clinical predictions of violence can provide clear and convincing evidence of dangerousness in the commitment context).

49. See, e.g., Cal. Code § 5250 et seq. (providing for a full judicial hearing after fourteen days of detention).

50. See Ralph Reisner et al., *Law and the Mental Health System: Civil and Criminal Aspects* 763–64 (4th ed. 2004) (summarizing research).

Chapter 8

1. See Paul Gianelli, "*Daubert* in the States," 34 *Criminal Law Bulletin* 154, 155 (1998)) (under the relevancy test, "if the expert was qualified, the underlying technique used by that expert was qualified"); Paul Gianelli, "The Admissibility of Novel Scientific Evidence: Frye v. United States, a Half-Century Later," 80 *Columbia Law Review* 1997, 1239 (1980) (noting that the "principal justification for the *Frye* test" is that it " 'assures that those most qualified to assess the general validity of a scientific method will have the determinative voice'," quoting United States v. Addison, 498 F.2d 741, 743–44 (D.C. Cir. 1974)). Professor Gianelli also notes how the general acceptance test obscured inquiry into reliability and pro-bative value issues. Ibid., 1224–28.

2. Some commentators have argued that *Daubert* is more consistent with a social constructionist view of science than the *Frye* test. More specifically, they contend that whereas the general acceptance test (and therefore, implicitly, the relevance test) legitimizes "elite, authoritative opinions" as "the sole arbiters of specialized knowledge," *Daubert* and *Kumho Tire* take a "realist-constructivist view of science." Joseph Sanders et al., "Legal Perceptions of Science and Expert Knowledge," 8 *Psychology, Public Policy & Law* 139, 149 (2002). In determining whether *Daubert* will make expertise more positivist in tone, however, the focus should be on what the legal fact finder is likely to hear, not on the source of the expert's expertise. For reasons outlined in the text, a reliability test clearly excludes more expert testimony than the other two tests.

3. Mark P. Denbeaux & D. Michael Risinger, "*Kumho Tire* and Expert Reliability: How the Question You Ask Gives the Answer You Get," 34 *Seton Hall Law Review* 15, 52, 59 (2003) (discussing handwriting and fingerprint evidence).

4. Paul C. Gianelli, "The Supreme Court's 'Criminal' *Daubert* Cases," 33 *Seton Hall Law Review* 1071, 1097–98 (2003).

5. Jennifer L. Groscup et al., "The Effects of *Daubert* on the Admissibility of Expert Testimony in State and Federal Criminal Cases," 8 *Psychology, Public Policy & Law* 339, 363 (2002).

6. Cf. Lloyd Dixon & Brian Gill, "Changes in the Standards for Admitting Expert Evidence in Federal Civil Cases Since the *Daubert* Decision," 8 *Psychology, Public Policy & Law* 251, 269, 277 (2002) (finding that post-*Daubert*, "judges have examined the reliability of expert evidence more closely and have found more evidence unreliable as a result" and that "*Kumho* appears to have confirmed a trend already under way in federal district courts to apply *Daubert* broadly rather than restrict it to hard science").

7. Wayne Lafave, *Criminal Law* 59 (4th ed. 2003) ("It is uniformly held that the defendant is obliged to start matters off by putting in some evidence in support of his defense—e.g., evidence of his insanity, or of his acting in self-defense, or of one of the other affirmative defenses.").

8. Denbeaux & Risinger, "*Kumho Tire* and Expert Reliability," 49–51, 56–58. See also David A. Stoney, "Fingerprint Identification: Scientific Status," in 3 David L. Faigman et al., *The Law and Science of Expert Testimony* 394–95 (2002) (describing "realistic" methodological models for measuring fingerprint identification expertise that are not "particularly easy" but are "feasible" and will provide information about the reliability of identification "when there is some minimal level of detail present in the fingerprints"). The same can be said for other forensic techniques on which the government relies. See, e.g., Alfred Biasotti & John Murdock, "Firearms and Toolmark Identification," in 3 Faigman et al., *The Law and Science of Expert Testimony*, 517 ("It is anticipated that objective quantitative criteria for identification will eventually become widely accepted and used because of the research already conducted and published."); Michael P. Risinger, "Handwriting Identification: Scientific Status," in 3 Faigman et al., *The Law and Science of Expert Testimony*, 481 ("Research can provide a warrant for believing that document examiners possess sufficient skills in regard to particular tasks to warrant admission, at least under test conditions.").

9. *Daubert*, 509 U.S. at 591 ("Fit is not always obvious, and scientific validity for one purpose is not necessarily scientific validity for other, unrelated

purposes."); 597 (the Federal Rules of Evidence "assign to the trial judge the task of ensuring that an expert's testimony both rests on a reliable foundation and is relevant to the task at hand"); *Kumho Tire*, 526 U.S. at 156 ("The trial court ha[s] to decide whether this particular expert had sufficient specialized knowledge to assist the jurors 'in deciding the particular issues in the case.'").

10. Denbeaux & Risinger, "*Kumho Tire* and Expert Reliability," 14.

11. Paul Cassell, "Protecting the Innocent from False Confessions and Lost Confessions—And from *Miranda*," 88 *Journal of Criminal Law & Criminology* 497, 502 (1998) (estimating the base rate for false confessions at between 1 in 2,400 and 1 in 90,000). As to the difficulty of determining a confession's falsity, compare Richard A. Leo & Richard J. Ofshe, "The Consequences of False Confessions: Deprivations of Liberty and Miscarriages of Justice in the Age of Psychological Interrogation," 88 *Journal of Criminal Law & Criminology* 429 (1998) (claiming to have found sixty cases of false confessions) with Cassell, "Protecting the Innocent," 587 (claiming that nine out of the twenty-nine cases reported by Leo and Ofshe that Cassell examined did not involve false confessions).

12. The only study of this type, conducted in 1996, involved seventy-five college students who were given a typing test on a computer and told not to touch the ALT key because it would crash the computer program and ruin the experiment. One minute into the test the computer program crashed; although the crash was caused by the experimenters, the subject was blamed. Using several modern interrogation techniques, the research team was able to get 69 percent of the subjects to falsely confess to causing the crash. But, as Professor Kassin, the principal investigator, recognized, far higher stakes are involved in a criminal investigation and, perhaps more important, the facts were such that the subjects could have honestly believed they caused the crash, as evidenced by the fact that over a third of the confessors stated they were responsible after simply being asked "What happened?" Saul M. Kassin & Katherine L. Kiechel, "The Social Psychology of False Confessions: Compliance, Internalization, and Confabulation," 7 *Psychological Science* 125, 127 (1996).

13. See generally Gary L. Wells, "Eyewitness Identification: Scientific Status," in 2 Faigman et al., *The Law and Science of Expert Testimony*, 391–422.

14. See, e.g., ibid., 404–07.

15. See Henry F. Fradella, "The Impact of *Daubert* on the Admissibility of Behavioral Science Testimony," 30 *Pepperdine Law Review* 403 (2003) (finding that exclusion of behavioral science testimony rarely occurs *except* when focused on eyewitness accuracy, the falseness of a particular confession or the credibility of a witness).

16. See, e.g., United States v. Brien, 59 F.3d 274 (1st Cir. 1995) (eyewitness testimony); United States v. Kime, 99 F.3d 870 (8th Cir. 1996) (eyewitness testimony); State v. MacDonald, 718 A.2d 195, 198 (Me. 1998) (false confessions). The following two cases make the point nicely. With respect to false confession research, consider State v. Free, 798 A.2d 83, 96 (N.J. 2002) ("Since Dr. Kassin cannot identify the degree to which the presence of one or more of these factors might cause a false confession, his opinions . . . would be of no assistance to the jury. What the jury would be left with . . . was accurately categorized by the Supreme Judicial Court of Maine as 'nothing more than an assertion that false confessions do occur.'"). With respect to eyewitness testimony, consider United States v. Hall, 165 F.3d 1095, 1104 (7th Cir. 1999) ("Expert testimony regarding

the potential hazards of eyewitness identification—regardless of its reliability—will not aid the jury because it addresses an issue of which the jury already generally is aware, and it will not contribute to their understanding of the particular factual issues posed.").

17. Jennifer L. Groscup & Steven Penrod, "Battle of the Standards for Experts in Criminal Cases: Police v. Psychologists," 33 *Seton Hall Law Review* 1141, 1153–55 (2003).

18. I think they are incorrect, because the testimony educates the jury in helpful ways, a fact that some courts recognize. See, e.g., Miller v. State, 770 N.E.2d 763, 774 (Ind. 2002) ("[False confession] testimony would have assisted the jury regarding the psychology of relevant aspects of police interrogation and the interrogation of mentally retarded persons, topics outside common knowledge and experience."); United States v. Mathis, 264 U.S. 321, 340 (3d Cir. 2001) ("[The eyewitness expert] attempted to provide information that, if itself deemed credible, might cause the jury to evaluate [the eyewitness's] testimony in a different light."). See generally D. Michael Risinger, "Preliminary Thoughts on a Functional Taxonomy of Expertise for the Post-*Kumho* World," 31 *Seton Hall Law Review* 508, 515–26 (2000) (describing "summarizational" and "translational" expertise which educates the jury about general scientific and technical knowledge).

19. Wells, "Eyewitness Identification," 415.

20. See, e.g., State v. McClendon, 730 A.2d 1107, 1115 (Conn. 1999) ("Leippe did refer to several areas of scientific inquiry concerning eyewitness identification, but . . . admitted, in sum, that 'we don't always know what factors are influencing' an eyewitness. He conceded that a controversy existed in the area of the statistical probability of false identification, the one kind of information inaccessible to the average juror.").

21. 5 Forensic Science Communications, available at www.fbi.gov/hq/lab/fsc/current/index. For 2002, the relevant congressional committee recommended another $8 million *over* 2001's appropriation (for a total of over $20 million). Ibid. There are at least ten government-sponsored scientific working groups in areas such as DNA analysis, bloodstain pattern analysis, firearms and tool marks identification, and drug analysis. Carol Henderson, presentation at panel on "Science after *Kumho Tire*: When Is Science Really Science?," AALS Meeting, Washington, D.C., Jan. 3, 2003.

22. The advisory committee notes to the revised Federal Rule of Evidence 702 indicate that courts often consider as a reliability-indicating factor the "nonjudicial uses" to which the basis of expert testimony has been put, suggesting that if there are no nonjudicial uses, reliability is suspect. See also Judge Kozinski's opinion in Daubert v. Merrell Dow Pharm., 43 F.3d 1311, 1317 (9th Cir. 1995) ("One very significant fact to be considered is whether the experts are proposing to testify about matters growing naturally and directly out of research they have conducted independent of the litigation, or whether they have developed their opinions expressly for purposes of testifying").

23. See http://www.fastlane.nsf.gov/a6/A6AwardSearch.htm (using keywords "eyewitness & identification," "confessions," and "insanity").

24. See David L. Faigman, "The Evidentiary Status of Social Science under *Daubert*: Is It 'Scientific,' 'Technical,' or 'Other' Knowledge?," 1 *Psychology, Public Policy & Law* 960, 971–77 (1995).

25. Joseph Sanders, "The Paternalistic Justification for Restrictions on the Admissibility of Expert Evidence," 33 *Seton Hall Law Review* 881, 940 (2003).

26. Katherine Goldwasser, "Vindicating the Right to Trial by Jury and the Requirement of Proof beyond a Reasonable Doubt: A Critique of the Conventional Wisdom about Excluding Defense Evidence," 86 *Georgetown Law Journal* 621, 636, 639 (1998).

27. Janet C. Hoeffel, "The Sixth Amendment's Lost Clause: Unearthing Compulsory Process," 2002 *Wisconsin Law Review* 1275, 1316–51 (2002) (using court decisions involving eyewitness, false confession, rape trauma syndrome, and polygraph expertise as a basis for arguing that courts apply *Daubert* inconsistently and often with little attention to reliability concerns).

28. Barry Scheck et al., *Actual Innocence* (2000) (eyewitness identifications were involved in 84 percent of sixty-three definitive DNA-based exoneration cases in the United States); Arye Rattner, "Convicted but Innocent: Wrongful Conviction and the Criminal Justice System," 12 *Law & Human Behavior* 283, 289–91 (1988) (out of 205 erroneous conviction cases, eyewitness misidentifications were responsible for 48.8 percent, a greater proportion than all other causes, including perjury (26 percent), coerced confessions (16 percent), and forensic science errors (3 percent)).

29. Innocence Project, *Convicted by Juries, Exonerated by Science: Case Studies in the Use of DNA Evidence to Establish Innocence after Trial* 15–18 (1996).

30. Cf. Ellen Yankiver Suni, "Who Stole the Cookie from the Cookie Jar? The Law and Ethics of Shifting Blame in Criminal Cases," 68 *Fordham Law Review* 1643, 1690 (2000) ("If police and prosecutors know that defendants have limited resources to investigate . . . and that even if defendants obtain resources to do so, evidence that they find will be unusable . . . police and prosecutors will have little incentive to explore alternative theories once they have reached a preliminary conclusion.").

31. Shari Seidman Diamond et al., "Juror Reactions to Attorneys at Trial," 87 *Journal of Criminal Law & Criminology* 17 (1996).

32. Sanders, "The Paternalistic Justification for Restrictions on Expert Evidence," 909–24.

33. Trial by document is prohibited by the Sixth Amendment's Right of Confrontation Clause. See, e.g., Coy v. Iowa, 487 U.S. 1012 (1988) (requiring face-to-face meeting with available witnesses).

34. Gary Melton et al., *Psychological Evaluations for the Courts: A Handbook for Mental Health Professionals and Lawyers* 188–89, 204–08 (2d ed. 1997).

35. Hoeffel, "The Sixth Amendment's Lost Clause," 77. See also Richard D. Friedman, "Squeezing *Daubert* Out of the Picture," 33 *Seton Hall Law Review* 1047, 1048 (2003) (test for defense evidence should be very lenient).

36. Roger Park, "*Daubert* on a Tilted Playing Field," 33 *Seton Hall Law Review* 1113 (2003). See also Joelle Anne Moreno, "What Happens When Dirty Harry Becomes an (Expert) Witness for the Prosecution?," 79 *Tulane Law Review* 1, 46–53 (2004).

Index